HOW TO CREATE AN
ECO GARDEN

HOW TO CREATE AN
ECO GARDEN

The practical guide to greener, planet-friendly gardening

Garden layouts and planting plans, step-by-step techniques, a directory of 80 plants and over 500 photographs and illustrations

JOHN WALKER

PHOTOGRAPHY BY COLIN LEFTLEY

*To Aunty Pat, and in memory of
my gran, Ellen Handley*

This edition is published by Aquamarine
an imprint of Anness Publishing Ltd
Blaby Road, Wigston
Leicestershire LE18 4SE

Email: info@anness.com
Web: www.aquamarinebooks.com;
www.annesspublishing.com

If you like the images in this book
and would like to investigate using
them for publishing, promotions or
advertising, please visit our website
www.practicalpictures.com
for more information.

Publisher: Joanna Lorenz
Senior Editor: Felicity Forster
Photography: Colin Leftley
Illustration Concepts: John Walker
Illustrator: Liz Pepperell
Copy Editor: Catherine Best
Jacket Design: Lisa Tai
Designer: Nigel Partridge
Production Controller: Wendy Lawson

ETHICAL TRADING POLICY

At Anness Publishing we believe that
business should be conducted in an ethical
and ecologically sustainable way, with
respect for the environment and a proper
regard to the replacement of the natural
resources we employ.

As a publisher, we use a lot of wood pulp
in high-quality paper for printing, and that
wood commonly comes from spruce trees.
We are therefore currently growing more
than 750,000 trees in three Scottish forest
plantations: Berrymoss (130 hectares/
320 acres), West Touxhill (125 hectares/
305 acres) and Deveron Forest (75 hectares/
185 acres). The forests we manage contain
more than 3.5 times the number of trees
employed each year in making paper for
the books we manufacture.

Because of this ongoing ecological
investment programme, you, as our customer,
can have the pleasure and reassurance of
knowing that a tree is being cultivated on your
behalf to naturally replace the materials used
to make the book you are holding.

Our forestry programme is run in
accordance with the UK Woodland Assurance
Scheme (UKWAS) and will be certified by the
internationally recognized Forest Stewardship
Council (FSC). The FSC is a non-government
organization dedicated to promoting
responsible management of the world's
forests. Certification ensures forests are
managed in an environmentally sustainable
and socially responsible way. For further
information about this scheme, go to
www.annesspublishing.com/trees.

PUBLISHER'S NOTES

Although the advice and information in this
book are believed to be accurate and true
at the time of going to press, neither the
authors nor the publisher can accept any
legal responsibility or liability for any errors
or omissions that may have been made, nor
for any inaccuracies nor for any loss, harm
or injury that comes about from following
instructions or advice in this book.

Great care should be taken if you decide
to include pools, ponds or water features
as part of your garden landscape. Young
children should never be left unsupervised
near water of any depth, and if children are
able to access the garden all pools and
ponds should be fenced and gated to the
recommended specifications.

PAGE 1: Honey bee on *Verbena bonariensis*.
PAGE 2: A border filled with insect-attracting
annual flowers rich in pollen and nectar.
PAGE 3 Left: Runner beans grown up coppiced
hazel poles maximize vertical cropping space.
Middle: The bee-attracting flowers of
fiddleback (*Phacelia tanacetifolia*).
Right: Red admiral butterfly on a single dahlia.
PAGE 4 Left: Versatile woven willow makes
an attractive and informal boundary marker.
Middle: Summer-fruiting redcurrants are a
prolific and easily grown soft fruit.
Right: An eye-catching garden path made
using a montage of recycled ceramic tiles.
PAGE 5 Top: A food garden comprising raised
beds made from long-lived, untreated oak.
Left: Self-seeded orange nasturtium, yellow
pot marigold and red orache.
Middle: Opium poppy (*Papaver somniferum*).
Right: A pretty living roof on a garden shed.

Contents

Introduction

Eco (or ecological) gardening is all about working in harmony with the intricate web of life of which we are ourselves a part. This book explains how to create and sustain a beautiful, biologically diverse and prolific garden while staying within and respecting nature's limits. Everyone, whatever the size of their plot, can garden in a more sustainable, planet-friendly and deeply enriching way.

Just going about our everyday lives comes with some environmental cost attached, and it can be hard, however enthusiastic we are, to find rewarding ways of doing our bit for the environment. We know that we should recycle, use our cars less, make our homes more energy-efficient and try to eat locally grown food. Yet all these 'green' activities, important though they are, can sometimes leave us feeling deeply unfulfilled.

▼ You do not need a large garden to enjoy a closer relationship with nature. This small and sunny plant-packed courtyard abounds with life.

However, when you step out into your own unique piece of paradise – your garden – all that changes. Here, working with nature, you can garden in a way that is both personal and intensely satisfying, but which also allows each person, in his or her own special way, to do that extra bit towards easing planetary burdens.

This book starts by looking at the connections between gardening and the world around us, and how reducing emissions of greenhouse gases (those responsible for global warming) from our gardens makes them more climate-friendly.

An introductory guide explaining how you can eco-fit your garden using planet-friendly features is followed by original and inspirational 'greenprints': detailed layouts and planting ideas for different types of eco garden, packed with information, including lists of plants and earth-friendly garden-making ideas.

All the basic information you need to begin eco gardening is found in the next section. This covers establishing a garden ecosystem, choosing tools,

▲ Blue *Salvia nemorosa* and yellow coreopsis are perennial flowers which will attract beneficial insects to your eco garden.

▼ Growing simple flowers such as annual cosmos (Cosmea) will boost your garden's biodiversity.

▲ Nectar-rich *Verbena bonariensis* flowers attract many beautiful garden insects, including butterflies such as this painted lady (*Vanessa cardui*).

compost (soil mix) and containers, how to sow seeds and feed plants, non-chemical ways of beating pests, tackling slugs, and using and controlling weeds.

Practical information and illustrated step-by-step instructions show you how to care for your soil and make great garden compost. Advice is given on improving and cultivating soil, choosing and using mulches, composting in bins (and in wormeries) and making soil-enriching leaf mould.

Using the two most renewable resources in your garden – sunlight and rainwater – is an effective way of helping reduce your garden's carbon footprint. Learn how to use sunny walls, greenhouses and polytunnels to capture pollution-free sunshine, together with how green manures (cover crops) use sunlight to improve your soil. Harvesting, storing and using rainwater are also covered in this section, which is richly illustrated and filled with practical advice.

Food gardening is at the heart of a successful eco garden. Discover why home-grown fruit and vegetables are the most planet-friendly foods you can eat, and what 'food miles' are. Instructive plans show how to transform an ordinary back garden into an abundant food-producing plot over a five-year period. There is also hands-on advice about growing vegetables and fruits (including in containers), and maximizing your vertical food-growing space.

The role of garden biodiversity and the vital part it plays in sustaining a healthy eco garden is clearly explained. There are useful tips and techniques for attracting a wide range of wildlife to your garden, some of which help in controlling plant pests. Building a pond, encouraging a 'wild lawn' and making an insect hotel are shown in clear step-by-step sequences.

Sustainable landscaping is defined alongside factors to consider when choosing landscaping materials, together with advice on more eco-friendly options and potential sources. There is information too on how to make water-absorbing paths, how to plant a living roof, and how to choose fences and screens.

A directory of eco-friendly plants suitable for the eco garden, from fast-growing, insect-attracting annuals to long-lived trees and shrubs offering food and shelter for garden birds, is fully illustrated with photographs and symbols highlighting bee- and insect-friendly plants. A comprehensive calendar of care gives key seasonal jobs in the eco garden.

This book's ambition is to encourage you do that extra bit for the environment, by inspiring you to garden in a more thoughtful, earth-friendly way. It would be easy to think that individual actions cannot make much impact, but there are tens of millions of gardeners across the globe. Working together, in our own diverse, beautiful and abundant gardens, yards and allotments, we can make a positive and rewarding difference, at the same time as deriving endless pleasure.

▲ Attracting beneficial insects is key to successful eco gardening. These old bamboo canes are being used by solitary bees as nesting chambers.

▼ Eco gardening offers simple solutions to common problems. These pretty willow-twig path edgings stop pigeons from walking on to the beds and eating precious crops.

Gardening and the environment

Everything we do in our gardens is an interaction with nature and the wider living world. We usually think of gardening as an unquestionably 'green' activity, and although it has many positive environmental benefits, we must not overlook its sometimes negative effects. Eco gardening is about creating ecologically sustainable gardens that bring positive benefits to the world around us.

▲ Home-grown food is ultra-local, and also free of chemical residues.

▼ The collective impact of how we go about our gardening can have repercussions for the natural world beyond our own garden gates.

Environmental stewardship

Gardeners have a closer relationship with nature than anyone. Farmers may cultivate a larger surface area of the Earth, but the gardener's bond with the soil, with plants, birds, animals and myriad other life forms, is a much more intimate and constantly changing one. In contrast with the vast, soulless monocultures that typify modern farming, each of our patches of ground is unique, with its own distinct character, often echoing our own aspirations and personalities.

In making and caring for a garden we are privileged to become custodians of that piece of land. What we grow, how we grow it and whatever else we do in the garden has knock-on effects – good and bad – on other living things. These effects might be felt in our own or our neighbours' gardens, across neighbourhoods, regions or countries, or throughout the wider world.

Eco gardening abides by and utilizes ecological principles in the way we make gardens and grow plants. It is the most globally accessible, enjoyable and personally rewarding form of environmental stewardship in which each and every one of us can play an ongoing and active part.

Our changing planet

Wondrous satellite imagery shows us how our species is quite literally changing the face of the planet: urbanization, rainforest clearance, desertification, intensive farming, disappearing lakes and rivers, massive pollution from oil spills and many other environmental changes are clearly visible from space. Technology also shows how global warming, driven by the burning of the fossil fuels, coal, oil and natural gas, is accelerating the speed of man-made climate change. All these human-driven activities are unsettling the delicate balance of life on Earth, resulting in profound, planet-wide changes to natural habitats and ecosystems, which are leading to loss of biodiversity and quickening rates of extinction.

Looking closer

Satellite images of our towns and cities also show us something else: a diverse interlinked network of home gardens, yards and allotments. If they could show us more than just a static snapshot, if they could highlight life itself, we would see all kinds of wild creatures, large and small, crisscrossing our gardens as they go about their business.

If we could see energy use in our gardens and the pollution it generates, we could identify 'hot spots' where fossil fuels are used to run powered garden equipment or heat greenhouses. The carbon dioxide and other invisible atmospheric pollutants released would also be clear. We would be able to see those gardens with large, manicured lawns that consume huge amounts of energy and finite resources in their upkeep.

We would also see where garden pesticides (insecticides, fungicides and weedkillers) were entering our environment – either as spray drifting on the breeze, or washing down into the drains and into our watercourses. We would see birds and animals eating caterpillars or slugs killed by garden chemicals which then enter the garden

▶ A greenhouse harvests free solar energy from the sun, but heating one (unless you use 'green' electricity from a renewable source) requires energy which causes pollution through the burning of finite fossil fuels.

▲ Composting worms are among the eco gardener's most valuable allies. They convert most garden and kitchen, and some household, waste into nutrient-rich garden compost.

▼ Some petrol-powered lawn mowers produce more air pollution during an hour's use than a brand new car does in a whole year. The carbon dioxide they emit contributes to global warming.

food chain. We might even see pesticide residues coating the vegetables and fruits growing in many gardens, and watch those same crops being harvested and prepared for a family meal.

Going green

But in that interlocking patchwork of growing space, we would see something else. Among the squares and rectangles of warning red – highlighting those gardens with high energy inputs, pollution and regular use of garden pesticides – would be many

▼ Wildflowers such as ox-eye daisy (*Leucanthemum vulgare*) can replace resource-hungry lawns.

others in welcome shades of green. These green-tinged gardens are buzzing with life. A wildlife pond is at the heart of each one. Part or all of the plot is devoted to the growing of fresh, residue-free and ultra-local food. Crops intermingle with self-seeded, beneficial insect-attracting flowers.

Lean-to greenhouses burst with crops grown using only free and renewable solar energy. Compost bins and worms work hard to keep anything that rots from landfill, transforming it instead into soil-enriching garden compost. Roofs harvest renewable rainwater that is stored in large, recycled tanks, dramatically reducing the use of tap water. Bare soil is mulched to trap moisture, encouraging a healthy, worm-rich underground ecosystem that locks carbon away in the undisturbed soil.

Instead of manicured, resource-hungry lawns, paths cut by human-powered push mowers meander through long, insect-rich grasses and wildflowers. Plants have been grown locally, using climate-friendly peat-free compost (soil mix) in biodegradable pots. Garden beds and path edges are made of rot-proof and maintenance-free recycled plastic boards. Other landscaping materials are reclaimed, or obtained from sustainable, renewable and ethical sources.

Climate-friendly gardening

Gardeners are already noticing the effects of global climate change. Hotter summers, wetter and milder winters, droughts and more frequent flooding are among the increasingly unseasonal weather events we are learning to adapt to. Eco gardening is a practical and positive way of making a personal contribution to lessening the future impact of a changing climate.

Global warming

What happens to our world's climate affects every living being on Earth. There is overwhelming scientific agreement that a build-up of carbon dioxide and other greenhouse gases in the atmosphere is due to human activities, most of all the burning of fossil fuels, coal, oil and natural gas. This invisible pollution acts like an insulating blanket wrapped around the planet, trapping heat energy from the sun, resulting in global warming. It is this heating effect that is causing climate change and the disruption of weather patterns worldwide. Some effects of climate change are already apparent; one of the most familiar is the melting of polar ice and glaciers. Unless we reduce carbon emissions, global temperatures will continue rising, leading to potentially dangerous changes. Climate-related disasters tend to hit the world's poorest people the hardest, those whose own gardening activities are often crucial to their day-to-day survival.

Eco gardeners can do more than just adapt to climate change by growing different types of plants, and by changing how and when we do things. We can also make choices that do not add to the problem, or can even help slow its pace.

▲ Trees and shrubs absorb carbon dioxide from the air as they grow, incorporating it into their woody tissues. Undisturbed grassy meadows also store carbon in the soil.

Reducing energy use

Using powered garden equipment requires energy and creates pollution, especially when petroleum is burned. The most eco-friendly garden equipment is powered by renewable electricity from a 'green' supplier – or from simple human effort. Fertilizers and pesticides (insecticides, fungicides, weedkillers) use energy in their production, packaging and transport. Weedkillers generate more carbon emissions than any other garden pesticides.

Locking up carbon

One way to reduce the amount of atmospheric carbon is to lock up some of it in your garden soil and in the plants you grow. Adding organic matter to your soil leads to a build-up of dark humus, which can store carbon for long periods. All plants absorb carbon dioxide from the air, storing it in their tissues, but trees and shrubs can store large amounts for long periods; large, fast-growing trees are most effective at locking carbon away in the woody parts of their roots, trunks and branches. Look after your trees: if they die, their carbon is released as they decay or when they are burnt.

▼ Melting polar ice is a visible symptom of accelerating global warming. Many everyday gardening activities routinely release greenhouse gases such as carbon dioxide.

▼ Many man-made garden chemicals are derived from crude oil and involve long, energy-intensive manufacturing processes which add carbon dioxide to our atmosphere. Synthetic weedkillers (chemicals which kill weeds) have an especially large carbon footprint.

▲ Much of our food now travels great distances, often by air, burning large amounts of fossil fuel energy. Home-grown, low-input food is climate-friendly.

▼ Garden and other biodegradable waste which is buried in landfill sites produces methane, a powerful greenhouse gas that is helping to increase global warming.

Growing food

The food you grow in your eco garden or allotment requires few energy inputs. Apart from constructing the garden, harvesting might be the most energy-intensive job you do. Food from your garden does not need synthetic, oil-derived fertilizers and pesticides to grow, will not require packaging, refrigeration and processing, or transporting thousands of miles – it might travel just a short distance from plot to plate. In contrast, modern food production uses energy and resources that generate greenhouse gases.

Making garden compost

When organic waste materials are buried in landfill they rot in the oxygen-starved conditions, releasing methane, a heat-trapping greenhouse gas 20 times more powerful than carbon dioxide. Eco gardeners see garden, kitchen and general household waste differently – as a valuable resource. Compost bins and wormeries will transform it into rich, soil-building garden compost, which also adds carbon to the soil.

Rethinking lawns

Because they remain undisturbed, and because their fibrous roots add organic matter to the soil, lawns can store carbon. But maintaining them can be energy- and resource-intensive, which cancels out any benefits. Applying synthetic weedkillers and fertilizers, using a petrol lawn mower and watering with tap water are all energy-intensive and emit carbon. Using nitrogen fertilizer can release nitrous oxide, another powerful greenhouse gas.

Climate- and wildlife-friendly lawns are those where most of the grass is allowed to grow long and wildflowers are given the chance to flourish. A push mower, or an electric model powered by 'green' electricity, is used to maintain any mown paths. To maintain a traditional lawn in an eco-friendly way, avoid using energy-intensive tap water, use only organic lawn feeds, set a high cutting height on your mower and leave any clippings on the lawn (they store carbon as they decay).

Consuming less

Gardening is now a globalized industry dependent on constantly encouraging gardeners to consume more and more mass-produced items, often regardless of whether they actually need them. Constantly creating new fads and trends is one way in which gardening consumption is maintained.

Even eco gardeners occasionally need to buy some everyday gardening essentials, such as peat-free compost (soil mix), pots, seeds and perhaps plants. But there is much we simply do not need. Most gardening products use resources and energy in their manufacture, which emits carbon pollution. They also create waste.

Asking ourselves if we really need some of these consumer products and avoiding non-essential ephemera is an important aspect of gardening with the health of our climate in mind.

▼ Being discerning at your garden centre can help reduce unnecessary consumption and reduce carbon emissions.

ECO GARDEN GREENPRINTS

The 'greenprints' in this chapter show attractive and creative ways of making a planet-friendly garden. 'Eco-fitting your garden' explains how to assess a garden's eco-friendliness, then shows what it might look like before and after an eco-fit. There are also detailed and original garden plans for making a city courtyard 'greener', the best way to grow food in an eco garden, ideas for a low rainfall garden or an intriguing 'rain garden'. The plans offer inspiration, information, practical advice and lists of suitable plants. Use and adapt the ideas here, either in whole or in part, to suit your own individual circumstances.

◄ Sweet peas (*Lathyrus odoratus*) are easy to grow, provide fragrant flowers for cutting over many months, and will attract pollinating insects such as bees to a food garden.

▲ Eco-friendly allotments buzz with life and can even include a pond.

▲ Thoughtful use of vertical space can transform a city courtyard garden.

▲ Careful plant selection can create a beautiful garden in dry climates.

Eco-fitting your garden

Eco-fitting your garden is all about making it more self-sustaining, less wasteful of valuable resources, more reliant on renewable sources of energy and friendlier to wildlife. Eco-fitting will turn a garden that was previously drab, uninteresting and lifeless into an outdoor space that is biologically diverse, beautiful and productive, and much more planet-friendly.

▲ Culinary herbs are attractive, easy to grow in a sunny position and will provide you with year-round pickings. Grow them near the house.

▼ In this decorative yet productive kitchen garden, crops and flowers are grown more informally and can be easily reached from the winding paths made of re-used paving stones.

What is garden eco-fitting?

Eco-fitting a garden is similar to retro-fitting a house: it is the updating of any existing elements and the addition of new ones that were not there when the garden was originally made. Before you set about eco-fitting, first spend some time noting down how environmentally friendly (or unfriendly) you think your garden might currently be. The basic tenets of eco-friendly gardening are:

- Recycle all garden waste through composting.
- Reduce garden energy use.
- Harness and use renewable sunlight energy.
- Harvest rainwater and use it wisely.
- Improve soil with garden compost and green waste.
- Create a thriving garden ecosystem by adding habitats and encouraging wildlife.
- Grow flowers to attract beneficial pest-controlling insects and boost biodiversity.
- Mulch to conserve soil moisture and stop weed seeds from germinating.
- Create areas for play and relaxation.
- Grow some of your own food.
- Use reclaimed, recycled and sustainable landscaping materials.
- Avoid the use of synthetic insecticides, fungicides and weedkillers.

▲ Increasing the number of insect-attracting flowers in your garden will boost the numbers of pollinators. This bumblebee is visiting a bloom of *Echinacea purpurea*.

You might already be implementing some of these eco-friendly practices, but much of the enjoyment of eco gardening is in deciding where you might add more. You do not have to carry out an eco-fit all at once – adding a lean-to greenhouse is a major undertaking, but simply growing more flowers to attract beneficial insects gives immediate rewards.

▼ Sunlight is free, renewable on a daily basis and causes no pollution. A lean-to greenhouse like this will instantly expand your gardening possibilities.

BEFORE AND AFTER ECO-FITTING A GARDEN

These illustrations show how any average back garden can be transformed into an eco garden by incorporating elements that help to make it more ecologically sustainable. The garden is 5m (16ft) wide and 10m (33ft) long. In summer the house wall receives full sun for most of the day. Adding the lean-to greenhouse creates a whole new multi-purpose space which can be used year-round in all weathers.

BEFORE

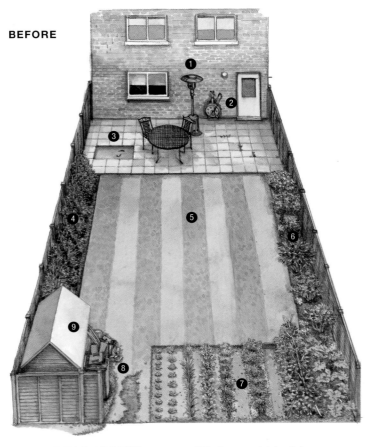

AFTER

BEFORE ECO-FITTING

1 A gas-powered patio heater releases the polluting greenhouse gas carbon dioxide.

2 Energy-intensive mains tap water is used for watering and for running a lawn sprinkler.

3 Goldfish dominate the small pond at the expense of wildlife.

4 An overgrown x *Cupressocyparis leylandii* hedge has been cut down, leaving ugly stumps. Its roots have starved the soil.

5 Lawn mowing uses fossil fuel, creating air and noise pollution, and more work.

6 Dry and bare border soil, routinely sprayed with weedkiller, has little appeal for wildlife. Double nectarless flowers attract few insects.

7 In the vegetable plot, crops grow in poor, dry soil. Synthetic fertilizers encourage sappy, pest- and disease-prone growth; plants are sprayed regularly with pesticides and slug pellets are used.

8 Valuable garden and kitchen waste is binned and collected for municipal composting.

9 Rainwater runs off the shed roof.

AFTER ECO-FITTING

1 A lean-to greenhouse warms up as it absorbs sunlight energy, creating a space in which to grow edible and ornamental plants; some slabs are removed to create soil beds. Heating is not used during winter, when only frost-hardy food crops are grown.

2 Herbs are grown near the house and are convenient to harvest.

3 Rainwater from the greenhouse roof is stored in linked water butts.

4 The lawn is replaced by a decorative kitchen garden. Vegetables, fruits and herbs intermingle with pollen- and nectar-rich flowers, which attract beneficial pollinating and pest-eating insects. The paths are made of reclaimed natural stone. Columnar fruits utilize vertical growing space.

5 An insect hotel attracts solitary bees and other useful insects.

6 Espalier apples and pears and currant cordons are now trained on the fence. The hedge has been removed and the soil improved.

7 Slug-eating frogs breed in a fish-free wildlife pond.

8 Log piles create a wildlife habitat.

9 A living willow 'fedge' encloses a grass play area, edged by uncut grass and wildflowers. A human-powered push mower is used.

10 Wood chips are used as a mulch between the stepping stones; weedkiller is not used.

11 Rainwater fills a recycled plastic water butt.

12 All garden and kitchen waste is composted in recycled wooden bins, then returned to the garden to improve the soil.

13 The rainwater-harvesting shed is planted with a pretty living roof, and a solar panel charges a battery to operate the shed light.

City courtyard garden

Although it might seem an unlikely setting for an attractive yet food-producing garden, this enclosed city courtyard, with its high walls, has been designed as an enchanting and eco-friendly outdoor space. Reclaimed and sustainable materials have been used, while the planting makes effective use of the light that is available, and of the plentiful vertical growing space.

About this garden

Measuring 8m (26ft) wide by 6m (20ft) deep, this courtyard at the rear of a city dwelling is surrounded by a brick wall 3m (10ft) high, painted to reflect light back into the garden. The area is not overhung by trees and during the summer months the wall facing the house receives full sun for most of the day. The garden stays warm well into the evening.

The more productive areas of the garden are concentrated where maximum light falls, and attractive shade-loving, mostly ornamental plants are used in the beds nearer the house. In mid-winter no direct sunlight falls on the garden.

Rainwater is harvested from a downpipe and stored in slim water butts fixed to the house wall (not shown). Kitchen waste is composted in a recycled plastic wormery, while garden waste is composted in a pair of wooden 'beehive' compost bins standing next to the house.

Using vertical growing space

Both permanent and short-term plantings maximize productivity of the wall space. Vertical surfaces, especially those receiving full sun, are an important growing area in small and enclosed gardens like this. The apple U-cordons were

▲ The decorative focus of this courtyard is a globe containing a fountain.

obtained as ready-trained plants; the cherry fan and pear espalier have been trained from young trees. They will be allowed to reach just below wall height, but will then be pruned to keep them within bounds. Because of the eventual height of the plants, any pruning or training, or picking out-of-reach fruit, is done from a ladder or from the paths using a long-handled fruit picker.

▼ In town and city gardens where planting in soil isn't an option, food crops can be grown in large, deep containers of peat-free compost (soil mix).

▼ This water butt is attractive yet functional and complements the pots.

PLANTS FOR SHADE
Bugle (*Ajuga reptans* 'Burgundy Glow')
Brunnera macrophylla 'Jack Frost'
Lily of the valley (*Convallaria majalis*)
Dicentra 'Pearl Drops'
Spurge (*Euphorbia amygdaloides* var. *robbiae*)
Winter hellebore (*Helleborus orientalis*)
Hosta 'Halcyon'
Greater periwinkle (*Vinca major* 'Variegata')

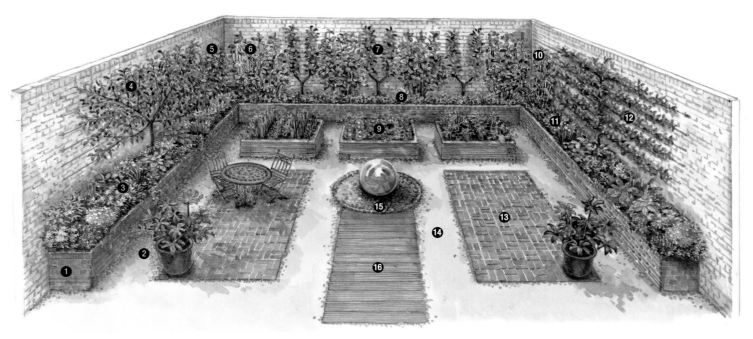

KEY ELEMENTS OF A CITY COURTYARD GARDEN

1 Beds 60cm (24in) deep and 50cm (20in) wide, made from reclaimed bricks, line the perimeter of the garden. They have drainage holes at their base, and are filled with a mixture of locally sourced green waste compost and good-quality topsoil.

2 Evergreen *Fatsia japonica* gives year-round interest.

3 Various shade-loving perennial plants and bulbs occupy the beds where little direct sunlight falls.

4 A Morello cherry trained as a fan; the branches are attached to taut horizontal wires spaced 30cm (12in) apart. Morello cherries are ideal for shaded walls.

5 Redcurrants are grown as single-stemmed vertical cordons and are attached to the vertical support wires.

6 Sun-loving climbing runner and French (green) beans, with white, red and purple flowers (and with pods in various colours) are grown between the apple U-cordons, up sticks tied to horizontal wires. Sweet peas for cutting mingle among the beans and attract bees which will pollinate their flowers.

7 Apple U-cordons, on dwarfing rootstocks, provide blossom in spring and fresh fruits in autumn; their leafless frameworks form an eye-catching structural element in winter, when their outline contrasts with the pale walls.

8 Summer-fruiting strawberries hang over the edges of the beds, making them easy to see and harvest as they ripen.

9 Three raised beds 1m (3ft) wide by 1.7m (5½ft) long and 45cm (18in) tall, made with untreated oak 'sleepers', occupy the sunniest part of the garden. Each bed is filled with a green waste compost/topsoil mixture and planted with cut-and-come-again baby-leaf salads, various small-growing 'baby' vegetables, and bush varieties of tomatoes and French beans. Pot marigold (*Calendula officinalis*) and poached egg plant (*Limnanthes douglasii*) are mixed among the crops to attract beneficial insects such as hoverflies, whose larvae feed on aphids, a sap-sucking pest.

10 Raspberry canes are tied to horizontal wires.

11 The sunniest ends of the perimeter beds are planted with perennial vegetables.

12 An espalier pear with five tiers is trained on horizontal wires spaced 45cm (18in) apart.

13 Reclaimed bricks create attractive all-weather areas for sitting and outdoor entertaining.

14 Recycled loose ceramic chippings help to reflect light back to the plants. They also allow water to soak in during rainstorms, relieving pressure on urban drainage systems.

15 An eco-friendly water feature creates a central focus; a water jet sprays inside a perspex globe, creating sound and movement, but no water is lost through evaporation. The pump is powered by a solar panel on the roof. The globe sits in a circle of recycled crushed brick.

16 A path of reclaimed timber, sourced from a local salvage yard, leads from the house doors.

▲ Raised beds made from untreated oak sleepers (railroad ties).

▼ Coppiced poles can be used to support edible climbers such as these runner beans.

PERENNIAL VEGETABLES

Tree onion (*Allium cepa* [Proliferum Group])
Garlic chives (*Allium tuberosum*)
Perpetual spinach (*Beta vulgaris* subsp. *cicla*)
Good King Henry (*Chenopodium bonus-henricus*)
Lemon balm (*Melissa officinalis*)
French sorrel (*Rumex scutatus*)

Intensive food garden

Vegetables, fruits and herbs you grow yourself, which can be harvested only a few steps away from your back door, are the least-travelled, most nutritious and planet-friendly foods you will ever eat. This large back garden is dedicated to producing as much food as possible, in every season. No synthetic garden chemicals are used, ensuring that all produce is free of pesticide residues.

▲ The eye-catching pods of mangetout pea 'Golden Sweet' are eaten whole.

▼ Timber is less flexible than recycled plastic boards for making raised growing beds, and will eventually need replacing when the wood rots.

About this garden

Every available space in this 8m (26ft) wide by 15m (50ft) long rear garden has been considered with eco-friendly food production in mind, but this has not precluded an unusual and pleasing overall design, breaking with the tradition of growing vegetables in straight rows. A geodesic dome greenhouse is the central feature around which the rest of the garden flows. Four main no-dig soil beds, edged with flexible recycled plastic boards, enclose the greenhouse, which is itself a highly productive year-round growing space.

Birds are a problem here because they eat the ripe soft fruits, so the farthest end of the garden has been converted into a bird-excluding fruit cage.

Bringing in beneficial insects

Pest control relies both on diligence in looking out for the early signs of pest attack, such as clusters of butterfly eggs, and on the efforts of beneficial insects; hoverflies, ladybirds and numerous other less obvious insects all eat or parasitize plant pests. To attract them into this garden, a band of pollen- and nectar-rich plants encircle the dome

ROTATING CROPS

Growing annual vegetable crops in a different part of the garden each year prevents a build-up of soil pests and diseases, and is called 'crop rotation'. In this garden, vegetables are grown in four outdoor beds and in the dome greenhouse. Crops are divided into groups, and then a different group is grown in each bed (or part of a bed under cover) every year. In this garden's outdoor beds, no crop group occupies a bed more than once every four years. The rotation groups used here are:

1 Brassicas (cabbage family): cabbage, kohlrabi, radish and relatives.
2 Legumes (pea and bean family): broad (fava) and green beans, peas and relatives.
3 Potato family: aubergines (eggplants), peppers (bell peppers) and tomatoes. All members of this family (except potatoes themselves) are grown in the dome greenhouse.
4 Root crops: beetroot (beets), carrots, parsnips; onion family: garlic, leeks, onions; and miscellaneous crops: courgettes (zucchini), sweetcorn (corn).

greenhouse, drawing beneficial and often beautiful insects to the heart of the garden. Some will enter the greenhouse through its vents, helping to control pests under cover.

▼ Gooseberries can be grown as bushes or cordons, or as fan-shaped bushes trained against a wall or fence.

▲ These just-hatched large cabbage white butterfly (*Pieris brassicae*) caterpillars can easily be controlled by squashing them between finger and thumb before they do much damage.

▲ The red admiral butterfly (*Vanessa atalanta*) is a frequent summer visitor to the purple, nectar-rich flowerheads of tall verbena (*Verbena bonariensis*).

KEY ELEMENTS OF AN INTENSIVE FOOD GARDEN

1 Garden shed with a living roof.

2 Rainwater is diverted to a wall-mounted butt.

3 Frost-tender annual crops are raised in a 2 x 3m (7 x 10ft) lean-to greenhouse.

4 Espalier apples, pears and fan-trained plums grow against the boundary fence.

5 'Stepover' apples edge the beds.

6 Legume (pea and bean family) crops.

7 Herb bed easily reachable from the paths.

8 Reclaimed bricks form the main 40cm (16in) wide all-weather paths; between beds the 30cm (12in) wide paths are made of wood chips.

9 Comfrey for making into liquid feed.

10 Made from old glazing units, this solar frame is used for early salad crops and melons.

11 Clumps of rhubarb are forced for early pickings.

12 The four main 1m (3ft)-wide curving vegetable beds are formed out of recycled plastic boards. Soil cultivation is minimal and all work is done from the paths. Crops are rotated between beds (see panel). This bed contains root crops, onion family and miscellaneous crops.

13 *Verbena bonariensis* attracts butterflies and bees.

14 Insect-attracting flowers encircling the greenhouse include astrantia, bedding dahlias, lungwort (*Pulmonaria*), ox-eye daisy (*Leucanthemum*) and pot marigold (*Calendula*).

15 The dome greenhouse, which is 4m (13ft) in diameter and 3m (10ft) tall, has a central bed 2m (7ft) in diameter and another bed 50cm (20in) wide on the perimeter, with a path between them. Tall cordon tomatoes and early climbing beans are grown in the centre. Crops are rotated (see panel).

16 Brassica (cabbage family) crops.

▲ In this two-bay compost bin, one side is gradually filled with layers of fresh material (left), while rotted-down mature garden compost is harvested from the other (right).

17 Early and maincrop blight-resistant potatoes.

18 Wildlife pond attracts slug-eating frogs and toads.

19 A cultivated blackberry is trained on the fence.

20 Acid-loving blueberries grow in a raised bed filled with peat-free ericaceous compost (soil mix).

21 Blackcurrants.

22 A large fruit cage protects fruit from birds. The garden fence forms three sides of the enclosed area, with netting over the top and front. The door is tight-fitting.

23 Two fan-trained Morello cherries flourishing in shade; the beds are edged with strawberries.

24 Red and white currants and gooseberries, grown as vertical cordons to maximize cropping space.

25 Summer- and autumn-fruiting raspberries grown on wires.

26 Wooden compost bins 1m (3ft) square, made from pallet timber, recycle garden waste.

27 Oyster mushroom logs part buried in the ground.

Eco allotment

Allotments are plots of rented land used for growing your own food. They vary in size, but an average-sized rectangular-shaped plot covers about 250 square metres (300 square yards). This eco-friendly plot is used to grow fresh, chemical-free organic food, and works closely with nature; a biodiverse living 'perennimeter' of perennial and annual flowers attracts copious garden allies.

▲ Tall sunflowers are ideal for a perennimeter. They provide nectar and pollen while their seedheads provide food for birds.

▼ The shed on this eco-aware allotment has a living sedum roof. Rainwater is harvested and stored in butts.

What is a perennimeter?

Derived from a combination of the two words perennial and perimeter, this is simply a wide, continuous bed on the outer edge (perimeter) of a plot. It is planted with annual, perennial and woody plants, including some crops, but also incorporates a range of wildlife habitats, including insect hotels, log piles and mulch.

Self-seeding annual flowers and annual vegetables such as lettuce spread randomly throughout the perennimeter. Perennial vegetables such as globe artichokes and insect-attracting herbs such as fennel are also grown. Tall sunflowers with large flowerheads provide pollen and nectar for bees and seeds for birds.

About this allotment

A series of highly productive no-dig raised beds are enclosed within a wildlife-rich perennimeter planted with insect-attracting flowers, fruit trees and bushes, offering various wildlife habitats. At the core of this plot, which is 10m (33ft) wide and 25m (82ft) long, is a wildlife pond – an aquatic ecosystem teeming with life.

GOOD PERENNIMETER PLANTS

Annuals and biennials (self-seeders):
Borage (*Borago officinalis*)
Pot marigold (*Calendula officinalis*)
California poppy (*Eschscholzia californica*)
Sunflower (*Helianthus annuus*)
Poached egg flower (*Limnanthes douglasii*)
Honesty (*Lunaria annua*)
Forget-me-not (*Myosotis sylvatica*)

Perennials:
Anise hyssop (*Agastache foeniculum*)
Chives (*Allium schoenoprasum*)
Ornamental thistle (*Cirsium rivulare* 'Atropurpureum')
Globe artichoke (*Cynara cardunculus*)
Bronze fennel (*Foeniculum vulgare* 'Purpureum')
Ox-eye daisy (*Leucanthemum vulgare*)
Catmint (*Nepeta racemosa* 'Walker's Low')
Verbena bonariensis

Shrubs:
Barberry (*Berberis darwinii*)
Bluebeard (*Caryopteris* x *clandonensis*)
Fuchsia magellanica
Hebe 'Great Orme'
Rock rose (*Helianthemum* 'Ben Ledi')
St John's wort (*Hypericum olympicum*)
Lavender (*Lavandula angustifolia*)
Russian sage (*Perovskia atriplicifolia*)

Apart from overwintering crops, many allotments are cleared after the main growing season, dug over and left bare in winter. This annual cycle of disturbance offers few opportunities for wildlife to take up residence. A perennimeter changes that by enclosing the food growing area within a permanent, undisturbed strip that is rich in garden-friendly biodiversity. Try not to be over-zealous in keeping a perennimeter too tidy; garden wildlife lives among decaying leaves, and birds feed on old seedheads.

KEY ELEMENTS OF AN ECO ALLOTMENT

1 Red and white currants and gooseberries grown as space-saving vertical cordons are spaced 1–1.5m (3–5ft) apart. Raspberry canes grow in groups around stakes.

2 Asparagus bed.

3 Pest-eating hunting spiders and ground beetles run through dry mulch on the perennimeter.

4 A polytunnel measuring 3 x 4.5m (10 x 15ft) provides a space for raising plants and extends the growing season, enabling year-round harvests. Adhesive guttering diverts rainwater into recycled storage tanks.

5 Rhubarb grown in its own bed.

6 Annual cut flowers grown from seed.

7 Perennial herbs such as lovage, mint and sage.

8 Each year some beds are sown with soil-building green manures (cover crops) to improve their fertility.

9 Space-saving columnar fruit trees (apples, pears, plums, cherries) on dwarfing rootstocks spaced 2m (7ft) apart.

10 An insect hotel provides crop-pollinating solitary bees with somewhere to make their nests.

11 Cardboard keeps cleared ground moist and weed-free until sowing or planting time.

12 Flowering perennimeter plants, plus any self-seeded annuals flowering in among the cropping beds themselves, attract beneficial insects which keep plant pests in check.

13 Annual crops are grown in family groups and rotated each year. There are sufficient beds here for a 10–20 year rotation.

14 Pollen- and nectar-rich sunflowers.

15 Patch of comfrey 'Bocking 14' used for mulching, composting, and liquid feeds.

16 Carrots in a bed surrounded by insect mesh are protected from carrot root fly attack.

17 Cold frame made from reclaimed double glazing units, used for hardening off.

18 Rainwater harvested from the shed roof is stored in linked recycled water butts.

19 Three-bay composter made from wooden pallets recycles all garden waste, including soft and sappy prunings.

20 Potting shed for raising plants and storing tools, and for shelter.

21 Temporary growing space created by laying a reclaimed glazing unit against the shed.

22 Home-made liquid feeds.

▲ Polytunnels are an all-weather, season-extending working space, and also somewhere to grow food crops such as winter salads.

23 Edible screen of summer-fruiting raspberries.

24 Pumpkins growing on a heap of rotting manure.

25 No-dig potatoes growing through a thick mulch, which do not need to be earthed up.

26 The plot-enclosing perennimeter.

27 Raised beds 1m (3ft) wide, 3m (10ft) long and 15cm (6in) deep, made with recycled plastic boards. Some are covered with insect mesh to deter pests. The beds are easily reached from the paths and soil is not trodden on or compacted.

28 Central path 90cm (36in) wide, with 50cm (20in) wide paths between beds, covered with hard-wearing and long-lasting wood chips.

▲ A small pond at the heart of an allotment will attract different kinds of wildlife. Some, such as frogs and toads, help control slugs.

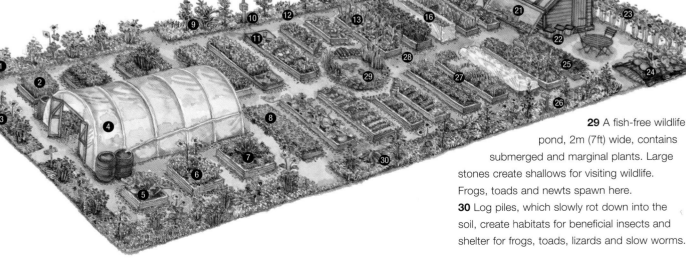

29 A fish-free wildlife pond, 2m (7ft) wide, contains submerged and marginal plants. Large stones create shallows for visiting wildlife. Frogs, toads and newts spawn here.

30 Log piles, which slowly rot down into the soil, create habitats for beneficial insects and shelter for frogs, toads, lizards and slow worms.

Dry garden

Creating a garden in a dry climate, where rainfall is low or restricted to only a short period each year, is challenging. Choosing plants that will thrive in dry conditions without additional watering is the key to achieving a beautiful, low-input, drought-proof garden. In this sun-baked terraced garden, eco-friendly reclaimed slate is used for the drystone walls.

About this garden
Measuring 12m (40ft) wide by 5m (16ft) deep, this front garden formed out of a sloping, rocky bank is made of three terraces, each 1.5–2m (5–7ft) wide. The retaining walls, 60cm (2ft) high, are made of local reclaimed and weathered slate from old demolished outbuildings, using traditional wall-building techniques. No mortar is used, allowing cracks and crevices in which plants can take root, as well as a habitat for lizards and other wildlife.

The area outside the door is paved with slate, and slate chippings are used as infill in any gaps. A pathway with steps made from reclaimed sea-washed pier timbers leads from the house, down through the garden, to the pavement below. Plants grow in the flat of the terraces, in cracks in the walls, next to rock outcrops, as path edging and in pots near the house. The plants in pots are watered, but none of the plants in the terraces receive any water other than during their first establishment phase.

Using existing features
The outcrops of bedrock are incorporated into the design. Where necessary, the walls are built over and around the bedrock, creating a striking contrast with the formality of the slate walls. Each terrace is filled with a mixture of sieved rock fragments and

the thin, poor soil removed during the construction of the garden, which guarantees good drainage all year round. The mixture is not improved with organic matter or fertilizer, as plants suitable for a dry garden are more resilient when grown in naturally infertile soil. A mulch of recycled slate chippings 5cm (2in) deep is spread over the terraces, preventing weeds from growing and providing an attractive foil to the plants. The middle section of the path is finished with a finer grade of chippings.

In the lower left-hand corner of the garden, a 'dry pond' has been sculpted into the soil and is lined with fine chippings, into which California poppy (*Eschscholzia californica*) happily self-seeds.

Planting in a dry garden
The most critical period for new plants in a dry garden is just after planting. They must root deeply and quickly to draw on moisture below the surface. To aid their establishment, make a 'watering basin' around the plant by mounding the soil up, away from the base of the plant, into a water-retaining lip at least 30cm (12in) across and 5cm (2in) deep, bigger for larger plants. The basin is filled with water immediately after planting, which then soaks down around the roots.

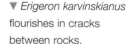

▲ These drought-tolerant cacti and succulents are grown in wooden planters filled with gritty, free-draining compost (soil mix).

▼ *Erigeron karvinskianus* flourishes in cracks between rocks.

▼ Bee-friendly French lavender (*Lavandula stoechas*) thrives in full sun.

▼ *Eschscholzia californica* will self-seed throughout a dry garden.

GOOD PLANTS FOR A DRY GARDEN

A = Annual
EP = Evergreen perennial
HP = Herbaceous perennial
S = Shrub
B = Bulb

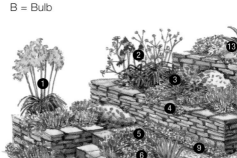

1 *Stipa gigantea* (EP)

2 *Kniphofia rooperi* (EP)

3 *Eryngium giganteum* (HP)

4 *Armeria maritima* (EP)

5 *Rosmarinus officinalis* (S)

6 *Eryngium bourgatii* (HP)

7 *Nepeta* 'Six Hills Giant' (EP)

8 *Euphorbia myrsinites* (EP)

9 Mixed thymes (S)

10 *Allium hollandicum* 'Purple Sensation' (B)

11 *Lavandula* 'Munstead' (S)

12 *Santolina chamaecyparissus* var. *nana* (S)

13 *Caryopteris* x *clandonensis* (S)

14 *Cistus* x *purpureus* (S)

15 *Euphorbia characias* subsp. *wulfenii* (EP)

16 *Agave americana* 'Variegata' (EP)

17 *Perovskia* 'Blue Spire' (S)

18 *Verbena bonariensis* (HP)

19 *Agapanthus campanulatus* (EP)

20 *Genista aetnensis* (S)

21 *Salvia officinalis* 'Purpurascens' (S)

22 *Yucca filamentosa* (S)

23 *Centranthus ruber* (HP)

24 *Yucca filamentosa* 'Bright Edge' (S)

25 *Sedum acre* (EP)

26 *Eschscholzia californica* (A)

27 *Stachys byzantina* (EP)

28 *Festuca glauca* (EP)

29 *Caryopteris* x *clandonensis* 'Worcester Gold' (S)

30 *Erigeron karvinskianus* (EP)

HOW PLANTS REDUCE WATER LOSS

Plants native to dry climates have evolved different ways of minimizing water loss through transpiration (the loss of water from the leaves). All these plants, which are suitable for a dry garden, use different techniques to survive in tough conditions.

◄ The silver-grey leaves of *Brachyglottis* are coated on their undersides in a thick down, which slows water loss.

◄ *Cytisus* (broom) has only small, insignificant leaves which it sheds in times of stess such as a drought, when it relies instead on its wiry green stems to carry out photosynthesis.

◄ The leaves of this variegated *Elaeagnus* are covered in silvery scales, especially on their undersides, which stop moisture loss through the breathing pores (stomata).

◄ This hebe has thick, leathery leaves which resist drying out. Hebes are evergreen shrubs bearing summer flowers. Some 'whipcord' species have scale-like leaves.

◄ Fleshy-leaved *Sedum* (stonecrop) stores water in its leaves, allowing it to survive long periods of intense drought. It thrives on the tops of stone walls.

Rain garden

There are good practical uses for harvested rainwater in a garden, but it can work creatively as well. Rainwater can easily be redirected so that it flows into and through the garden, rather than being lost down a drain. In this way it creates different features that can be attractively planted and become beneficial to wildlife. In this 'rain garden', water links together the various elements.

▲ Siberian iris (*Iris sibirica*) grows well in rich and constantly damp soil.

About this garden

Sloping gently away from the house, this back garden, which is 7m (23ft) wide by 15m (50ft) long, utilizes the rainwater captured by the house roof. The water travels via a modified downpipe, carrying rainwater from the house roof into a raised rainwater or stormwater planter, which overflows into a wildlife pond. Next, the water flows along a swale to the main rain-garden area. Swales are elongated, usually curving shallow depressions in the ground, which carry and hold rainwater while it soaks into the earth. Here the swale carries water to the main planted area, which is a shallow, tear-shaped depression. The swale's slightly raised sides are left unmown and contain wildflowers. These grassy, wildlife-friendly areas extend around an area of close-mown lawn.

Environmental benefits

Rain gardens not only use water creatively, but bring environmental benefits. By diverting rainwater away from the drainage network, and allowing it to soak into the ground, as it would do naturally if the ground were not covered by impermeable hard surfaces (roads, buildings or paved garden areas), rain gardens can help to alleviate the risk of flooding in towns and cities.

▼ Plants growing on the margin of a wildlife pond, fed by a rainwater planter, create valuable habitats.

RAIN-GARDEN PLANTS

Coneflower (*Echinacea purpurea*)
Hemp agrimony (*Eupatorium cannabinum*)
Meadowsweet (*Filipendula ulmaria*)
Yellow flag iris (*Iris pseudacorus*)
Loosestrife (*Lythrum salicaria*)
Giant cowslip (*Primula florindae*)
Ornamental rhubarb (*Rheum palmatum* 'Atropurpureum')
Black-eyed Susan (*Rudbeckia fulgida*)

▲ Coneflower (*Echinacea purpurea*) is a good choice for the main planting area in a rain garden.

▼ Primrose (*Primula vulgaris*) thrives in the long grass beside a swale, and will soon spread by self-seeding.

KEY ELEMENTS OF A RAIN GARDEN

1 Rainwater from the roof feeds into a water-holding planter (see panel 'Rainwater or stormwater planters'). The plants grown here can be perennials or small shrubs that prefer moist soil.

2 When the rainwater planter is full following a heavy storm, excess water overflows, via a spout, into a semi-circular wildlife pond.

3 In the pond, large stones are used around the margin to create shallow areas where wildlife can safely gain access to the pond to drink, bathe and breed. Marginal plants, such as dwarf reedmace (*Typha minima*), give wildlife cover.

4 Any excess water from the pond overflows into the swale, which is planted with moisture-loving plants. Cuckoo flower (*Cardamine pratensis*), marsh marigold (*Caltha palustris*), ragged robin (*Lychnis flos-cuculi*), snake's head fritillary (*Fritillaria meleagris*) and water avens (*Geum rivale*) are all suitable.

5 From the swale, water feeds into the main rain-garden planting area, which is approximately 3m (10ft) across and contains moisture-loving plants (see panel on previous page). Soil excavated from the depression is mounded up around its edge to form a lip, which retains water in a temporary pool; the lower stems of plants are submerged in the rainwater for a short time after a storm, but it does not harm them, and eventually soaks away into the ground. The cross-section shows how this part of the rain garden works.

6 The grass along the swales and around the planting area is left unmown and contains wildflowers such as bird's foot trefoil (*Lotus corniculatus*), red campion (*Silene dioica*) and primrose (*Primula vulgaris*). The grass is cut with a scythe in late summer, after the wildflowers fade.

RAINWATER OR STORMWATER PLANTERS

These above-ground structures contain soil and plants, and intercept roof water from a downpipe outlet carrying water from the roof. They are usually at least 45cm (18in) deep, made out of brick or similar materials, and are built against a waterproofed building wall, or constructed separately, slightly away from it. This ensures that moisture does not cross into the walls and bridge any damp-proof membrane.

They are filled with a coarse drainage layer such as crushed brick, followed by a layer of soil or compost (soil mix) at least 15cm (6in) deep, in which the plants grow. When it rains, any water flowing out of the downpipe hits several large stones, reducing its force. Once the planter is full, any overflow can be directed into a pond, bog garden or swale. Following rain, water gradually soaks away into the underlying soil. Some planters are sealed and excess water is directed into the existing drainage network.

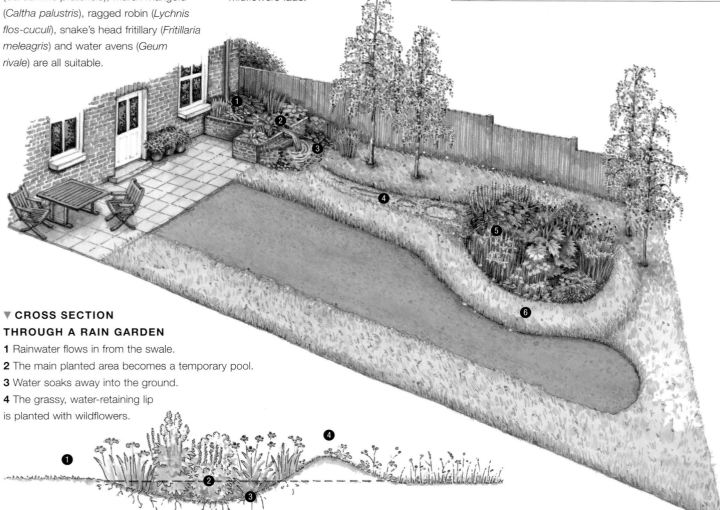

▼ CROSS SECTION THROUGH A RAIN GARDEN

1 Rainwater flows in from the swale.

2 The main planted area becomes a temporary pool.

3 Water soaks away into the ground.

4 The grassy, water-retaining lip is planted with wildflowers.

ECO GARDEN BASICS

Eco gardening is all about working in harmony with nature, using ecologically sustainable and renewable resources and minimizing any negative effects on the world around us. This chapter encourages you to think differently about your own garden and to see it as a dynamic, living ecosystem. To help the eco garden flourish, advice is given on basic practicalities, from choosing tools, compost (soil mix) and containers with low environmental impact to concocting home-made plant feeds. Safe, non-chemical ways of dealing with pests, including slugs and snails, and tackling tough weeds without resorting to weedkillers, are covered too.

◀ This striking pink oriental poppy (*Papaver orientale* 'Kleine Tänzerin') is just one of the plants you can grow from seed once you have have acquired basic eco gardening skills.

▲ This versatile weeding tool allows you to hoe off young seedling weeds.

▲ Raising your plants from seed is eco-friendly and reduces 'plant miles'.

▲ Tunnels of fine mesh can be used to protect plants from egg-laying pests.

Establishing an ecosystem

The first step in eco gardening is to start looking at your garden differently. Rather than viewing it as a collection of different, unconnected elements and of problems to solve, as you might have done in the past, think of it as an interconnected, dynamic community of living organisms, large and small, interacting with their surroundings. In an eco garden you are part of that community.

What is an ecosystem?

Put simply, an ecosystem is a collection of living things and the physical surroundings in which they live and interact with each other. Mature oak woodland, which supports a wide variety of life, is a good example of a natural ecosystem.

In oak woodland, birds make their nests and feed on grubs and insects, which themselves are feeding on the oak leaves. Bird droppings fall to the woodland floor where they are broken down, along with fallen leaves, by worms and other soil life, becoming part of the soil that supports and feeds the tree roots. The fissured bark of the trunk is home to insects and other creatures, which are eaten by birds or mammals. After dark, bats, which roost in cracks in the trees' trunks and branches, feed on night-flying insects, while owls hunt small mammals over the woodland floor.

Learning from nature

In an eco garden our aim is to look at the way nature works and then weave together as many different kinds of life and physical habitats as

▼ Seating areas allow you to take time out to observe your garden's vibrant ecosystem at close quarters.

possible, so that they work together for the benefit and health of the whole garden. With a guiding hand from us, nature puts in place its own checks and balances. Increasing the variety of life in an eco garden – its biodiversity – helps it to become a vibrant ecosystem in its own right.

Weaving the garden web

Everyone can encourage birds into the garden by providing nesting habitats, food and shelter. Small birds such as blue tits will hunt for pests such as caterpillars, feeding them to their chicks, while thrushes will eat snails. Beneficial insects such as hoverflies, whose larvae eat aphids, are attracted by growing flowers rich in pollen and nectar.

Pollinating solitary bees are drawn to insect hotels, where they will breed. Perennial stinging nettles attract aphids, which ladybirds will eat when they emerge from hibernation. Nettles are also eaten by the caterpillars of several butterflies. Adding a pond will dramatically increase the life in your garden. Slug-eating frogs and toads will use it to breed, as will newts and dragonflies. Birds, small mammals and bees will all drink there.

Your garden might already contain some mini ecosystems, such as a compost bin, where garden and kitchen waste is turned into a rich material for improving soil. Adding garden compost to soil feeds earthworms and the soil micro-organisms which create humus – the decomposed organic matter that makes soil dark.

◄ One way to make your garden's ecosystem more attractive to pollinating insects is to grow nectar- and pollen-rich plants. Bumblebees visit the clusters of sweet-scented tall verbena (*Verbena bonariensis*) flowers for their copious nectar.

▲ Nectar-rich foxglove (*Digitalis purpurea*) will self-seed in your eco garden.

▼ Soil is a dynamic, living ecosystem in its own right, and contains myriad life.

THE LIVING GARDEN

Combining a range of habitats and their accompanying life is the basis of of successful and rewarding eco gardening. In this garden the different elements overlap, creating a thriving ecosystem where living things are constantly on the move and interacting with each other.

1 Insects flock to the shed's living roof.
2 Shrubs such as firethorn (*Pyracantha*) provide autumn and winter food for a wide variety of garden birds.
3 A dense, spiky holly bush is an ideal nest site for blackbirds and thrushes.
4 Bats feed on night-flying insects.
5 Birds roost and nest in trees.
6 Hedgehogs often hibernate in deep piles of dry leaves left in undisturbed corners.
7 Insect hotels placed in a warm and sunny spot invite in beneficial and pollinating insects.
8 Slow worms, common and glass lizards, frogs and toads live among piles of logs.
9 Compost heaps are self-contained mini ecosystems and help feed the soil.
10 Mature sunflowers provide food for seed-eating birds such as goldfinches.
11 Sparrowhawks will prey on smaller birds.
12 Nest boxes attract birds.
13 Multipurpose weeds such as nettles attract pest-eating insects and feed

▲ A habitat hotel attracts insects such as solitary bees and wasps, lacewings and ladybirds.

butterfly caterpillars, and their young sappy shoots can be turned into liquid plant feed.
14 Letting grass grow longer, allowing useful weeds to flower and introducing wildflowers boosts beneficial insect numbers.

▲ Even a small pond soon becomes the focus for much garden wildlife.

15 In this food garden, flowers grown among the crops attract beneficial insects that prey on or parasitize plant pests.
16 Soil underpins the whole garden ecosystem and teems with invisible microbial life.
17 A pond is a self-contained mini ecosystem. Frogs, toads, newts, salamanders, beetles and dragonflies will breed there, while birds, mammals and insects will drink in the shallows.
18 Ground beetles thrive in longer grass and travel at night, feeding on slugs and the eggs of cabbage root fly.

Choosing tools

To create and maintain your eco garden you will need a basic set of quality tools. If they are carefully looked after and maintained, and repaired when necessary, many tools should last a lifetime – or even longer. When buying new, choose tools which have been hand-made by craftsmen as locally as possible, using sustainable materials such as wood from well-managed forests.

Old or new?

Used garden tools can often be found for sale in antique and secondhand shops. If these will do the job, they are an excellent choice for the eco gardener, because they help reduce the demand for new tools and for the resources and energy required to manufacture them.

Cherished tools are often handed down from one generation to another – a good example of reuse in action. Older tools are sometimes superior to their modern equivalents, having better balance or longer handles which are easier to use.

Choose the best

It can be difficult to find out where many new tools have been made. In general, cheap tools are likely to have been mass-produced overseas and will be short-lived, whereas more expensive tools of known provenance can last a long time. Always ask suppliers where their tools have actually come from. Tools made primarily from metal and wood are preferable to those containing a lot of plastic.

▼ In time you will gather your own collection of comfortable and easy-to-use garden tools and equipment.

Whenever you choose tools, spend some time trying them out so you can get a feel for how they will perform. There are several factors to consider. Does the tool feel heavy or light? Is a long or a short handle going to be easier to use (are you short or tall)? What is the balance like? How easy are any adjustments? Does it offer good grip?

Tools and their uses

Some tools are very specific in what they are used for, while others can accomplish many different jobs.

Preparing the soil

• A spade is used for digging, moving soil and compost (soil mix) around, loading a wheelbarrow, spreading compost and chopping up weeds and garden waste. Stainless-steel blades (and tines on forks) do not rust and are easier to use and clean. Wooden handles are warmer and more comfortable to hold than plastic.

• A fork is used for breaking up clods after digging, loosening the soil surface, turning the soil over, mixing garden compost into the soil and spreading mulch. A fork can also be used for loosening the soil around weeds, for picking up and carrying manure, weeds or garden debris, and for loading a wheelbarrow.

• A rake is used for breaking down lumps of soil to create a fine crumbly surface (tilth) suitable for sowing seeds. It can also be used to rake out stones, gather up weeds and make grooves (drills) for seed sowing. Rakes with thin metal tines are used for gathering fallen leaves.

Planting and weeding

• A trowel is used to make holes for planting small plants or bulbs and for sowing larger seeds.

• A hand fork is used for breaking up the soil among other plants and loosening and lifting small weeds.

• A push or Dutch hoe is used for weeding. The sharp blade kills weed seedlings by cutting them off just below the soil surface as the hoe is pushed over the ground. Use during dry weather in borders and among food crops.

▲ These sturdy and cared-for tools made of wood and metal may not look especially modern, but still work perfectly well after decades of use.

▼ High-quality tools may involve more of an initial outlay, but with care will often last a lifetime.

Taking cuttings

• A clean sharp-bladed pocket knife is useful for taking different types of cutting, as well as for cutting string and removing dead flowerheads. It is also useful for harvesting crops.

Pruning and trimming

• Secateurs (pruners) are used for cutting out shoots of woody plants such as shrubs, removing dead flowerheads and cutting back faded perennials. The bypass type (shown here) cuts like scissors, while the anvil type works by pressing a sharp blade against a solid surface. Always keep the blades sharp, and wipe them clean after use to avoid spreading disease. Use a biodegradable oil to lubricate the moving parts.

• Long-handled pruners (loppers) are a more powerful tool than secateurs, as they can be used with both hands to cut through the thicker branches of trees and shrubs. Some have telescopic handles.

• Shears are used for trimming soft growth on hedges and for clipping back long grass, where they do less damage to wildlife than a powered line trimmer. They work with a scissor action. Shears can also be used for chopping up soft weeds prior to composting.

▲ Sturdy trowels and hand forks made from wood and metal will give many years' service.

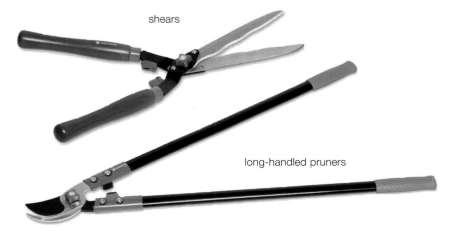

shears

long-handled pruners

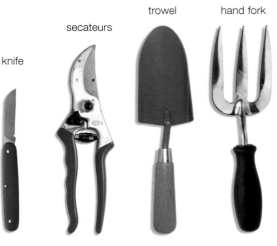

knife

secateurs

trowel

hand fork

spade

fork

rake

push or Dutch hoe

USING COPPER TOOLS

Copper rings and tape deter slugs and snails and are widely used as barriers to protect plants. Using copper tools for cultivating soil and for planting and weeding is also thought to impart deterrent qualities, and gardeners who use tools made of copper, such as this trowel and weeder, often find that their plants are less prone to slug and snail damage. Another theory is that copper tools do not disturb the soil's natural magnetic fields, unlike those made from iron. You can buy copper spades, forks and hoes.

copper tools

Choosing compost

To raise plants from seed and to grow them in pots and containers, you will need compost (soil mix). There are many different kinds available and they all have some environmental impact, but you can reduce this by avoiding those containing peat and choosing peat-free mixes instead. Alternatively, you could try making your own potting compost using low-impact materials.

What is compost?

Compost (soil mix) as used for sowing seeds and for filling containers is different from the garden compost that comes out of a compost bin. Seed, cutting, potting and multipurpose composts are specially made and are sold in plastic bags. These mixtures are free of weed seeds, pests and diseases, and contain plant foods. Always buy fresh compost, avoiding bags that are torn or waterlogged.

Garden compost might contain weed seeds, pests or diseases, so avoid using this for sowing seeds and raising seedlings, and use a peat-free compost instead. Garden compost can be included in a home-made compost for potting up larger plants with well-established roots.

Planet-friendly compost

Ecologically sustainable composts are those which do not deplete non-renewable resources such as peat, and cause minimal environmental impact in their manufacture and transport.

The most eco-friendly compost is the kind you make yourself using materials such as leaf mould or garden compost mixed with some purchased peat-free compost, as shown in the sequence above right, 'Mixing your own compost'. Good-quality and pest-free sieved soil can also be used.

▼ Garden compost is sieved before being used in home-made potting compost (soil mix).

MIXING YOUR OWN COMPOST

1 Make up a 50:50 mix of peat-free compost (the black bucket contains coir) and sieved leaf mould or garden compost. Add a handful each of seaweed meal and pelleted chicken manure per bucketful to boost growth.

2 You can either mix the two ingredients together on a sheet on the ground, using a clean spade to blend them together, or, for smaller quantities, put them in an empty compost bag and tie off the top. Allow room for mixing.

3 To mix, roll the bag over repeatedly so that the ingredients combine (you can also turn the bag from end to end). When the original ingredients cannot be identified, mixing is finished and the compost is ready for use.

USING A COIR BLOCK

1 Coir is a crumbly, fibrous by-product derived from the husks of coconuts. Although some energy is used in transport, it can be compressed into blocks and dried, reducing its carbon footprint. Start by placing a dry block in a large container.

2 Different-sized blocks produce different volumes of compost. Pour warm tap water over the block and leave it to expand. This 650g (1½lb) block produces approximately 9 litres (2 gallons) of compost when fully moist and expanded.

3 After several hours, any hard dry lumps can be broken up by hand and allowed to soak up water. Plant nutrients can now be added to the moist coir and thoroughly mixed in. Coir is used for seed sowing, rooting cuttings and potting on plants.

TYPES OF COMPOST

▲ Coir – made from an imported coconut industry by-product, it is available bagged or as dry and compressed bales or blocks.

▲ Peat-free – made from garden waste which is composted at high temperatures. Composted bark or coir are sometimes added.

▲ Reduced peat – the peat content is reduced by adding varying proportions of composted bark, wood fibre or green waste compost.

▲ 'Green' peat – made from silt washed from upland bogs and collected from water supply filters, so it does not lead to peat bog destruction.

▲ Composted bark – made from fine chips of conifer bark, this material keeps home-made potting compost (soil mix) open and free draining.

▲ Leaf mould – rotted leaves 2 or 3 years old. Use it finely sieved in home-made seed and potting compost (soil mix).

▲ Garden compost – made in a compost bin. Sieve to remove any large lumps and use in home-made potting compost (soil mix).

THE PROBLEM WITH PEAT

Peat-based compost (soil mix) is made from peat, which is the part-decomposed remains of mosses, taken largely from lowland sphagnum peat bogs. When bogs are drained, unique natural ecosystems are destroyed and the peat releases carbon dioxide (CO_2), the main greenhouse gas causing climate change.

Undisturbed, peat bogs act as 'sinks' for atmospheric carbon, absorbing huge amounts. Using up peat, which is a fossil fuel, is causing the destruction of one of the Earth's most important ways of storing carbon safely. Extracting peat is unsustainable because we are using it faster than it forms (1mm/¹⁄₁₆in per year).

Consistent, good-quality and completely peat-free composts are now widely available.

▲ An Irish peat bog following drainage.

Types of container

Globally, most plant pots and trays are made of plastic or polystyrene, which are manufactured from oil using fossil-fuel energy. Plastic recycling is increasing, but the different types often make this difficult. You can become more eco-friendly by reusing and recycling existing containers, making your own pots, and using biodegradable and compostable containers.

Why containers matter

Pots, trays, tubs, window boxes and other types of container help the gardener to raise, move around and grow many different plants. The choice of container sets off a reaction along the manufacturing chain, which has environmental impacts. For example, when you choose plastic pots, you set in motion a process that is almost completely reliant on oil, a finite resource. This process releases carbon dioxide, a greenhouse gas that is driving climate change.

When gardeners start to reuse plastic pots or, even better, make their own from materials such as newspaper that will rot down in the soil, they reduce the demand for both oil and energy.

Pots made from peat should be avoided (always check the label for what pots labelled as 'biodegradable' are made from). Peat is a fossil fuel and is harvested from ancient and irreplaceable natural ecosystems.

▼ Using everyday materials such as plastic food containers, toilet-roll tubes and egg boxes reduces demand for non-renewable resources such as oil.

HOW TO MAKE BIODEGRADABLE PAPER POTS

1 A wooden pot-maker and sheets of newspaper is all you need to make low-impact plant pots.

2 Tear the newspaper into strips of varying size according to the size of pot you want to make.

3 Lay the strips of newspaper on a flat surface and roll them around the pot-maker.

4 Fold the overlapping paper over and firm it down on to the bottom. This forms the pot base.

5 Carefully slide the newly formed pot from around the pot-maker. It is now ready to use.

6 Slightly overfill the paper pot with peat-free all-purpose compost (soil mix) and tap to settle.

7 Sow seeds by placing them on the compost and pushing them in.

8 As seedlings start to grow, the moistened paper pot will start to break down.

9 When roots grow out through the now rotting paper, plant out or pot on.

▲ When roots start to grow through a biodegradable pot, it can be planted in the soil. There is no need to remove the pot or disturb the roots. Soak any dry pots thoroughly before you plant them.

Reusing and recycling

Plastic pots and trays have many benefits. They are lightweight and easy to clean and store. If you have a good stock of plastic pots and trays, the most eco-friendly thing you can do is to keep using them. Kept well away from the sun (which turns them brittle), they will last for years.

To divert gardening plastic from landfill, ask your friends to pass any pots or trays on to you, or ask at your garden centre – they often have piles of pots which they otherwise have to pay to dispose of. If you have a surplus, offer them to a local school gardening project.

When plastic pots become brittle and shatter, it is time to recycle them. Take them to a local recycling station or check whether your garden centre runs a take-back scheme. Washing them clean first aids the recycling process.

Plastic pollution – a growing problem

Environmental pollution by plastic is a serious global problem. When plastic containers (and other gardening materials made from plastic) degrade in sunlight, they usually break up into small fragments which enter the soil and our waterways. These

BAMBOO FIBRE POTS

Attractive pots made from bamboo fibres are 100 per cent biodegradable. They can be reused many times and have a average life span, provided they do not become cracked or broken, of two to three years. When they do start to deteriorate, they can be broken up into small pieces and buried in the compost bin, where they will break down into organic matter.

Although their manufacture requires some energy input, the basic raw material – bamboo fibre – is a sustainable material that also absorbs and then locks up carbon dioxide from the atmosphere when the bamboo plant, which requires few inputs, is growing.

'microplastics', especially those found in marine environments, can absorb toxins which pass into the food chain when they are eaten by fish, birds and animals – and ultimately, us. Our major oceans now contain huge masses made up of plastic garbage.

Reusing and recycling plastic containers, making your own low-impact pots, and choosing compostable types all help to reduce both visible and more insidious invisible pollution.

TYPES OF ECO POT

Those marked with an asterisk* can all be planted into the soil and will rot down naturally.

▲ Pots made of coir, a sustainable by-product of the coconut industry, bound with natural latex.*

▲ Roots grow out through the base and sides of these pots, made from a mixture of paper and coir.*

▲ Toilet-roll tubes are ideal for raising vegetables and add organic matter to the soil.*

▲ Pots made of cattle manure release nutrients after planting, encouraging healthy growth.*

▲ 'Bioplastic' pots are a less eco-friendly option as they will only break down in landfill.

▲ Individual cell trays made from recycled paper pulp. They are easy to separate by pulling them apart.*

▲ Bamboo fibre pots can be added to your compost bin/heap when they finally wear out.

▲ Sturdy and attractively coloured pots and saucers made from rice husks, bamboo and straw.

Sowing seeds

Growing from seed is the starting point for many plants, and is an easy, economical, rewarding and eco-friendly way to raise many flowers, vegetables and herbs. When you grow your own plants from seeds, rather than buy them, you eliminate the 'plant miles' that they might otherwise travel, and you can choose pots, trays and compost made from sustainable materials.

Choosing seeds

Inside each seed is all the information needed to grow a whole new plant, plus enough stored food to kick-start the process. Seeds can be bought at garden centres, by mail order, or you can save your own from many flowers and vegetables.

In an eco garden the aim is to try and reduce unnecessary use of energy and resources, so the most eco-friendly seeds are those you save yourself. The next best choice is seeds which have been grown organically, with no chemical inputs, perhaps following ethical and fairtrade guidelines, and as locally to your garden as possible.

However, most seeds are still mass-produced, often overseas, in countries where seed production is more reliable and where the use of pesticides and fungicides is routine. These are usually sold in brightly coloured packets and listed in glossy catalogues, both of which use considerable amounts of energy and resources, such as paper and inks for printing and plastic envelopes for mailing. Many seeds are sold in foil and/or plastic packets which, unlike paper packets, cannot be recycled and do not rot in a compost bin or heap.

Seed treatments

Always make sure seeds are free from treatment with insecticides and fungicides by checking the information on the back of the packet. Some seeds are coated with harmless clay, or with brightly coloured materials to make sowing easier. Chemical treatments and special coatings both require extra inputs, so choosing quality seeds that are free of any added extras is the best choice for an eco garden.

Store seeds in a cool, dark and dry place. A metal tin with a tight-fitting lid is ideal. Never leave them in sunshine or next to a heat source such as a radiator. If you do not sow all the seeds at once, fold over the top of the packet, but do not seal it tightly and avoid using adhesive tape. Some seeds retain their ability to germinate (viability) for longer than others.

▲ Dust-like seeds, such as lobelia, can be mixed with silver sand to make sowing easier, and are not covered.

▲ One of the easiest ways to sow seeds accurately is to drop small pinches of them evenly over the compost (soil mix) surface.

USING SEED MATS

1 Seed mats are circular discs of biodegradable material impregnated with pre-spaced seeds. To grow a seed mat, lay it in a pot of compost (soil mix), cover and water.

2 Seedlings appear and grow at an even spacing, so there is no need to thin them out. These are 'baby leaf' salad mixtures which can be cut several times.

▲ Seeds can be sown individually in small cells of compost, then potted up.

▲ Large seeds (these are calendula) can be sown one or two per cell by pushing them into the compost (soil mix) with a dibber. If two germinate, remove the weaker seedling.

▲ An empty plastic compost bag turned inside out (black side outwards) will warm up in the sun, making it an effective and cost-free solar-powered seed propagator.

Handling seeds

Seeds vary in size from almost dust-like (such as lobelia) to those large enough to hold between a finger and thumb (such as broad or fava bean). There are different sowing methods, and it is worth trying out various techniques to find what works best for you.

You can sow a group of seeds together in a pot, then move the individual seedlings into their own pots or trays by 'pricking out'. Alternatively, sow them singly, or in small groups of 2–3 seeds, straight into pots, multi-cell trays or small plugs of coir compost. Where two or more seedlings appear, remove the weakest at the two-leaf stage by carefully pinching it off at compost level.

SIMPLE SEED SOWING

1 Choose a compost (soil mix) suitable for seed sowing. Overfill the pot, tap it several times to settle, and then use a straight piece of wood to scrape off any excess.

2 Using a flat-ended piece of wood (or similar flat-bottomed object), gently firm down the compost, ensuring it is level and even over the whole area and is 5mm (¼in) below the rim.

3 Using the 'tap' technique, place some seeds on a strip of card and then gently tap the card with your finger, scattering them evenly over the compost surface.

4 Use some fine compost to cover the seeds, sieving it first if necessary. The compost should be deep enough so that it just covers the seeds to no more than their own depth.

5 Use a watering can with a fine spray to moisten the compost. Label the pot with the plant's name and date of sowing, and then put it in a suitably warm place to germinate.

6 When young seedlings push up through the compost, move them into a sunny spot to prevent them becoming drawn and 'leggy', and 'prick out' when large enough.

HOW TO HOLD A SEEDLING

To move seedlings into their own pots or multi-cell trays, loosen the compost (soil mix) underneath them, then carefully take hold of one of the seed leaves (cotyledons) and lift the seedling from the compost. Never hold seedlings by their fragile stems, which can be easily damaged, making them prone to attack by fungal diseases. Make a hole in the pot or cell (with a dibber or your finger), then lower the roots into it, gently firm the compost around them, and water in.

▶ To lift and move a seedling, hold it gently by one of its seed leaves (coytledons).

Feeding your plants

Like us, plants need feeding as they grow. In an eco garden it is always best to use plant feeds made from natural, sustainable materials of animal or vegetable origin, which feed plants gradually over a long period. Quick-fix, energy-intensive synthetic fertilizers are often made from non-renewable resources. You can make your own liquid feeds using garden plants or weeds.

Why feed plants?

When seeds first germinate, a small reserve of food helps them produce their first roots and seed leaves (cotyledons). As they grow, seedlings draw water and nutrients from the soil or compost (soil mix) and use energy from the sun to produce stems, leaves, flowers and fruits.

The three main plant nutrients are nitrogen (N) for leaves, phosphorus (or phosphate) (P) for roots and potassium (or potash) (K) for flowers and fruits. These nutrients are often referred to as NPK. Most purpose-made plant foods contain all three in varying amounts, sometimes with other essential nutrients such as calcium, magnesium or iron and with trace elements (micronutrients), which plants only need in small amounts.

Choosing a plant food

Plant foods for the eco garden are made from different materials, some of which are shown on the opposite page. Some, such as bonemeal, are made from animal remains, while others, such as comfrey pellets, are made from the comfrey plant. Human urine can be used as a free and readily available liquid feed. Try to avoid foods made from mined rocks or minerals, as these

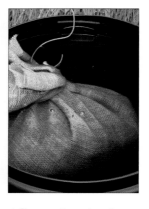

▲ Russian comfrey (*Symphytum* x *uplandicum*) leaves can be steeped in water for a liquid 'tea' high in potassium (K). Dilute one part 'tea' in ten parts of water.

are becoming increasingly unsustainable in the long term and are often transported over long distances, which requires fossil fuel energy.

Soil to which garden compost has been added regularly will usually contain plenty of nutrients, so it may be unnecessary to add extra plant food. But if you are growing plants in a new garden or allotment where the soil is in poor condition, then extra feeding with an appropriate food may be beneficial. For example, to feed leafy brassicas

▲ Suspending a hessian (burlap) sack of well-rotted farmyard manure in a water butt makes a nutrient-rich 'tea' which can be used diluted (one part 'tea' in ten parts of water) at every watering.

▼ Human urine makes a nitrogen-rich liquid feed, especially for leafy outdoor crops. Use it fresh, diluted one part urine in ten parts water. Water around the roots, avoiding the leaves.

MAKING NETTLE LIQUID FEED

1 Chop fresh nettle (*Urtica dioica*) stems into a bucket. Pack them down and cover with water.

2 Place a heavy flat stone over the bucket to weigh the nettles down, then leave for 2–4 weeks.

3 The resulting strong-smelling slurry is rich in plant nutrients. Keep covered to exclude flies.

4 Make up a solution of one part nettle feed to ten of water, then use to feed established, leafy plants.

▲ Feed plants through their leaves by lightly spraying them on both sides with seaweed extract. Do this in the early morning/evening to avoid scorching.

such as cabbages, use chicken manure, which is high in nitrogen. For flowering and fruiting crops, choose a potassium-rich food such as vinasse.

Foods such as seaweed meal (or crumb) are good general-purpose plant foods for an eco garden because they come from a renewable source (seaweed), contain a range of different nutrients, encourage beneficial soil micro-organisms and increase organic matter in the soil.

If you prefer to avoid using animal-derived products in your garden, plenty of other choices exist. Always try to use plant foods from an organically accredited, sustainable source.

How to feed

Pelleted, granular or powdered plant foods are spread over the soil surface and worked in (wear latex gloves and check the application rate). Do this 4–6 weeks before you sow or plant so that the nutrients are available when your plants start to grow.

Liquid feeds are especially useful for plants in containers, but can also be used to feed those growing in soil. You can buy ready-formulated organic liquid feeds, which should be diluted first, or make your own, as shown in the sequence 'Making nettle liquid feed'. Always follow the recommended dilution rates (usually 1 part feed to 10–20 parts of water). Never use liquid feed on dry, wilting plants or their roots could be damaged – water them thoroughly first and feed after they have fully recovered.

Plants can also absorb nutrients through their leaves. Foliar feeding, usually using seaweed extract, is a good way to give any plants that are growing slowly, or showing signs of leaf yellowing, a fast-acting tonic which also improves their general health. Water or spray the entire leaf surface, top and underside, at least once a week. Foliar feeding is not a substitute for improving your soil, or for using other feeds when necessary.

PLANET-FRIENDLY PLANT FOODS

Those marked with an asterisk* are not of animal origin.

▲ Composted chicken manure – pelleted, easy to use, rich in nitrogen plus other nutrients and good for all-round use. Strong odour.

▲ Comfrey pellets* – made from the leaves of comfrey and rich in NPK, trace elements and natural plant growth hormones.

▲ Bonemeal – ground sterilized animal bones which slowly release phosphorus as they break down. Wear latex gloves when handling.

▲ Seaweed meal* – dried seaweed containing trace elements and plant growth stimulants. Encourages soil micro-organisms.

▲ Dried blood – a by-product from abattoirs, high in nitrogen and useful for giving leafy crops a boost in spring.

▲ Vinasse* – pelleted vegetable-origin by-product of the sugar industry, rich in potassium and useful for fruiting crops.

▲ Sheep wool pellets – these release plant nutrients as they rot down, and their fibrous texture helps to deter slugs and snails.

▲ Alfalfa pellets* – made of alfalfa combined with comfrey and seaweed, for general garden use. Stimulates soil microbial life.

Pest barriers and deterrents

An effective, eco-friendly way of preventing pest damage to your plants, especially food crops, is to put physical barriers between plants and pests. You might need to protect your whole garden from larger pests, such as rabbits, with a fence, or prevent butterflies from laying their eggs on your cabbages by using netting. Pests can also be deterred using some simple techniques.

▲ Garden fleece excludes pests and is simply draped over crops and anchored in slits made in the soil.

▼ Plastic netting suspended above this bed of cabbages stops butterflies from laying their eggs on the leaves.

Keeping out larger pests

Rabbits cause serious damage to plants by eating them. Installing a 90cm (36in) boundary fence of wire mesh, with holes 25mm (1in) or less in diameter, is the best way of rabbit-proofing your garden. There should be no gaps and the mesh must be buried 15cm (6in) deep.

Birds will eat both vegetables and fruits. They sometimes peck at crops such as onion sets after planting (usually out of curiosity) but will leave most crops alone once they start growing. To protect vulnerable seedlings and young plants from birds, use lengths of wire mesh bent into tunnels and laid along crop rows. Fruit crops are especially prone to attack by birds and also by squirrels. Both can strip fruit bushes and trees in hours.

If you grow fruit, it is best to assume that both birds and squirrels will be a problem, and build a permanent walk-in fruit cage. This is a metal (or wooden) frame covered with UV-stabilized plastic netting. If you grow only a small amount of fruit –

▲ Insect mesh lets air and rain pass through but stops pests from laying their eggs on or near crops.

perhaps strawberries in a raised bed – you can cover them with a smaller, temporary cage when they are most vulnerable.

Although plastic netting keeps out birds, squirrels will quickly learn to bite through it, and covering a sturdy frame with wire mesh might be necessary to keep them off the crop.

Using netting, mesh and fleece

The adults of winged insect pests search out suitable plants on which to lay their eggs, which then hatch into larvae that feed on plants or crops. Protecting plants with a physical barrier, through which the adult pest cannot fly, crawl or push, prevents any egg-laying from taking place.

How you use a barrier depends on which part of a plant is most vulnerable. Cabbage white butterflies will land and lay their eggs on the leaf undersides of cabbages, cauliflowers or other brassica crops, and the whole plant – or group of plants – must be covered with no gaps left.

If butterflies are the main problem, plastic netting of the kind used for covering a fruit cage is an effective solution and should be suspended above the crop, using sticks, canes and/or twine, making sure that no leaves are left exposed.

To keep out other, smaller pests, such as carrot and cabbage root fly, which attack the roots of carrots and brassicas, use a barrier with smaller holes (less than 2mm/1⁄16in in diameter) through which the adult flies cannot pass. This sort of insect mesh is usually made from long-lived polyethylene, is porous to light, air and water and comes in varying lengths and widths.

Mesh can be used to make a permanent carrot fly barrier by putting a fence 60cm (24in) tall around individual soil beds. The adult flies do not fly any higher than this, so the crop is protected. With other crops, the mesh can simply be draped over them and its edges buried.

Garden fleece is made from polypropylene, a finely spun-made porous material with tiny holes. It is laid over crops to protect them from small pests such as flea beetle, and the edges must be anchored in the soil. This type of fleece can also be draped over frost-sensitive plants at night.

Soil barriers

Physical barriers will protect plants from soil-dwelling pests. Adult cabbage root flies lay their eggs around the base of brassicas, such as cabbages. The grubs then eat the roots, weakening and, in severe attacks, killing the

▼ Twigs among these kales scare any birds trying to land, while the barrier stops them walking in off the paths.

plant, which wilts and turns yellow. A collar 15cm (6in) wide, made of cardboard or old carpet fitted around the stem, prevents egg-laying.

Empty food cans with both ends removed (leaving no sharp edges) work in a similar way and will also protect plants from soil-dwelling cutworms (moth caterpillars), which feed on roots and bite through stems at soil level.

Using deterrents to scare pests

Where using netting is not feasible, larger pests, such as pigeons, can be deterred by pushing thin twiggy sticks 60–90cm (24–36in) long into the soil among any at-risk plants. This gives them a harmless fright as they try to land. A barrier of thin sticks, pushed into the soil around the edge of a bed of vulnerable plants, stops birds from walking on to the bed from the path. A combination of twiggy sticks and barriers can be extremely effective. Scarecrows give only limited, short-term protection.

▲ A fruit cage is an effective way of protecting ripening crops from birds and small mammals.

▼ Food cans pushed into the soil around these kohlrabi are protecting them from cutworms.

Slugs and snails

Of all garden pests, slugs and snails are potentially the most damaging. They attack many different plants, above and below ground, quickly causing extensive damage. As well as adopting less slug- and snail-prone gardening techniques and growing slug-resistant plants, other ways of dealing with them include encouraging natural predators, using traps and protecting plants with barriers.

When do they do damage?

Slugs and snails are active mostly at night when it is cool and moist, especially during wet weather. They move by secreting a layer of sticky mucus over which they slide – the familiar glistening slime trails. During the daytime, when temperatures are higher and the air is drier, slugs tend to retreat into the soil and under stones. Snails have shells, which makes them easier to spot, and tend to hide in cracks and crevices. Most damage tends to occur during spring, summer and autumn, but slugs and snails often feed during a mild winter and stay active in greenhouses.

Achieving a balance

No garden can be made entirely slug- and snail-free. These pests are constantly on the move, can travel surprising distances and breed rapidly. Eco gardens try to achieve a healthy and balanced ecosystem, and slugs and snails are part of that system. They provide food for wildlife such as birds, frogs and hedgehogs, and some larger slugs eat decaying plant material, so they play a part in the composting cycle.

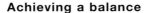

▼ A simple way to trap slugs is to lay flat stones around your garden, with some bran scattered underneath. Check them daily and dispose of any resting slugs.

◄ Snails carry a hard shell and can often be found hidden in crevices or among plants such as these hostas, with their damaged leaves.

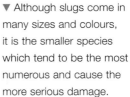

▼ Although slugs come in many sizes and colours, it is the smaller species which tend to be the most numerous and cause the more serious damage.

Dealing with slugs and snails is always a balancing act, and using a mixture of different techniques usually gives the best results. Generally, the younger a plant is, the more alert you need to be in protecting it. Seedlings and transplants, especially of vegetables, are particularly vulnerable.

Growing as many plants as possible in pots and then planting them out is an effective way to make your garden less prone to slug and snail damage. Larger plants are able to shrug off and recover from damage more easily, so there is less chance of the whole plant or crop being wiped out.

USING A BEER TRAP

1 Sink the lower half of a purpose-made beer trap in the soil and half fill it with fresh (or stale) beer.

2 Fit the lid of the trap, which helps to keeps out rain and allows removal of captured slugs and snails.

3 Slugs and snails drink the beer, then fall in and drown. Their dead bodies can be composted.

Capture, trap or kill

The simplest way to deal with slugs and snails is to catch them, which is best done in the evening by torchlight. They can be dropped into salty water, which kills them, or, if you prefer to leave them unharmed, gathered and released well away from your garden. Wear gloves during slug hunts (or use barbecue tongs) as they are very sticky.

Because they retreat to cool dark spots, a simple way of trapping slugs is to lay flat pieces of stone and wood around your garden and to check underneath them each morning, disposing of any slugs. Beer traps use the beer's pungent scent to attract slugs and snails and drown them.

Natural predators

Birds, frogs, toads, slow worms, hedgehogs and ground beetles are among the garden creatures that feed on slugs and snails. Songbirds eat snails and piles of their broken shells can be found in your garden. All these natural allies can be encouraged by making a pond and by providing suitable habitats for birds to roost and nest in.

You can also introduce naturally occurring parasites by treating the soil around slug-prone crops such as potatoes with microscopic eelworms (nematodes). This biological control is perfectly safe and effective on all but heavy soils.

▼ Slug- and snail-resistant barriers at least 2.5cm (1in) wide can be used to protect vulnerable plants. Wool pellets, human hair and bran disrupt the pests' movement, so they avoid crossing them. Ceramic shards have sharp edges, while hygroscopic granules and sawdust and myrrh dry out the pests' slimy mucus.

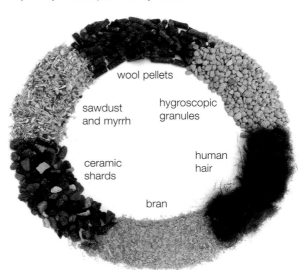

wool pellets

hygroscopic granules

sawdust and myrrh

ceramic shards

human hair

bran

PROTECTING PLANTS FROM SLUGS AND SNAILS

▲ **Copper rings** – long-lasting collars that, like copper tape and matting, give pests a tiny electric shock. Push the rings into the soil surface.

▲ **Copper tape** – this is adhesive and can be used around pots (fixed just below the rim) or on the legs of greenhouse staging to stop pests crawling up.

▲ **Copper-coated matting** – stand plants on this in a greenhouse or cut it up and use it as collars around individual plants grown outdoors.

▲ **Moat** – slugs and snails will not cross water, so protect plants with a small moat or one put around an entire garden bed.

▲ **Gel barrier** – sticky gels made of safe and natural materials provide a temporary barrier around plants and eventually break down into the soil.

▲ **Salt collar** – card collars impregnated with salt, which repels slugs and snails, can be placed around crop plants. Compost them after use.

The eelworms, which occur naturally in soil, invade the slugs' bodies and kill them from within. One advantage of using this kind of biological control is that as the affected slugs die underground, their bodies release more eelworms back into the soil, which will go on to infect more slugs.

Using barriers

Stopping slugs and snails from physically reaching your plants can be very effective, especially in the vegetable garden. Barriers work in different ways and can be short-term or more permanent features. Materials such as copper give slugs and snails a tiny electric shock, while others, such as hair or wool, create a fibrous barrier that they cannot cross.

▼ These eco-friendly, non-toxic slug pellets, made from iron and phosphorus, are effective at killing slugs and snails but do not harm wildlife, including songbirds.

Companion and mixed planting

In an eco garden we can mimic the vibrant diversity of natural ecosystems to help protect plants from pest attack, rather than relying on artificial chemicals. Clever and thoughtful planting combinations can help to confuse or deter pests, and can also encourage the natural predators and parasites which feed on them. Experiment with different combinations to find out what works for you.

Mixing everything up

Eco gardeners who observe nature for inspiration will tell you that one of the most important techniques for keeping pests at bay, without resort to synthetic chemicals, is to mix everything up. Essentially, this means that, whenever possible, it is best to grow plants together in a jumbled, relaxed and intermingled way.

This is how nature works and it is the foundation for what is called companion or mixed planting. It can be done in a deliberate and planned way, by growing two different crops side by side, or in a looser, more random way, by letting self-sown flowers grow among crops.

Although many different recommendations for companion planting exist, a good first step is to grow lots of insect-attracting flowers, rich in pollen and nectar, throughout the garden.

▼ Growing flowers in the beds of your greenhouse will entice beneficial, pest-controlling insects to come inside.

Attracting predators and parasites

Growing plants, especially vegetables, in isolation, in long rows or blocks surrounded only by bare soil, deprives them of the benefits of being close to other plants and makes them more vulnerable to pest attack. Once established, pests multiply rapidly, and if unchecked by any natural controls they can quickly overwhelm and damage crops unless chemicals are used.

Rather than growing vegetables as a single-crop monoculture, sow or plant fast-growing annual flowers such as pot marigold (*Calendula officinalis*) or poached egg flower (*Limnanthes douglasii*) in the spaces among them. When these bloom, they attract an array of beneficial insects, from minute parasitoid wasps, which lay their eggs inside aphids and caterpillars, eventually killing them, to hoverflies, whose larvae eat sap-sucking aphids.

By tempting the adults of these garden-friendly insects closer to crops, we let nature take charge by establishing a balance between pest and predator (or parasitoid). Do not expect completely pest-free plants. For beneficial insects to thrive,

▲ This nasturtium (*Tropaeolum majus*) 'trap plant' lures pests away from these Brussels sprouts.

▼ Nectar-rich flowers such as fennel (*Foeniculum vulgare*) attract hoverflies and other beneficial insects.

▲ These single-flowered French marigolds (*Tagetes patula*) deter whitefly from attacking tomatoes, but also draw hoverflies, the larvae of which eat aphids, into the greenhouse.

some pests (their food supply) must always be present, but in a balanced garden ecosystem they should not cause serious problems.

Confusing and deterring pests

Crops such as cabbages growing in bare soil are easily located by flying pests. Undersowing with a green manure (cover crop), such as trefoil (*Medicago lupulina*), at planting time soon covers the soil in a living green carpet which confuses pests by making it harder for them to find the crop plants. A carpet of annual weeds works in the same way, but they will need removing before they begin flowering and produce seeds.

Some plants release strong odours and other volatile compounds which keep pests away from crops. In greenhouses and polytunnels, French marigolds (*Tagetes patula*), with their pungent smell, are grown next to tomatoes to deter whitefly. Growing flowers among crops under cover will help attract beneficial predators and parasites that might not otherwise find their way in.

In the garden, growing one row of carrots to every four rows of onions helps to prevent carrot root fly attack, because the smell of the growing onions masks the scent of the carrots, and confuses the adult carrot root flies (which use the scent to find the carrots). Pungent herbs such as coriander (cilantro) can be used in a similar way, sown between crop rows or between plants grown in blocks.

▲ As well as confusing adult flying pests, such as cabbage butterflies, the trefoil (*Medicago lupulina*) growing among these brassicas helps to improve the soil.

Using trap plants

Plants which are attractive to certain pests can be used to divert them away from food garden crops. Nasturtium (*Tropaeolum majus*) attracts both aphids and cabbage white butterflies, which will lay their eggs on its leaves. It is important to check trap plants regularly and squash eggs or larvae when they appear, or pull up and compost the whole plant, along with any pests. Trap plants can either be planted deliberately among crops, or you can allow any self-seeding plants to grow on and flower.

▼ Growing onions with carrots reduces attacks by carrot root fly, because the onion smell makes the carrots harder to locate.

A MULTI-BENEFIT PLANTING COMBINATION

This trio of sweetcorn (corn), *Verbena bonariensis* and buckwheat (*Fagopyrum esculentum*) is an example of thoughtful companion planting that benefits the crop, the wider garden and the soil. The tall sweetcorn, which produces edible cobs, is planted in a block along with verbena and the whole area is sown, after planting, with seeds of the green manure (cover crop) buckwheat. The purple nectar-rich verbena flowers appear among the sweetcorn stems and attract insect predators, helping to control any aphids attacking the sweetcorn. Below the verbena, the white buckwheat flowers are a magnet for pollinating and nectar-seeking beneficial insects, helping to boost biodiversity throughout the garden, while its deep, fibrous roots improve the quality of the soil.

► Thoughtful planting combinations can simultaneously be productive, assist in pest control and help improve soil.

Using and controlling weeds

We usually think of weeds only as causing problems in the garden. Many do, but others can be surprisingly useful and valuable assets. As well as giving clues to the kind of soil in the garden, weeds can help attract and feed wildlife, be used for mulching and making home-made liquid plant feeds, and as raw materials for producing garden compost.

What are weeds?

Any plant growing where it is not wanted, and which competes for light, water and nutrients with the plants we do want to grow, is called a weed. Often, weeds are described as 'plants growing in the wrong place'. A patch of creeping thistle (*Cirsium repens*) colonizing waste ground might be growing in the 'right' place, but when its creeping roots invade a garden, it becomes a weed.

Weeds are grouped according to the length of their life cycle, which varies according to the timescale (weeks, months or years) over which they germinate, grow, flower, produce seed and die.
• Annual weeds germinate, grow, flower, produce seeds and die within one year. Some, such as chickweed (*Stellaria media*) can repeat the whole cycle several times in a year and are called ephemerals. Annual weeds are usually a problem on bare, freshly disturbed ground.
• Biennial weeds germinate and produce a leafy clump or rosette in their first year, then lie dormant over winter. The following year the plant flowers, produces seeds and dies. Biennials are often found where the soil is undisturbed. A good example is ragwort (*Senecio jacobaea*).
• Perennial weeds, such as Japanese knotweed (*Reynoutria japonica*), grow for many years, often

▼ This bare soil is being colonized by fast-growing annual weeds, but they can easily be controlled with a hoe.

indefinitely. Some have tough, woody stems, while others, such as dandelion (*Taraxacum officinale*), survive as fleshy roots. Many perennial weeds can still flower and produce seeds, but also spread in other ways. They are often found in neglected gardens and overgrown allotments.

What can weeds tell us?

Looking carefully at the weeds in your garden will give you an idea of what type of soil you have, its fertility and its pH (how acid or alkaline it is). Chickweed (*Stellaria media*) suggests a rich, fertile soil, while creeping buttercup (*Ranunculus repens*) thrives in moist, poorly drained soil. Sheep's sorrel (*Rumex acetosella*) is a common lawn weed found on acid (low pH) soil. Thickets of perennial weeds, such as bramble (*Rubus fruticosus* agg.) show that a garden has not been cultivated for some time.

Magnets for wildlife

Most weeds are wild plants and have evolved alongside insects and other garden wildlife in mutually beneficial ways. Hogweed (*Heracleum sphondylium*) produces flat flowerheads to attract

▲ Allowing some weeds to share your garden brings many benefits. Hogweed (*Heracleum sphondylium*) attracts pollinating and pest-controlling insects.

▼ Stinging nettle (*Urtica dioica*) is used as a summer food plant by the caterpillars of several species of butterfly.

▲ The fresh, sappy shoots of stinging nettle (*Urtica dioica*) can be cut and quickly turned into a rich, home-made and eco-friendly liquid plant food.

insects, which help with pollination and seed production. These same insects, such as hoverflies, are welcome in the eco garden because their larvae feed on aphids, which are sap-sucking plant pests.

Perennial stinging nettle (*Urtica dioica*) is a multipurpose weed which can be grown in clumps around the garden. In spring its leafy shoots attract aphids, which are a valuable food source for beneficial insects such as ladybirds emerging from winter hibernation. Later, in summer, red admiral and small tortoiseshell butterflies lay eggs on the nettle leaves, which the caterpillars eat. Clumps of stinging nettles also provide shelter for for ground-dwelling garden predators such as frogs and toads.

Mulches, plant feeds and composting
Freshly pulled up leafy weeds can be spread on the soil between crops as a temporary mulch, to stop more weeds germinating. Stinging nettles

▲ Sheep's sorrel (*Rumex acetosella*) is often found in lawns where the soil is acid (has a low pH).

(*Urtica dioica*) can be cut and steeped in water to produce a nutrient-rich brew which is diluted and used to feed plants, while most fresh and leafy weeds, except tough perennials, are ideal for adding to the mix in a compost bin.

ECO-FRIENDLY WAYS OF DEALING WITH WEEDS

▲ Stop the spread – remove weeds before flowering. This dandelion has airborne seeds.

▲ Cut off seedlings – use a sharp hoe to sever the stems of young weeds just below the soil surface.

▲ Pull them up – remove shallow-rooted weeds by hand. Do this before they become well established.

▲ Loosen and lift them – use a fork to free the soil around deep roots, then ease them out.

▲ Remove fragments – each piece of great bindweed (*Calystegia silvatica*) root can regrow.

▲ Grow dense crops – crops such as pumpkin cast shade, preventing weed germination.

▲ Use ground cover – low and spreading plants make an attractive, weed-suppressing blanket.

▲ Sow a green manure – fast-growing buckwheat smothers weed seedlings and improves soil.

▲ Use landscape fabric – this stops light reaching the soil and prevents weeds, but lets rain through.

▲ Rake them out – moss is a lawn weed which can be removed using a spring-tine rake.

Tackling tough weeds

Almost all weeds can be successfully composted, and most can be added straight to a compost bin or heap, where they are an important source of 'greens'. However, perennial weeds, with tough, fleshy and creeping roots (rhizomes) and runners, need to be dealt with first to make sure they are completely dead before being composted. There are several ways to achieve this.

Dry them out

Whenever you pull or dig up weeds, try to leave them out in the hot sunshine for several days, perhaps spread out over a paved area, so they weaken, shrivel and die. Annual weeds are easily killed this way and can then go straight into the compost bin, although it is a good idea to wet them first to speed up rotting.

The leafy tops of perennial weeds such as dock (*Rumex*) will dry out and die in hot sunshine, but this will not be enough to kill their thick roots. If you add these roots to a compost bin the weeds will begin to regrow, even in darkness, and will survive for many months – they could still be alive when you empty the bin.

Another advantage of letting weeds dry out is that their bulk and weight reduces, which makes gathering them up and moving them around easier.

▶ Perennial weeds can be buried in the core of a large 'hot' compost heap like this, where they are 'cooked' by high temperatures which will also kill weed seeds.

KILLING TOUGH WEEDS BY 'BAGGING'

1 Moistening a pile of freshly uprooted weeds (these are dock [*Rumex*]) with a mixture of water and human urine helps speed up the rotting process.

2 Chop the weeds up, if necessary. Turn an empty compost bag (with no large holes that will let in light) inside out and pack the weeds into it fairly tightly.

3 Once the bag is full, but not too tightly compacted, tie off the top. Prick over the surface of the bag with a garden fork in order to allow in some air.

4 The bagged weeds will rot more quickly if you put the bag in a sunny spot, so that it heats up. If you keep the bag in a shady spot, breakdown takes longer.

5 Check progress. Pale shoots like this indicate that not all the weeds are completely dead. After 3–12 months the bag should contain rich dark compost.

▲ Laying weeds out loosely in the baking sun dries them out and kills them. Chop thick roots into small pieces first.

▲ These Japanese knotweed (*Reynoutria japonica*) roots are shrivelling in hot sun but will need drowning to kill them.

▲ Dock (*Rumex*) roots are tough and resilient, but soon rot down in a compost heap if they are smashed with a hammer first and then left out to dry in the sun for a few days.

Chop them up

Crushing tough weed roots and breaking them into smaller pieces makes killing and then composting them much easier. Small amounts of thick, tough roots can be smashed using a hammer, or larger numbers can be passed through a shredder. Thick clumps of roots can be chopped up using a spade. Drowning is a highly effective way to kill them.

Perennial weeds with masses of thinner roots, such as couch grass (*Elytrigia repens*), can be spread on a lawn and passed over with a mower. Leave the chopped-up fragments in the sun until they feel crisp and dry, then compost them. If any regrow inside the bin, put them back in the sun.

Problem perennial weeds can also be buried in the core of a large hot compost heap, where they are killed by being 'cooked' at high temperatures.

Foolproof solutions

Some persistent weeds will try to cling to life whatever you do, but fortunately there are two ways to tackle them that guarantee success. You might want to treat all tough weeds this way. It is still a good idea to weaken weeds in the sun, but crushing and chopping them first is not essential.

• Submerging problem weeds in a container of water will cut off their air supply and drown them. This is an easy and relatively quick method, which kills most weeds in four to six weeks, and is shown in 'Drowning weeds in a bucket'. The dead remains can be added to the compost bin to rot down.

• Sealing weeds inside a plastic bag starves them of light and they will eventually die, although this takes longer than drowning – usually three to twelve months. The bag used must not let in any light. If left long enough, the dead weeds will turn into dark, crumbly compost which can be worked straight into your garden soil. See 'Killing tough weeds by 'bagging'.

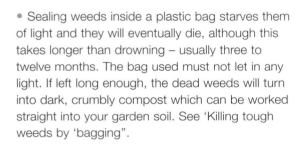

▶ Shoots of rosebay willowherb (*Chamerion angustifolium*) can be chopped up with a spade, left to wilt and composted.

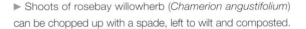
DROWNING WEEDS IN A BUCKET

1 Fill a bucket (or barrel) with any tough perennial weeds, especially those with tap and creeping roots or rhizomes. They should be packed down tightly and then completely submerged underwater.

2 Put a brick or a heavy stone on top of the weeds to weigh them down and make sure they stay below water level, which cuts off their air supply (this stops them from regrowing).

3 The weeds are fully dead when they turn yellow and brown and are decaying. The pungent liquid can be poured around crops as a liquid feed, while the remains can be put straight into your compost bin.

SOIL CARE AND COMPOSTING

Good soil stewardship and making garden compost are at the heart of eco gardening and also bring significant environmental benefits. This chapter looks at how and when to improve your soil, together with the materials, tools and techniques you can use. There is advice on using labour-saving mulches and how to make an instant vegetable garden using the sheet mulch technique. The importance of the garden compost cycle is explained, as well as how to make planet-friendly compost in your garden compost bin or heap, in a home-made wormery or by gathering autumn leaves and turning them into leaf mould.

◄ Garden compost is used to feed and sustain your garden's soil. It can be made in a simple bin made from recycled wooden fencing panels.

▲ Fallen leaves can be collected and will rot down into soil improver.

▲ Wood bark, spread over the soil around ornamental plants, helps prevent weeds.

▲ Kitchen and household waste can be added to your compost heap or bin.

Improving your soil

Adding plenty of organic matter to your soil on a regular basis is the best way to improve it. Your soil will be easier to cultivate, while your plants will be healthier and more resistant to pest or disease attack. Improving soil has wider environmental benefits, too – dark soils with a crumb-like structure can lock up and store atmospheric carbon and so help reduce global warming.

The importance of organic matter

Organic matter is the rotted-down remains of animal waste and vegetable matter. When added to soil, it helps to glue together tiny rock fragments to form crumbs and create a good soil structure. As organic matter is broken down further, by earthworms and soil micro-organisms, it eventually forms humus – a stable kind of soil carbon that gives the majority of soils their typical dark brown-black colour. By locking carbon into your soil, you can help reduce the build-up of the greenhouse gas carbon dioxide (CO_2), which is primarily responsible for causing climate change. Biochar can also be used to store carbon in soil (see panel 'What is biochar?').

Organic matter breaks up heavy clay soil, making it more workable, faster draining and quicker to warm up in spring. Adding it to a lighter, fast-draining sandy soil improves its structure and helps it retain water and nutrients. Soil improved with organic matter is rich in microbial life, releases nutrients gradually to plants as and when they need them, and promotes strong, healthy growth.

Types of soil improver

Organic matter used for soil improvement comes from well-rotted animal waste, such as cattle or horse manure, garden or green waste compost or leaf mould. Other soil improvers include spent (preferably organic) mushroom compost and clean, fresh seaweed.

Try to obtain animal manure from an organically accredited farm to be sure it is not contaminated with drugs or agricultural chemicals. Fresh manure

◀ This dug-away slice through soil is darker toward the top, where most plant roots, humus and soil life, including earthworms, are found. Lower, the paler soil is less fertile, with fewer roots.

▲ Spread a 2.5–5cm (1–2in) deep layer of well-rotted garden compost evenly over the soil surface, then fork it in to a depth of no more than 15–30cm (6–12in).

▲ Coarse grit is used to open up heavy soils and improve their drainage.

WHAT IS BIOCHAR?

Biochar is a kind of charcoal used as a soil conditioner or for adding to potting mixes (soil mixes). It improves fertility and also stores carbon, helping to reduce global warming. Biochar is porous, absorbs water, increases the availability of plant nutrients and encourages beneficial soil micro-organisms.

When woody plants (such as trees) grow, they absorb the greenhouse gas carbon dioxide from the air and store it in their tissues as carbon. When dry wood is burned without oxygen present, much of the carbon is left as stable biochar. Mixed with soil or compost (soil mix), biochar does not decompose and so its carbon remains stored away indefinitely.

Although the best ways of using biochar to store carbon are still being researched, its soil-enhancing properties have been known to gardeners for thousands of years.

biochar

▲ A good population of earthworms is a sign of healthy soil. Earthworms tend to be slower-moving than composting worms and less brightly coloured.

▲ Animal manure (this is from horses) adds organic matter and plant foods to your soil. You should let it rot down before use.

should be stacked in a heap, covered with a rainproof sheet and left to rot down for at least a year before being used. This also gives any chemical residues a chance to break down.

Garden compost can be used straight from your bin. Green waste compost is made from garden waste composted at high temperatures to kill weeds and pathogens, and is often available locally. It can be a cost-effective way of quickly improving your soil if garden compost is in short supply.

Soil improvers contain different levels of plant nutrients. Well-rotted animal manure and garden compost have medium to high levels of plant nutrients and are best used in spring and summer. Leaf mould has low levels of nutrients and be can added to the soil at any time.

Using soil improvers

Organic matter can be incorporated during soil cultivation, such as when digging, or it can be spread over the soil and worked in using a garden fork. Mix it into the upper 15–30cm (6–12in) layer of darker soil only. This is the topsoil, where most soil life and roots are found.

Add as much soil improver as you can, especially if the soil is poor and plants are not growing strongly. The more you add, the sooner you will encourage a thriving soil ecosystem, indicated by an increasing number of earthworms and other soil life. If the soil is already dark and crumbly and plants are growing well, use improvers such as garden compost more sparingly. Sharp grit worked into heavy soil will also improve drainage, although it does not add organic matter.

▲ Soil improver made from composted garden and food waste is available from garden centres, or may be available in bulk – occasionally for free – from your local council.

Soil improvers can also be used as a weed-suppressing mulch spread over the soil surface, where they will rot down and be incorporated by earthworms and other soil organisms. This is a useful technique for raised beds or for a no-dig garden where the soil is left as undisturbed as possible.

Green manures as soil builders

The dense, fibrous roots of green manures (cover crops) improve soil by adding organic matter as they grow. Some, such as grazing rye, not only prevent nutrients from washing out of the soil, they also build a crumbly soil structure and form humus when they eventually decompose.

◀ This rich garden compost, made from a mixture of bracken and old straw, is dark and crumbly, and is now ready to use for improving soil and as a surface mulch.

▶ Grazing rye is a green manure (cover crop) with fine and much-branching soil-improving roots. It can be sown in autumn and will grow steadily during the winter months.

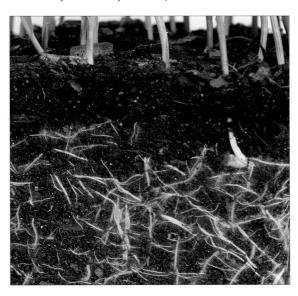

Soil cultivation

In nature, soil is rarely disturbed on a regular basis, but in an eco garden we usually need to work with it in order to improve it, to remove tough weeds and to prepare it for seed sowing and planting. Soil is cultivated in different ways, by turning and breaking it up during digging, by forking in soil improvers and by raking it down to a fine, crumbly tilth in order to sow seeds.

Why cultivate soil?

There are different reasons for cultivating soil. In a brand new garden, digging the soil is a good way to relieve compaction, allowing the gardener to find out what condition it is in and to remove any debris. Digging or forking soil also makes it easier to extract deep-rooted perennial weeds and allows organic matter to be incorporated, which improves the structure of the soil.

Once soil has been loosened and cleared of large stones, any sizeable clods need breaking down further with a fork or a rake, ready for sowing seeds or planting out young plants. If there are any low and/or high spots in your garden, use a rake to make a more level surface.

In your eco garden the aim should be gradually to minimize soil cultivation. Although you might initially need to dig over most of your garden or allotment to improve a heavy or poor soil, over time you can gradually scale back on soil

▼ When adding well-rotted manure like this to the trench during single digging, always break up any large lumps before turning the soil on to it.

HOW TO DIG YOUR SOIL

1 To 'single' dig your soil, take out a rectangular trench one spade blade (spit) deep and two spade blades wide. Store this at the end of the area to be dug.

2 Spread some organic matter over the base of the trench, then use the spade to invert the soil into the trench, burying any annual weeds. Break up any hard clods.

3 Use a fork to spread more organic matter evenly over the base of the trench and on the sloping face of the disturbed soil which has just been turned over.

4 Dig over the next section, again using the spade to turn the soil and bury any weeds (chop up any clumps). Finally, use the stored soil to fill in the last trench.

DIGGING – A BALANCING ACT

We usually only see bare, exposed soil when agricultural land is ploughed, when trees are uprooted during storms – or when we dig. Exposed soil is soon colonized by fast-growing weeds and then other plants. This is nature's way of 'healing' breaks in the 'skin' of living soil. We often need to cultivate soil at the outset in order to reap long-term benefits. However, in most situations the need for regular digging declines and the soil can be allowed to return to a mostly undisturbed and more natural state.

▲ Digging disrupts the soil ecosystem but is often necessary to improve soil.

▲ Try to work from paths whenever possible to avoid treading on and compacting the soil. Use a fork to loosen the soil before seed sowing.

▼ If you need to reach the centre of a wider bed or border, lay a wooden plank on the soil to spread your weight and work from that.

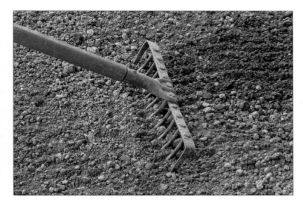

▲ Use a rake to break up clods of soil, to rake out any large stones and debris ahead of sowing and planting, and to move soil around to even out bumps and hollows.

cultivation (and on work). Undisturbed soil that is rich in humus helps to store carbon and reduce greenhouse gases in the atmosphere.

A food garden, for example, can be laid out as a series of permanent beds separated by paths. Because you walk only on the paths, the soil in the beds does not become compacted and digging is unnecessary. Any cultivation – such as forking in organic matter or raking ahead of sowing – is done from the paths. Working from a temporarily laid board is another way to avoid compacting soil.

Digging and forking

Digging with a spade loosens, lifts and turns over the top 25cm (10in) of soil (the approximate length of a spade's blade). The technique is shown in the sequence 'How to dig your soil'.

Heavy clay soils are usually dug in late autumn or early winter. The freeze/thaw action of frost and winter weather in general breaks down large clods ready for raking in spring. Lighter sandy soils can be dug at almost any time, but spring cultivation allows weeds to be removed and organic matter to be added ahead of sowing or planting.

A fork can be used like a spade to turn the soil, but light soils tend to fall through the tines. Use a fork to break down any large clods in spring, to work in organic matter or plant foods and to loosen the soil surface ahead of sowing or planting. In a food garden, lightly forking the soil, using just the tips of the tines, is all the cultivation needed to prepare the soil for sowing larger seeds (such as broad beans) and planting out. In beds or borders of ornamental plants, use a fork to work in soil improver and to remove weeds.

Cultivating soil when it is wet, frozen or covered with snow damages its structure. If the soil sticks to your boots, it is too wet to dig, fork or rake.

Using a rake

The tines on a rake head, as it is moved back and forth over the soil, break up any clods to create a fine, crumbly tilth. A rake is also useful for removing large stones or debris and for gently moving soil to fill any hollows. Use a rake on larger areas or from the paths between permanent beds.

Avoiding powered cultivators

Powered cultivation equipment requires energy and resources. Burning petrol or diesel as fuel uses a finite non-renewable resource (oil) and releases the greenhouse gas carbon dioxide, along with other airborne pollutants. To make your eco garden as climate-friendly as possible, cultivate soil whenever you can using quality tools powered by renewable and physical human energy.

▼ This three-tine cultivator is used to break up any compacted soil between growing crops, for incorporating plant foods, and also for uprooting any seedling weeds.

Choosing and using a mulch

Laying a mulch is one of the easiest, most effective and eco-friendly of all gardening practices. As well as being a chemical-free and labour-saving way of controlling weeds, mulching can help improve the soil, reduce your water use and give your beds and borders an attractive finish. There are many different types of mulch to choose from, and they are often freely available and plentiful.

What is a mulch?

A mulch is any material that is laid on the surface of the soil, either in the garden or in a greenhouse or polytunnel. Mulches can be natural organic materials, such as grass clippings or leaf mould; biodegradable materials, such as newspaper or cardboard; or synthetic, non-biodegradable materials such as black polythene.

In the eco garden it is best to use mulches made from plant remains, or from inorganic recycled materials such as stone chippings. Any non-synthetic mulch obtained (and preferably made) as locally as possible will usually have the smallest environmental footprint. Many mulches are made from recycled waste materials, such as tree bark or seashells. Depending on the type, mulches can be effective for just a few months or many years.

Manufactured synthetic mulching materials, including woven weed control fabrics, are energy-intensive and usually derived from oil. Shredded rubber tyres are sometimes used as a mulch, but the possible release of toxins means they are best avoided. Do not use peat – its extraction destroys habitats and contributes to global warming.

▼ Organic mulch can be spread, in an even layer, around established plants at any time. Remove any weeds first and make the mulch at least 2.5–5cm (1–2in) deep.

PLANTING THROUGH A RECYCLED PAPER MULCH

1 Paper mulch (supplied on a roll) can be laid over the soil. It stops weeds from germinating and conserves moisture. Plant through cross-shaped holes.

2 Fold the paper back and make a hole using your fingers or a trowel. Place the plant (this is pak choi [bok choy]) in the hole and firm the soil around its roots.

3 To settle the plants in, pour water into the hole. The paper will start to rot down as the plants grow, and can eventually be dug into the soil or composted.

Laying a mulch

Mulching generally keeps soil in the same condition as it was when the mulch was laid. If you need to cultivate or improve soil, do it before mulching. You can plant through a mulch, but it is difficult to add soil improver once a mulch, especially a permanent inorganic one, has been put in place.

The thickness of a mulch depends on the material used. Denser mulches such as grass clippings or seaweed should be about 2.5–5cm (1–2in) deep,

▼ Cardboard is a useful mulch for temporarily covering bare soil until sowing or planting, preventing weed growth.

◄ Laying stones as a mulch over the compost (soil mix) in containers helps to prevent drying out through evaporation, but you can water as normal.

PLANET-FRIENDLY MULCHES

▲ Grass clippings – check that the lawn has not been treated with chemical weedkiller. Use around vegetables in summer.

▲ Slate chips – these can be riddled from old spoil heaps and used as an attractive and permanent mulch in borders.

▲ Bark – useful for mulching around shrubs, it is long-lasting, available in coarse or fine grades and breaks down slowly into the soil.

▲ Seaweed – smothers weeds and improves the soil as it quickly rots. It is good for covering bare soil during autumn and winter.

▲ Hay – store outdoors for several months before using. It is easy to lay in thick, heavy and overlapping, light-excluding sheets.

▲ Mineralized straw – easy to use and lasts for up to two years before rotting down into the soil. Ideal for mulching food crops.

▲ Scallop shells – recycled crushed seashells. Use for mulching containers or as a slug-deterring mulch around vegetables.

▲ Wood chips – shred any woody garden prunings and use them as a long-lasting mulch around trees, shrubs or hedging plants.

▼ Straw has been used as a thick mulch around these Brussels sprouts, and helps to attract predatory beetles and fast-moving hunting spiders. It also makes good temporary paths.

while straw can be up to 15cm (6in) deep at first, as it will settle. Where a light-excluding weed control fabric is used, the mulch layer can be much thinner.

The ideal times to mulch larger areas are in autumn and from late spring onwards, when the soil is warm and moist. In a food garden, you can mulch as you plant. Never spread a mulch when the ground is cold, frozen or covered with snow.

The benefits of mulching

Mulches work hard in the eco garden in different ways, bringing many potential benefits:
• Mulches stop light reaching the soil, so weed seeds cannot germinate. A thick layer smothers and kills seedling and many annual weeds (but not tough perennial weeds).
• The soil beneath a mulch dries out more slowly, so less frequent watering is needed.
• During heavy, compacting rain, a mulch helps to protect the soil structure and prevent a hard surface crust from forming.

• Soil life, especially earthworms, flourish under a mulch, and they pull it underground as it rots.
• Dry, loose mulches such as straw attract beneficial garden predators such as hunting spiders and ground beetles.
• As they rot, natural mulches enrich the soil with organic matter and plant nutrients. They are used extensively in a no-dig garden where the soil is left largely undisturbed.
• Mulching with lime-rich spent mushroom compost helps make acid soil more alkaline.
• The fruits of strawberries and bush tomatoes are kept clean by a straw mulch.
• A thick mulch such as straw insulates soil from temperature extremes, keeping it warmer in winter and cooler in summer.
• Plants in containers dry out less quickly if the compost is mulched with stones.
• Decorative mulches such as shells and slate chips can be used as a background foil for ornamental plants.

Sheet mulching

Clearing an overgrown garden or allotment of weeds without resorting to energy-intensive chemical weedkillers usually involves plenty of hard work. Sheet mulching offers a simpler, easier and earth-friendly solution which can be used on a small or large area. Its greatest advantage is that it allows the gardener to grow vegetable crops at the same time as clearing an overgrown plot.

What is sheet mulching?

A sheet mulch is similar to other mulches but is more heavyweight in the way it works. It is used to clear whole areas of all but the most stubborn perennial weeds. Sheet mulches are thick and heavy, and are made of layers of different materials laid one on top of the other on the ground, as shown in the sequence 'How to lay a sheet mulch'. This use of a deep layered mulch is sometimes called 'lasagne gardening'.

Some sheet mulch materials smother and kill existing weeds, while others help to improve the soil and prevent weed seeds from germinating.

How a sheet mulch works

Laying the thick mulch layer instantly arrests weed growth by cutting off light, killing annuals and weakening any perennials with spreading or deep tap roots. Stubborn weeds are easy to remove if

▲ Six months after being sheet mulched, this previously weedy allotment is now a productive food garden laid out as 1.2m (4ft) wide beds. So far no digging has taken place.

REMOVING TOUGH WEEDS

Some tough, mostly perennial weeds are not killed by a sheet mulch and will eventually push up through it. To remove them individually, part the mulch, loosen them using a fork and lift out as much root as possible. If they regrow, repeat the process.

After several months, any dense patches of persistent weeds will become obvious. To tackle them, scrape the area clear of mulch and cultivate the soil, removing as many of the weed roots as possible. The mulch layer can then be relaid, as deep as you can make it, or the soil can be planted with a weed-suppressing crop such as potatoes.

▲ Removing a dandelion.

they break through the mulch – see panel 'Removing tough weeds'. Although it takes time and effort, sheet mulching is far quicker and easier than digging over large areas and removing weeds manually.

As the mulch gradually settles on to the soil, the layers of organic mulching materials, together with any dead weeds, start to rot down. Earthworm activity increases immediately beneath the mulch and the covered soil is less prone to drying out.

The best times to sheet mulch are in autumn, or mid- to late spring, when the soil is warm and weeds are just beginning to grow. Never mulch during winter when the soil is cold – it could keep the soil temperature low for many months.

HOW TO LAY A SHEET MULCH

1 Start by cutting down any weeds using a sickle, or, for larger areas, a scythe. Dig out any tough, woody weeds such as bramble (*Rubus fruticosus* agg.).

2 Gather enough large sheets of cardboard to cover the area, then lay them out so that their edges are overlapping by at least 30cm (1ft).

3 To anchor the light-excluding cardboard layer, spread a 10–15cm (4–6in) deep layer of organic matter (this is green waste compost) over the sheets.

4 Add a top layer of straw roughly 15cm (6in) deep. In summer, fresh (weedkiller-untreated) lawn mowings can be used as a topping, or in autumn, fallen leaves.

5 These 'Desiree' potatoes were grown by pushing the seed tubers into the organic layer and covering with newspaper and straw. They are ready to harvest.

Planting through the mulch

Once the mulch is in place you have two choices. You can either leave the area undisturbed for the next six to twelve months, or plant through it with suitable vegetable crops to create an instant vegetable garden. Although the soil will not have been cultivated or improved, unless it is heavily compacted it will still grow good crops.

If you decide to grow crops through the mulch, this is a good time to mark out any permanent beds and paths. You then tread only on the paths, preventing soil compaction. Crops can also be planted in rows, although this will compact the soil across the whole area that has been mulched.

To plant, use a trowel to dig down to the soil surface, loosen it and mix it with some of the organic matter from the mulch. You can also add some garden compost or similar soil improver. Pot-grown vegetable plants are then planted into the soil pockets and the mulch is drawn back, but without burying the plants. Seed potato tubers are pushed into the soil below the mulch and covered – there is no need to plant them any deeper.

Whether or not you choose to grow crops immediately after mulching, six to twelve months later the soil should be quite weed-free. You can then cultivate and improve the soil, either across the whole area or in beds, or continue with a no-dig approach where soil cultivation is kept to a minimum. Other crops, such as fruit trees and bushes, can then be planted.

Sowing seeds

Sowing smaller seeds is difficult because very young seedlings are easily overwhelmed by the mulch materials, but you can sow larger seeds such as those of runner beans by scraping back the mulch layer first and making a hole in the soil surface. Fill the hole with a mixture of soil and garden compost so it sits level with the mulch layer, then sow into it.

To sow smaller seeds, especially those of root crops such as carrots, set aside an unmulched, relatively weed-free area, cultivate the soil in the usual way and then sow seeds direct.

▼ These summer cabbages are growing through a sheet mulch laid in spring. The bed is 1.2m (4ft) wide and, like the 45cm (18in) wide paths, is mulched with fresh straw.

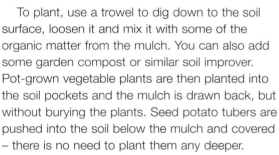

The importance of composting

Turning freely available and valuable resources that we usually think of as waste into garden compost benefits both your garden and our wider environment. By setting up your own compost cycle you will be helping to relieve pressure on landfill and reduce greenhouse gas emissions, while creating a rich soil improver that boosts soil biodiversity and encourages healthier plants.

▲ Egg boxes, toilet-roll tubes, cereal packets and other card food packaging can all be used to make garden compost. Any flat boxes should be scrunched into balls.

What is composting?

Making garden compost is simply encouraging the breakdown (rotting) of once-living materials until they form a crumbly, dark brown material which is used to improve your soil. This process is carried out by more obvious creatures, such as composting worms, and by mostly unseen bacteria, fungi and other soil-dwelling organisms.

Composting materials come from various sources. In the garden they might be weeds, grass mowings or crop remains, or fallen leaves which are used to make leaf mould. Household materials include vegetable and fruit peelings, used teabags, shredded paper, cardboard and food packaging. Even clothing made from natural and biodegradable materials, such as cotton, will rot down.

THE GARDEN COMPOST CYCLE

Your own garden and home is a rich source of raw materials for making garden compost. Here you can see how composting materials (the input, shown in blue) and the resulting compost (the output, in green) flow around your garden, and some of the ways in which they can be used.

1 Scrunched-up cardboard food packaging, egg boxes, toilet-roll tubes and other cardboard.
2 Kitchen waste, including peelings, coffee grounds and non-meat cooked food.

3 Torn-up newspaper or shredded office paper.
4 Garden waste, including weeds, soft prunings and faded bedding plants.
5 Use leaf mould as a mulch and soil improver for raised vegetable beds.
6 Add sieved leaf mould that is two to three years old to home-made potting compost (soil mix). During sieving, remove any stones or twigs along with any tree seeds, such as acorns.

7 The roots, stems and leaves of any harvested vegetable crops.
8 Autumn leaves from a neighbour's lawn for making leaf mould.
9 Lawn mowings – your own or a neighbour's. Check that no lawn weedkiller has been used. Use mowings fresh when they are still green and easy to combine with other materials.

10 Comfrey produces green leaves for adding to your compost bin, and can be cut repeatedly during summer. Chopping leaves up first using a spade makes them easier to mix with other composting materials.
11 Mature garden compost improves all soil types.

12 Mix sieved garden compost with leaf mould to make a home-made potting compost.
13 Soak a hessian (burlap) sack of garden compost in water overnight to make 'compost tea', then dilute it and use immediately as a plant tonic.

▲ Sieving home-made garden compost removes any larger and part-rotted materials, which can be returned to your garden compost cycle.

▲ Mature and well-rotted garden compost should be dark and crumbly. It can be spread over the soil and then forked in.

If something will rot, it can usually be used to make garden compost. Non-living materials such as glass, metal, plastic or wood are not compostable and should be taken to your nearest recycling centre.

Environmental benefits

Transporting garden and household waste requires fuel to truck it either to landfill sites (large holes in the ground) or to air-polluting incineration plants, while bonfires of garden waste can release cancer-causing chemicals. Composting waste where it is produced requires minimal transport, other than by wheelbarrow, and does not pollute.

Although waste separation and recycling is improving, large volumes of garden and household waste are still sent to landfill sites. When once-living materials are buried and compressed, they will rot, but because air (oxygen) is absent, they produce methane, which is a potent greenhouse gas contributing to global warming. Well-aerated compost heaps and bins do not generate methane.

Making garden compost utilizes these valuable resources and improves your soil while causing little or no harm to the environment.

Large-scale composting

If you cannot make your own compost, perhaps through lack of space, any garden or kitchen waste should be left out for collection, or taken to your nearest green waste collection site.

At a large-scale composting facility, the materials are chopped up and mixed together, then arranged in elongated hot heaps or 'windrows', which reach high temperatures.

▼ Lawn mowings (from lawns which have not been treated with weedkiller) are a valuable composting material, but they need mixing thoroughly with coarser garden waste.

COMMUNITY COMPOSTING

Working with other gardeners to make garden compost can be very rewarding. As well as using composting materials that might otherwise have been sent to landfill sites from a number of gardens, the work can be shared and there is a valuable social dimension. Community composting projects can be set up in towns, cities or rural areas. Funds may be available to help with the purchase of tools and equipment, such as this riddle being used to sieve compost before selling it back to the local community who donated the raw ingredients.

▲ Community composting equipment.

This speeds up the composting process and kills any weed seeds, pests or diseases. The resulting compost is sieved to grade it and to remove any contaminants, and is then used as a soil improver or mulch. Green waste compost is often the most readily available source of organic matter in towns and cities. Buying it encourages the ongoing recycling of garden waste.

▼ Many local councils have large-scale composting facilities which turn garden waste diverted from landfill into soil improver using hot, steaming 'windrows'.

Cool composting

Making garden compost using the 'cool' method is easy and straightforward. All you need, depending on the size of your garden, is the space for one or more compost bins. These can be made cheaply from wooden pallets, or you can buy bins made of timber or recycled plastic. You also need a steady supply of composting materials known as 'greens' and 'browns'.

▲ Soaking cardboard makes it easier to tear into smaller pieces for composting.

▼ In this 'cool' bin, made from wooden pallets, waste rots down over many months, and also provides a wildlife habitat.

What is cool composting?

Adding a mixture of once-living materials little and often to a compost heap or bin, where they rot down slowly over six to twelve months or longer, is known as cool composting. The composting materials are not turned or disturbed regularly and the contents of the heap or bin do not usually heat up. Fresh materials are added to the top of the heap or bin and they are gradually broken down by larger soil organisms such as compost worms, which move into the bin from the soil, and by soil micro-organisms.

As the contents of a heap or bin gradually rot down, its level falls and you can add more materials. This happens faster in summer, when it is warmer, and slows down or stops during winter. If you have composting worms in your bin, they will disappear deep into its contents during freezing spells, returning when temperatures rise. The fully decomposed materials eventually accumulate at the base.

▲ To keep plenty of air in your compost bin and create spaces for composting worms, scrunch up food packets and cardboard first by crushing them into loose clumps.

Heaps versus bins

You can make cool compost by simply mounding materials up in a round or square heap. A good size is 1.2–1.5m (4–5ft) wide. A disadvantage of heaps is that the sides tend to dry out and rot down very slowly. You can overcome this by covering the heap with a sheet to keep it moist, and this also prevents nutrients from washing out.

A simple recycled plastic compost bin with a lid is ideal for cool composting. In a bin the composting process is contained, it is less prone to drying out and most of what you add turns into garden compost. Two bins make composting easier because when one is full, you can start filling the next. Bins standing in the sun warm up and encourage faster composting.

Composting materials

For cool composting to work well, the materials you use must be a balanced mixture of 'greens' and 'browns' (examples are shown in the panel).

'Greens' are softer, sappier materials containing water (they are not always green in colour). They help to kick-start the composting process by providing food for micro-organisms. 'Browns' are tougher, drier materials that break down more slowly and help to absorb any excess moisture.

As a general rule, try to add a 50:50 mix of greens and browns every time you add fresh material to a bin or heap. Do not worry if the proportions vary occasionally, but avoid adding too many greens (such as lawn mowings) at once, or they will form a slimy, bad-smelling mass. Scrunching browns such as paper and card by crushing them into loose ball-shaped clumps introduces air and keeps the mixture open.

Moisture

Dry materials will not rot. Kitchen waste can be mixed with paper or card and moistened before it is added to the bin or heap. When adding a lot of dry plant material, spray it over with water first and soak any tough and dry 'browns', such as cardboard, in water first.

Compost bins are prone to becoming too wet, whereas heaps tend to be drier. Never soak the contents of a bin, or leave the lid off during prolonged spells of rain. Waterlogged bins turn slimy, smell and do not break down. If the contents become soggy, loosen the top layers with a fork and remove the lid to allow them to dry out.

What not to compost

Cool composting does not kill weed seeds or some plant diseases, and is not suitable for composting cooked food waste. Mature weeds and diseased plants can go into a 'green waste' recycling bin, along with cooked food scraps – or use them to feed composting worms in a wormery. Cat or dog faeces should never be composted because of potential health risks.

Do not add materials that will not rot, such as glass, plastic or tin cans, but recycle them instead.

▲ To encourage the natural breakdown process, a compost activator can be added to your bin.

▼ The shoots of young and leafy stinging nettles (*Urtica dioica*) can be chopped up and used as 'greens'.

WHAT ARE 'GREENS' AND 'BROWNS'?

'Greens':
- Vegetable and fruit peelings, banana skins.
- Tea leaves or bags and coffee grounds.
- Weed leaves, stems and roots (not tough perennials unless they have been killed).
- Chopped-up stinging nettles and comfrey leaves.
- Soft hedge trimmings and faded cut flowers.
- Lawn mowings.

'Browns':
- Woody prunings and evergreen hedge clippings.
- Scrunched cereal or pizza boxes and other food packaging.
- Straw and hay.
- Tough (chopped) stems of weeds, herbaceous plants and vegetables.
- Shredded newspaper and scrunched envelopes (remove plastic windows first).
- Occasional handfuls of autumn leaves.

'greens' and 'browns'

MAKING AND HARVESTING COOL COMPOST

1 To make slow, 'cool' compost, regularly add a 50:50 mixture of 'greens' and scrunched 'browns' to a recycled plastic compost bin with a lid.

2 This bin is used for composting mostly kitchen and household waste. Greens and browns are mixed together before being added to the bin.

3 Keep adding to the bin until the level inside reaches the top and it eventually stops sinking. Carefully lift the bin off to reveal its contents.

4 Fresh composting material is always at the top, while the well-rotted compost is at the bottom, with various stages of decay in-between.

5 Remove the still-to-rot upper layers (put them back in the now empty bin), then harvest the lower layers of mature compost for use as required.

Composting with worms

Colourful and fast-moving compost worms are one of nature's wonders. They can turn all kinds of different materials, including kitchen scraps, into a special kind of garden compost that is rich in plant foods and beneficial microbes. You do not need a garden or any special skills to keep these worms and it is easy to make a living space – a wormery – for them.

What are compost worms?

There are different kinds of compost worm and they are found naturally in compost bins, manure heaps and decaying organic matter. Smaller than earthworms, they are red or orange with paler stripes and move much faster when exposed to light. One of the commonest is *Eisenia fetida*, often called brandling or tiger worm. You can collect your own worms, get a handful from a neighbour's compost bin, or buy them by mail order.

Feeding your worms

Almost anything of organic origin that will rot will be eaten by worms, from paper and cardboard to vegetable scraps and peelings, dead flowers and leaves. Cooked food scraps, which should not go into a garden compost bin, can be fed to worms. They cannot eat hard materials, such as bones.

Worms need feeding little and often. They eat what you give them as it starts to decompose, so a wormery needs to contain some fodder in all the different stages of rotting. They will start eating fibrous food such as cardboard almost immediately, but soak it in water first.

▼ Thrashing composting worms are often found in compost bins and heaps, and can also be housed in a home-made wormery.

Using a wormery

A wormery is any type of suitable container in which worms are kept. It can be a simple box or bin with a lid which is fitted with a tap to drain off excess liquid, as shown in the sequence 'Making your own wormery'. More sophisticated designs have removable stacking layers where the worms gradually move upwards, leaving the finished compost in the lowest stack, so you do not need to actually handle them.

Worms do not like to be too hot or too cold, so keep your wormery out of direct sun, and in winter move it to a sheltered spot. Never let it freeze solid, become waterlogged or dry out completely, or the worms will die. If waterlogging occurs, empty the contents of the wormery on to some dry newspaper and leave it to dry out for a few days before putting it back.

◀ This recycled plastic stacking wormery is simple to use: once the worms have converted the first layer into compost, a second stack is added and the worms move up into it.

▼ Fragments of worm-worked paper, card, kitchen scraps, and worms, can be seen in this material from a thriving wormery.

▼ To make a root and foliar feed, put some worm compost in a fine mesh bag and submerge in water, then dilute the resulting 'tea' in ten parts of water.

MAKING YOUR OWN WORMERY

1 Use a lidded plastic box approximately 50cm (20in) long, 40cm (16in) wide and 30cm (12in) deep. Drill plenty of holes several centimetres apart around the top of the box.

2 To drain off the nutrient-rich liquid produced by the worms, drill a hole at one end of the box and fit it with a simple on/off tap with a tight-fitting, leak-proof seal.

3 Avoid waterlogging by putting a 5cm (2in) deep layer of lightweight plastic foam chips in the base of the box, then cover them with a sheet of fine wire mesh.

4 Line the box with some old garden fleece and add a 7–10cm (3–4in) deep layer of moist 'bedding' – a mixture of shredded news/office paper, and some straw or hay.

5 Introduce some composting worms to their new home. A handful taken carefully from another wormery or a compost bin will soon establish a thriving population.

6 Add a thin layer of food for the worms to eat. Use a mixture of fruit and vegetable peelings, used teabags and some moist torn-up cereal packets.

7 Cover the food layer with a further thin layer of 'bedding' material and then cover with a sheet of cardboard to exclude light and prevent drying.

8 Position the wormery so that the end with the tap is slightly lower than the other. Keep the lid in place at all times to keep out rain and flies. Keep it out of full sun.

9 After 4–6 weeks the initial food will be rotting down and the worms will be actively breaking it down. You can now start to add more food every week.

10 The liquid produced by a wormery is rich in plant nutrients and growth stimulants. Dilute it in ten parts of water and use as a root/foliar feed.

Harvesting the compost

In a stacking system you remove the worm compost when it is ready. A simple box-type wormery should be emptied out when it is full. Start by removing any fresh food on top and the rotting layer just below, with as many worms as possible, and put both in a container. To separate any remaining worms from the mature compost deeper in the box, take it out, mound it up in the sunshine, then follow the technique shown in the sequence 'Collecting worm compost'.

Worm compost is a rich source of plant nutrients and growth stimulants, so use it sparingly. It can be forked into your garden soil to improve it, used to top-dress plants in containers, added to home-made compost (soil mix) and used as a liquid feed.

COLLECTING WORM COMPOST

1 Remove the dark and crumbly worm compost from the wormery and mound it up in a sunny spot.

2 After the worms have burrowed away to escape the light, scrape off the surface layer of compost.

3 Repeat until all the compost is collected. Any worms that are left can go back into the wormery.

Leaf mould

Leaf mould is a type of garden compost made entirely from the fallen and decayed leaves of trees. It is simple to make and the raw materials are easy to collect, requiring few energy inputs other than the muscle power required to use a spring-tine rake. Nature and time do most of the hard work, so it is worth trying, even in a small garden, to make as much as you can.

What is leaf mould?

As leaves rot down they turn into a rich source of organic matter that can be used for improving soil, for mulching and for making your own potting compost (soil mix). This dark, crumbly material, which is usually free of weed seeds, is called leaf mould, and takes up to three years to make. During this time fungi, worms and other organisms break the leaves down, so that by the time you come to use it, they have been transformed into a soft, spongy material. Leaves do not need high temperatures to rot down, but they do need to be kept moist, especially during summer.

The leaves of plants that naturally shed their leaves each autumn (deciduous plants) are the best ones to use. Dead evergreen leaves and the needles from pine trees should be avoided.

Collecting leaves

Fallen leaves can be collected from lawns, paths, driveways, roadsides and roof gutters. In towns and cities, avoid gathering leaves from busy roads

because they might be contaminated with litter, such as broken glass, and pollutants from vehicle exhausts. When collecting leaves from a park or other open space, avoid any animal faeces. If your own supply of leaves is limited, try asking neighbours for theirs – most will be glad to have their lawns cleared and may even bag them up for you.

◄ Using two flat sections of board makes the overall 'grab' of your hands much larger and speeds up leaf gathering, once you have raked them into heaps first.

▼ Mature leaf mould is easy to use and also pleasant to handle.

BAGGING LEAVES

▼ It takes from one to three years for freshly fallen leaves (top) to rot down down into crumbly leaf mould (bottom). These are oak leaves.

1 Gather up fallen leaves and put them in an empty black-side-out plastic compost (soil mix) bag. If the leaves are dry, wet them thoroughly first to help kickstart their decay.

2 Push the leaves down into the bag but do not pack them too solidly. You will always get far less leaf mould out than leaves put in. Tie the top of the bag securely with string.

3 To let air into the bag, which is needed for the leaves to rot down well, use a garden fork to puncture some evenly spaced holes over the entire surface of the bag.

4 Put the bag in an unused corner of the garden and leave it for 1–3 years, until the contents have turned into crumbly leaf mould and the original leaves are no longer recognizable.

A spring-rake – one with long wire tines – is the best tool for gathering leaves into heaps. You can then pick them up using a leaf grabber, which can simply be two pieces of flat wood, held one in each hand, that make the overall 'grab' of your hands larger. For small numbers of leaves, hands work just as well, but wear gloves if necessary.

Making leaf mould

The simplest way to make leaf mould is to pile leaves up in a mound in an out-of-the-way part of the garden, perhaps beneath a tree. Make sure they are moist, then cover them with old plastic potting compost bags, split open, black side up, and use stones to hold them in place. Compostable sacks made from natural fibres such as jute are used by stacking the leaf-filled sacks together in a mound (both sacks and leaves rot down).

Small numbers of leaves can be put into empty potting compost bags to rot down in an unused corner of the garden. Large reused polypropylene builders' bags are ideal for collecting large volumes of leaves and, if you have the space, can be left in the bag, with the corners tied together, to rot down.

The tidiest way to create leaf mould is to make a simple cage of wire mesh fixed between four wooden posts to form a square, which stops the leaves blowing about. The mesh allows air into the leaves. Make the cage 1m (3ft) square and 1m (3ft) deep, or larger if you have lots of leaves. Having two cages means that when one batch of leaf mould is ready, it can be emptied out to make way for the next batch of fresh leaves. Cages can also be circular and should be at least 1m (3ft) in diameter.

Using leaf mould

Although it contains few plant foods, mature leaf mould of two to three years old is an excellent soil improver that adds large amounts of organic matter, helping to boost microbial soil life and encourage healthier plants. It helps lighter soils to retain moisture during dry spells and makes heavier soils easier to work. To incorporate leaf mould, spread a layer 5–7cm (2–3in) deep and fork it in no more than 10–15cm (4–6in) deep.

Leaf mould that is only one to two years old, still showing the remains of partially decayed leaves, can be spread over the soil surface as a mulch 2.5–5cm (1–2in) deep. Being mostly weed-free, it is suitable for using around established vegetables and plants growing in borders.

Mature leaf mould, which is fine and crumbly, can be used in home-made compost, but it needs to be sieved first to remove any twigs, stones and large lumps. Mixed with sieved garden soil and worm compost or garden compost, it makes a rich growing medium for use in containers.

▲ These circular leaf mould cages are 2m (6ft) wide. The one on the left contains one-year-old leaves, showing how the level drops down as the leaves rot.

USING BIODEGRADABLE LEAF SACKS

1 Woven leaf mould sacks made from jute fibre let in air and moisture and rot down along with the leaves you put in them. Pack them with moist leaves, preferably after rain.

2 When the bag is full, tie it off with the cord supplied. Check the weight of the bag as you fill it, as large quantities of damp leaves can be heavy. Move full bags around in a wheelbarrow.

3 Decide where to make your leaf mould and stack the bags together (the jute quickly rots). Covering them with a plastic sheet keeps them moist and encourages breakdown.

HARVESTING SUNLIGHT AND RAIN

For your garden to be ecologically sustainable, the energy and resources that it draws upon should always be derived from sources that are replenished naturally. This chapter looks at how using rainwater and renewable energy from sunlight will make your eco garden as planet-friendly as possible. Advice is given on how to capture and use the sun's energy, using walls, greenhouses and polytunnels. The importance of using rainwater rather than mains tap water is explained, and advice is given on harvesting it.

◄ All of our gardening activities are powered, in different ways, by the free and abundant energy received from the sun – both now and in the past.

▲ This solar-powered lean-to greenhouse is attached to a house wall.

▲ An eight-sided mini greenhouse is very efficient at capturing sunlight.

▲ Rainwater is free to collect and helps reduce reliance on mains tap water.

Renewable gardening

Using renewable, constantly replenishing natural resources will help you create and maintain a climate-friendly eco garden. You can capture solar (sunlight) energy using walls, greenhouses and polytunnels, and to use pollution-free 'green' energy to run essential garden appliances. Using rainwater reduces the garden's reliance on tap water and helps protect freshwater ecosystems.

▲ Sunlight makes plant growth possible and we can use it in different ways in an eco garden.

▼ One way to make your garden 'greener' is to run electrically powered equipment using energy from a renewable source, such as a wind farm.

What are renewable resources?

Any resource that is not permanently depleted by regular use and can be replenished is described as 'renewable'. The most familiar resource is renewable electrical energy produced by solar, wind and wave technology.

The most abundant renewable garden energy source is sunlight, which powers the growth of plants and can be used in different ways: we can capture it in structures such as greenhouses to create a season-extending growing environment, or we can grow green manures (cover crops) which capture it as they grow and help to improve soil. Food crops absorb and store sunlight energy in leaves, fruits, roots and tubers, which we then eat to give ourselves energy.

Water is essential for plant growth. Rainwater is a free, valuable and renewable resource which is easily harvested and stored. It is far more eco-friendly than tap water, which undergoes a series of energy-intensive processes during its extraction, purification and supply. Restricting your use of tap water helps to avoid the depletion of sources of fresh water, which can damage increasingly vulnerable ecosystems such as lakes and rivers.

▲ This photovoltaic solar panel generates 'green' electricity that charges the batteries of a garden security light.

Non-renewable fossil fuels

Although it can be generated using clean, non-polluting technologies, most electricity currently comes from the burning of non-renewable fossil fuels, coal and natural gas in large power plants, plus some from nuclear reactors.

Fossil fuels are derived from the fossilized remains of plants that grew hundreds of millions of years ago, during the Carboniferous Period, when Earth's atmosphere was rich in carbon dioxide. Huge forests grew on land, using sunlight to drive photosynthesis – the natural process by which plants absorb carbon dioxide to make roots, stems, leaves, flowers and fruits. Eventually, this mass of vegetation died down, forming deep layers of carbon-rich rotting plant material. Marine algae also combined sunlight energy with carbon dioxide before dying and sinking to the ocean floors. During subsequent geological changes these plant-based remains sank deep into the earth, where they became fossilized.

There are two key problems in using fossil fuels. The first is that they are non-renewable and becoming depleted; demand is already outstripping the rate at which new sources are discovered. Second, burning fossil fuels to generate electricity pollutes the atmosphere

by releasing carbon dioxide, the main greenhouse gas responsible for global warming. Together with other greenhouse gases, this is now adversely influencing Earth's climatic systems, leading to more extreme weather events worldwide. Switching to non-polluting and low-carbon sources of 'green' energy is urgently needed to avoid dangerous climate change.

Garden energy use

Fossil fuels are extracted not just to generate electricity, but also to manufacture a range of different products, including those used in gardens. Synthetic garden insecticides, fungicides and fertilizers are all derived from and made using fossil fuels. Powered garden tools, such as lawn mowers, electric propagators, outdoor and greenhouse heaters and other equipment all use energy derived from fossil fuels both to make and to run them. Many familiar gardening products, such as plastic plant pots, are made from oil.

By using fossil fuels in everyday gardening activities, we are using up the ancient sunlight energy that is stored away in gradually depleting reserves of oil, coal and natural gas.

Climate-friendly gardening

Switching to low-carbon gardening will make your eco garden more climate-friendly. The best way to do this is to rely far less on ancient sunlight, and to use new (or current) sunlight effectively. The solar energy falling on your garden is a free, non-polluting and renewable alternative to using fossil fuel energy. The following practical steps will all help to reduce your garden's reliance on fossil fuels and maximize its use of new sunlight:

▼ Boosting garden biodiversity by growing nectar-rich tall verbena attracts bees and beneficial pest-eating insects that remove the need for fossil fuel-derived pesticides.

● Use sunny walls, greenhouses and polytunnels to capture and harvest solar energy to grow earlier/later crops and more tender plants.
● Boost your garden's biodiversity, letting beneficial insects keep plant pests in check rather than using oil-derived chemical pesticides.
● Use home-made liquid feeds made from plants such as comfrey (*Symphytum* spp.) instead of fossil fuel-derived fertilizers.
● Grow green manures (cover crops) which capture new sunlight, and use them to increase the fertility of your soil and lock up carbon.
● Keep garden equipment use to a minimum; replace petrol-driven machines with rechargeable, battery-powered alternatives and switch to a supplier of 'green' electricity. Use rechargeable devices powered by electricity-generating photovoltaic panels.
● Reduce the size of your lawn, stop using synthetic weedkillers or fertilizers and use a human-powered push mower.

▲ This lean-to greenhouse harvests free sunlight energy and creates a warm, season-extending all-year growing space.

▼ Using rainwater in your garden is a more planet-friendly option than using energy-intensive tap water.

Using a sunny wall

House and building walls and garden fences that receive full or even partial sunshine provide a wonderful opportunity for raising and growing a wide range of edible and ornamental plants. The area in front of a wall, as it heats up in the sun, becomes a warm, sheltered and sun-powered microclimate which can be used in a number of different ways.

Heat for free

When the sun shines on a brick, stone or other solid wall, it absorbs the sun's energy and warms up, which also heats the air next to the wall. You can feel this for yourself by standing next to a wall on a calm and sunny day. This effect is most noticeable from spring to autumn when the sun is high in the sky, but even in winter, in a sheltered spot, such as the corner of a walled garden, the sun's low rays can raise the temperature a few degrees above the rest of the garden. In an eco garden this pollution-free natural energy is put to good use.

At night, when the sun has set, walls act like storage heaters and release the heat energy they captured during the day. Touch a wall after dark and feel the warmth. This keeps the area next to the wall slightly warmer than the rest of your garden, so it is a good idea to move frost-sensitive plants near to the wall on cold, starry nights.

Growing on a wall

Sunny walls can be used in different ways. If you have plenty of space, a walk-in lean-to greenhouse is one option, but where space is limited, perhaps in a small courtyard or on a balcony, smaller structures are more suitable. The most important

▲ This sunny courtyard wall is enlivened by a wide range of plants in various containers and hanging baskets, which make use of the sheltered microclimate.

factor is to work out the best ways of using the growing space you have. Taking photographs will remind you of where any sun falls.

You might choose to fix a mini greenhouse to the sunniest part of your wall, to fit strong shelves to the wall as high as you can comfortably reach, or to use a temporary tiered structure made from wood and bricks. Reclaimed glazing panels laid against the base of a wall make a simple but effective growing space, and this also prevents them going to landfill.

Crops such as aubergines (eggplants) and peppers need warm conditions, so growing them in large pots against a sun-soaked wall is ideal. Climbing beans make use of vertical growing space, while hanging baskets, which are sited above other plants, can be fixed to the wall for growing flowers or trailing edible crops such as bush tomatoes.

Because plants growing on or near a wall are usually in containers, you will need to pay careful attention to watering, especially when summer temperatures soar. Water containers thoroughly in the evening, when it is cooler. On hot days, seedlings and young plants may need several waterings, or even moving into the shade for the hottest period.

▼ This window box is planted with various sun-loving and aromatic herbs, such as sage and basil, which scent the house when the window is opened.

▼ Unwanted secondary and double glazing panels laid against a sunny wall make a temporary growing space for raising seedlings and young plants.

Attracting beneficial wildlife

The warm conditions created by a sunny wall are enticing to garden wildlife, especially beneficial insects such as hoverflies, the larvae of which eat aphids, so encourage these and other useful insects by growing plenty of plants rich in pollen and nectar among your other plants. Solitary bees are valuable pollinators and will breed in home-made nest boxes fixed to your wall. Frogs and toads will often live in the damp spaces between pots.

▼ Warm conditions near a sunny wall help attract welcome insects such as this hoverfly, the larvae of which eat aphids.

MAKING THE MOST OF A SUNNY WALL

1 Sweet peas will bloom earlier when grown next to a sheltered wall.

2 Nest boxes attract pest-eating birds.

3 Climbing runner beans grown in a recycled plastic trough are trained up strings. In summer they shade the kitchen from hot midday sun and some pods can be picked through the window.

4 Single-flowered pot marigolds (*Calendula*) entice beneficial insects.

5 Heat-loving crops such as aubergines (eggplants) and peppers grow best in large pots 30–45cm (12–18in) in diameter.

6 Food cans filled with hollow plant stems or bamboo canes provide nesting sites for wild solitary bees, which pollinate crops.

7 Use a permanent mini wall greenhouse to germinate seeds in spring, then during summer to grow single stem (cordon) tomatoes in a growing bag. From autumn onward, use it to protect overwintering salads from bad weather.

8 Make a temporary sowing and growing space using wooden planks and bricks stacked next to a wall. Put pots and trays on the shelves. On cold nights, drape garden fleece over the front. In summer, use for fast-growing salad leaves and sun-loving herbs such as basil.

9 Bush tomatoes in hanging baskets are easy to pick. To avoid them drying out rapidly, use baskets at least 40cm (16in) in diameter, lined with plastic compost bags.

10 Grow heat-loving herbs such as thyme in a a well-drained window box.

11 Hang up onions and garlic to dry off against the hot brickwork.

12 Rest glazing panels against a wall to make a warm and protected short-term growing area. Hold them in place with bricks.

Greenhouses and polytunnels

Powered by the sun's renewable energy, greenhouses and polytunnels will increase the range of plants you can grow in your eco garden. The covered and sheltered growing space they provide allows you to propagate plants and to raise crops that do not thrive outdoors. These structures also extend the growing season – you can grow plants earlier and harvest them later.

▲ A greenhouse is a separate garden microclimate with diverse uses. This one has automatic top vents and captures rainwater.

▼ The soil beds in a greenhouse should be easy to reach from the paths without over-stretching.

Extending the growing season

Using a greenhouse or polytunnel creates a separate microclimate where plants (and you) are protected year-round from wind, rain, frost and snow, although temperatures inside can fall below freezing during winter.

In spring, many vegetable crops can be sown in containers while the soil outdoors is still too cold and wet. They are transplanted outdoors when conditions improve, giving earlier harvests than from plants sown directly into the soil. In autumn, the covered conditions protect crops from frosts, extending their productivity for many weeks.

Polytunnels are especially useful for providing year-round food. In autumn they can be sown with hardy winter salads and oriental vegetables, which can be harvested regardless of the weather outdoors.

Capturing sunlight

We use greenhouses and polytunnels to harvest energy from the sun. As the sun's rays warm up the soil, paths and other surfaces inside a structure, they warm the air, which raises the temperature. Opening vents and doors during the daytime regulates temperature by letting warmer air out and cooler air in. At night, any heat-absorbing surfaces release their warmth, so closing doors and vents traps this heat, keeping the night temperature above that outdoors.

A greenhouse consists of a metal or wooden framework glazed with glass, polycarbonate or acrylic (virtually unbreakable plastics). Toughened glass is strong and shatters into small, rather than sharp, fragments when broken. The framework is usually made of aluminium or western red cedar, and sits on a solid base. Greenhouses range from mini wall-mounted types to larger models in various shapes and sizes, including square, rectangular, octagonal, or even geodesic domes. A lean-to greenhouse is one fitted against the side of a building; covering a solid, heat-absorbing wall makes a lean-to highly efficient in capturing solar energy.

A polytunnel is a series of galvanized metal hoops fixed in the ground, covered by a plastic skin. There are doors at each end and some have top vents.

▼ Polytunnels usually cover more area for less cost compared with greenhouses. Here a central bed is used to grow a row of 2.1m (7ft) tall cordon tomatoes.

▲ Louvre vents are positioned near the base of a greenhouse's sides. They allow in cool air, lowering the inside temperature.

▲ Always fit a greenhouse roof with guttering, and harvest rainwater in one or more water butts. Polytunnels can also be fitted with guttering systems.

The tunnel sides are either sloping or vertical, which increases the growing space. Skins need replacing every five to seven years (they can be recycled). Polytunnels are generally less expensive than greenhouses and cover a larger area.

Positioning and layout

Greenhouses and polytunnels need an open spot in full sun; orientate them east–west so they receive maximum sunlight. Plants can be grown in soil beds or containers in a greenhouse. Plants grown in beds can root deep into the soil and are not as vulnerable to drying out as container-grown plants. Polytunnel crops are usually grown in soil.

Make your soil beds where there is most vertical growing space, so that these beds can be planted with tall crops such as cordon tomatoes. This often means creating a central bed with permanent paths either side, rather than having one central path. Greenhouses can also be sited on hard or paved surfaces, with everything grown in containers. To utilize vertical space, tiered staging is used to stand pots, trays and plants on.

Equipment and care

Plants under cover rely on the gardener to control temperatures and supply them with water.

A thermometer will monitor day and night temperatures. In summer, lay shade netting over the roof and sides of a greenhouse to prevent high temperatures, but remove it on dull days. In winter,

▼ In summer, use shade netting to prevent greenhouse temperatures from soaring on sunny days, but remove it in winter, when light levels are low.

▲ This versatile aluminium staging has removable trays, allowing taller crops to be grown inside the framework.

lining the inside of a greenhouse with bubble-wrap plastic helps retain whatever warmth it can capture from the winter sun. Vents and doors can be opened manually; automatic vent openers work at a preset temperature. On hot days, wetting the paths increases humidity and has a cooling effect.

Heating

The most eco-friendly greenhouse or polytunnel receives no additional heating beyond that provided by the sun. This means that it is important to work with the seasons and to avoid plants needing year-round high temperatures or high humidity. In spring and summer, grow plants that need higher temperatures and plenty of sunshine, and in autumn and winter, grow those that need less light and lower temperatures.

Using a gas or paraffin greenhouse heater, or one using electricity generated by burning fossil fuels, will contribute to global warming. The most climate-friendly way to keep a greenhouse (or preferably just part of it) frost-free is to use a fan heater powered by 'green' electricity. Set it to operate only if the temperature falls low enough. Polytunnels are not normally heated at all.

Green manures or cover crops

Despite their rather curious name, green manures are actually living plants that capture renewable sunlight energy and turn it into soil-enriching organic matter. They are easy to grow and have numerous benefits, especially in a food garden where garden compost and other soil improvers are in short supply. It is worth trying different green manures to discover which work best for you.

What are green manures?

Often called 'cover crops' because they are used as a living blanket over otherwise bare earth, green manures are plants grown specifically to improve and enrich the soil, rather than for their edible or ornamental value. Even small areas of bare soil are worth sowing with green manures, and they can be grown outdoors or under cover. The benefits of using green manures are listed below:

• They use sunlight energy and carbon dioxide from the air to form stems, leaves and roots. When incorporated into the soil, they add organic matter, which is decomposed into carbon-rich humus. By absorbing atmospheric carbon dioxide and locking it away in your soil, green manures help make your eco garden more climate-friendly.

• Some plants 'fix' nitrogen from the air, releasing it later for use by leafy, nitrogen-hungry crops.

• Overwintering green manures absorb plant nutrients, which stops them being leached out of the soil, returning them later when they are dug in.

▼ These courgettes (zucchini) are undersown with nitrogen-fixing red clover (*Trifolium pratense*).

• They protect the soil during winter, preventing damage to its structure caused by heavy rain.

• Some draw nutrients from deep in the soil, then release them, as their roots, stems and leaves rot down, for other plants to make use of.

• Deep-rooted green manures can help to break up heavy and/or compacted soils.

• Some can be cut and used as a mulch, or as extra 'greens' for composting.

• They smother seedling weeds.

• Some have flowers that attract beneficial insects.

Nitrogen fixers

Green manures from the Leguminosae (Fabaceae) or pea family have root nodules containing bacteria which can 'fix' nitrogen from the air. When these nitrogen fixers are incorporated into the soil, the nodules rot down, slowly making the nitrogen they contain available for crops to use. This avoids the need to use nitrogen fertilizers. Field beans (*Vicia faba*) and winter tares (*Vicia sativa*) are two hardy legumes that are grown over winter and then incorporated into the soil in spring before planting nitrogen-hungry leafy crops such as cabbages and

▲ A few plants of fast-growing fiddleneck (*Phacelia tanacetifolia*) can be left to flower to attract bees and hoverflies.

▼ As well as adding nitrogen and organic matter to the soil, red clover's flowers provide nectar for friendly insects.

GREEN MANURE SOWING TIMES

Autumn to early winter:
Field beans*
Grazing rye
Winter tares*

Spring and summer:
Alfalfa*
Buckwheat
Fiddleneck
Mustard
Red clover*
Trefoil*

* = Nitrogen fixers

▼ The roots of these green manures from the pea family have fleshy, creamy-pink nodules containing nitrogen-fixing bacteria.

▲ Alfalfa (*Medicago sativa*) is a nitrogen-fixing green manure which can be cut for use as a summer mulch around food crops, or as 'greens' for composting.

other brassicas. Clovers (*Trifolium* spp.), trefoil (*Medicago lupulina*) and alfalfa (*Medicago sativa*) are also nitrogen fixers.

Choosing and using green manures

To find out which green manures are suited to your garden, sow small patches of each type to see how well they perform, and ask other gardeners locally what works for them.

Green manures can be grown for just a few weeks, or for several years; fast-growing leafy mustard (*Sinapsis alba*) can be dug in after only three weeks, while alfalfa can be grown for several years in an unused spot as a perennial green manure. As well as improving the soil with its deep roots, alfalfa suppresses weeds and can be cut during summer for use as a mulch material or nutrient-rich composting 'greens'.

Seeds of green manures are sown in drills or scattered and raked in. Large field bean seeds can simply be pushed into the soil. Taller-growing vegetables can be undersown with red clover (*Trifolium pratense*) or trefoil; green manure seeds are sown after planting the crop. For example, courgettes (zucchini) can be undersown with red clover, which is left to grow as an overwintering cover crop once the courgettes are finished.

Incorporating green manures into the soil

Start incorporating green manures while they are soft and sappy (not woody). Chop them down using a spade, sickle or shears, let them wilt, then dig them into the soil to at least 15cm (6in) deep or they might regrow. Alternatively, the chopped plants

▲ Buckwheat (*Fagopyrum esculentum*) is a fast-growing, deep-rooting green manure for growing in summer. Its flowers attracts swarms of pest-controlling hoverflies.

can be covered with a dense, light-excluding mulch and will rot down into the soil. After digging in a green manure, allow at least three weeks before sowing seeds or planting out young plants.

GREEN MANURES AND THEIR BENEFITS

Field beans: These have thick, nitrogen-fixing roots which break up heavy soil. Cut the tops in spring for mulching or composting.

Buckwheat: The plants are fast-growing and weed-smothering, and break down quickly after incorporation. Let some plants flower to attract beneficial insects.

Grazing rye: This absorbs and holds on to nitrogen during winter, then releases it for spring-planted crops. The fibrous roots add organic matter.

Mustard: This grows quickly and produces copious organic matter from its leaves and roots. Incorporate it into the soil before it flowers.

Winter tares: This is ideal for overwintering, and is very hardy and deep-rooting. It grows well on heavier soils and fixes large amounts of nitrogen.

▲ Seedling green manures (left to right): field beans, buckwheat, grazing rye, mustard, winter tares.

Water in the garden

Water plays many valuable roles in a garden: seeds and plants need it to grow, it creates a habitat for wildlife and it can delight the senses by creating sound and movement. Together with sunlight, rainwater is the most abundant and renewable resource anyone can harvest. Using it instead of energy-intensive tap water will help reduce the impact of an eco garden on the wider environment.

▲ Crops such as tomatoes need a regular supply of water to grow.

▼ Tap water contains nutrients and chemicals which can upset the delicate balance of life in a pond, so always top up using rainwater.

A limited resource

Fresh water is a finite natural resource. Human activity in many parts of the world is consuming this precious resource faster than it is being replenished. All living things – including plants – require water to exist. Less than 1 per cent of all the fresh water on Earth is available for use; the remainder is either sea water or water that is held in a frozen state, mostly at the Poles. As human populations expand and urbanization spreads, the demand for safe, drinking quality (potable) water is growing, intensifying pressure on the natural world.

To supply our homes, fresh water is extracted from our environment, then sanitized in large purification plants before being piped to our taps, which all requires energy and resources. Storing large amounts of fresh water in reservoirs can destroy entire ecosystems and displace human communities, while extracting water from rivers and lakes can have an adverse impact on aquatic systems. Drawing water from underground aquifers can lower water tables, degrading otherwise fertile land. Fresh water is also used for agriculture and horticulture, and for many industrial processes.

▲ Using mains tap water to water hanging baskets and other containers is less eco-friendly than using rainwater.

Domestic water use is increasing, with a growing amount being used in gardens. The essence of eco gardening is to create a beautiful and self-sustaining garden with minimal impact on the wider world. Reducing your garden's reliance on mains tap water is one of the best as well as one of the easiest ways to achieve that.

How gardeners use water

Water is essential for plants to carry out photosynthesis and respiration (the biological processes by which they grow, flower and fruit) and to absorb mineral nutrients from the soil through their roots. As gardeners, we use water in many different ways, for example:
• Watering seedlings and pot-grown plants.
• Settling in new pot-grown plants or bare-root transplants after planting outdoors.
• Regular watering and feeding of established plants and crops (outdoors and under cover).
• Moistening soil grooves (drills) before sowing seeds.
• Making and diluting purchased or home-made liquid plant feeds, and applying foliar feeds.
• Creating and topping up wildlife ponds, bog gardens, water features and bird baths.
• Watering and feeding hanging baskets and container-grown plants (indoors and out).

- Keeping compost bins or heaps moist.
- Moistening soil so that it is easier to cultivate.
- Washing the mud and dirt from hands, boots, tools and from harvested root crops.
- Damping down paths in greenhouses and polytunnels to cool them and raise humidity.
- Cleaning greenhouses, polytunnels and paths.
- Blasting away pests with jets of water.
- Applying nematodes (biological controls) to plants or soil (using a watering can).
- Scrubbing pots and containers.
- Providing a low pressure supply to automatic and semi-automatic watering systems.
- Creating sound and movement (water features).
- Making attractive and eco-friendly 'rain gardens'.
- Watering and liquid-feeding lawns.
- Using powered (jet) washers to clean garden furniture, patios, decking areas and other surfaces.

Abundant and cost-free rainwater serves almost all of these uses, but sheer convenience means it is often easier to turn on a tap (which also has a financial cost attached if your water is metered). Fully automatic watering systems often need the high pressure of mains water in order to work

▲ Roof water flows through a downpipe into this recycled plastic water butt, which is fitted with an overflow pipe into a drain.

▲ Made from a recycled copper tank, this intriguing garden fountain is fed from a recirculating water reservoir.

effectively, but fortunately these are among the most efficient watering methods. Other non-garden (but often substantial) uses include filling paddling or swimming pools and washing vehicles.

SOURCES OF WATER IN A GARDEN

A typical garden provides water from various sources. Some comes directly from the sky as rain, hail and snow, while some is recycled tap or 'grey' water. Much of the water moving through a garden ultimately enters the local drainage and/or sewage network. In an eco garden, our goal is to harvest, intercept, divert and store as much usable water as possible.

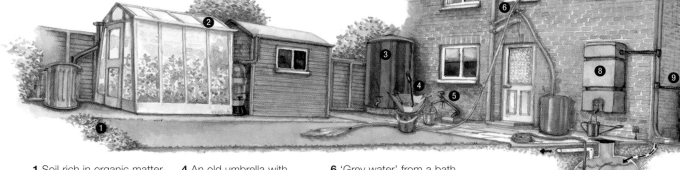

1 Soil rich in organic matter holds and stores water.
2 Greenhouse and shed roofs intercept rainwater to fill tanks or water butts.
3 Downpipes can be plumbed directly into large (recycled) plastic tanks (fit some fine mesh over the inlet pipe to filter out debris).

4 An old umbrella with holes in it captures small but useful amounts of water during rainstorms.
5 Fit outlet pipes from kitchen sinks and bathrooms with a diverter so that you can easily redirect suitable 'grey water' into a can, bucket or tank.

6 'Grey water' from a bath can easily be siphoned to the garden.
7 House and garage roofs are the single biggest source of rainwater in a garden.
8 Space-saving wall-mounted water butts store rainwater, which can be used for filling watering cans.

9 Rainwater diverters fitted to downpipes are easily plumbed into several linked water butts. When one butt is full, it overflows into the next.

10 In drier climates, an underground rainwater storage system can be a substantial but worthwhile investment; the water is pumped out as needed.

Harvesting and storing water

Harvesting and storing as much rainwater as you can is straightforward and costs very little. It is the most planet-friendly way to meet your eco garden's water needs. Almost any kind of container can be used for storage; water tanks or butts are popular and convenient and are often made from recycled plastic. Some waste household water or 'grey water' can also be used for watering.

Water in the soil
Soil is one of the most overlooked stores of water in a garden. Once it is improved with garden compost or other sources of organic matter, it can absorb and retain large amounts of water, which plants can then use. Although it can absorb large quantities of rainwater during heavy rainfall, soil will eventually dry out, especially during prolonged dry spells or drought, at which time plants will need a further supply.

▲ A greenhouse roof provides a good source of collectable rainwater.

▼ Here, rainwater is being piped to a wooden barrel from which a watering can could be filled.

Capturing water
Most harvestable water falls on the roofs of buildings, sheds and greenhouses. This normally runs into the gutters, then the downpipes, and on into the drainage network. You can intercept rainwater by tapping into the flow of water in the downpipe. A rainwater diverter is easily fitted to a downpipe, as is shown in the sequence 'Fitting

▲ If you find you are using more water than you are harvesting, water butts can be easily be linked together to increase your storage capacity.

a rainwater diverter'. On smaller structures such as sheds, a downpipe can simply feed water into an open tank through a lid, or be plumbed directly into a large water tank. To filter out any debris, recycle a fine-meshed nylon sock by securing it over the tank inlet pipe with a jubilee or hose clip. Ensure that any overflow water is directed into a drain, or perhaps to a pond or bog garden.

Polytunnels can be fitted with adhesive 'guttering' to harvest rainwater (there may be no other water source nearby).

Water storage
Rainwater can be stored in any watertight container. Custom-made plastic or metal tanks or water butts usually come pre-fitted with a lid and an outlet tap, and sometimes a base to raise them off the ground so that a watering can fits under the tap. Wall-mounted water tanks save on space. Choose recycled containers or those made from recycled materials. Lids prevent evaporation and deter both algal growth and breeding insects.

The amount of water stored will depend on the size of the garden and how much water it needs: food gardens will use more than deeply mulched

▲ Roofs offer the greatest potential for harvesting rain.

borders of ornamental plants. Greenhouses and polytunnels also increase garden water use. Aim to store as much rainwater as possible; you can always add extra capacity by linking together additional water tanks.

For safety, all water storage containers, especially larger ones, should have secure, tight-fitting lids and sit on a firm, solid base (not soil) that is able to carry their weight when full. For larger tanks, this might mean building a brick or block base. Drain the containers in winter to stop them from cracking, as water expands as it freezes. They can be scrubbed out while empty.

FITTING A RAINWATER DIVERTER

1 Check the fitting instructions carefully, then cut away a section of an existing downpipe and fix the bottom part of the diverter in place.

2 Fit the downpipe to the bottom of the diverter and attach it to the wall. The downpipe will still carry rainwater to the drain when the water butt is full.

3 This diverter comes with a handy leaf trap which fits inside it and gathers up any leaves and other debris which washes down from the gutters.

4 Fit the top part of the diverter into the bottom section. This design with its wide opening can accommodate either a round or square downpipe.

5 Use a short length of hosepipe to connect the diverter to a butt (it should be below the top of the butt so that any unharvestable water drains away).

6 To check the leaf trap, simply slide the top section of the diverter upwards. The trap will need emptying out at least once a week during autumn leaf fall.

USING 'GREY WATER'

'Grey water' is any domestic waste water other than sewage, including kitchen and bath or shower water. It is readily available and useful for garden watering. It should not contain excessive detergent, fat or highly perfumed toiletries (use eco-friendly biodegradable products). Never use chemical-laden dishwasher or washing machine water.

Use 'grey water' immediately; it quickly smells unpleasant if stored. Never bring it into contact with any edible part of a plant, including root crops; use it around fruit trees, and only with care around other crops. Avoid using it under cover and rotate its use around different areas of the garden.

Kitchen and bathroom waste pipes can be fitted with special water diverters for filling watering cans or buckets. The water from an upstairs bathtub can be siphoned through a garden hose straight down to the garden, or into a temporary holding tank. It is not suitable for automatic or semi-automatic watering systems.

▶ Use 'grey water' straight from a bowl.

▲ Water-capturing methods can be very simple. This old galvanized metal water tank is fed by a downpipe running from the shed roof. Various plants have grown up around it, making it an attractive feature in its own right.

Watering techniques

There are various ways of getting stored rainwater or tap water to the roots of your plants. They range from the simplest – using a watering can – to installing a fully automatic irrigation system which does most of the work for you. Low-tech watering methods, involving minimal use of energy and resources, and often using recycled materials, are good choices for an eco garden.

Why watering matters

When plants run short of water, the most visible symptom is wilting: the leaves, stems and flowers flop and sag. This occurs when there is too little water available in the soil or compost (soil mix) to sustain healthy plant growth.

When plants run short of water, they become stressed and can suffer from various problems. Food crops become less productive, resulting in smaller plants, lower yields and the premature dropping of flowers and fruits. Plants are more prone to pests and diseases, and to nutrient deficiencies. Annual plants will 'bolt' (flower prematurely) while only small, and trees and shrubs may shed their leaves early.

Using water wisely

The first rule of watering is to reduce the need for it as much as possible. This keeps stored water in reserve for periods of real need, and it saves time. Choosing climate-appropriate plants, improving soil with organic matter and not disturbing it in dry weather, using mulches, removing weeds (which compete for water), shading seedlings from hot sun and sheltering plants from drying wind, all reduce the need for watering. When it does become necessary, apply these simple rules:

▼ Eco-friendly seaweed crumb mixed with compost (soil mix) helps retain moisture. The same quantity of crumb is shown dry (left) and after wetting.

* Only water if needed.
* Water in the early morning or evening.
* Prioritize seedlings and new plants (use tap water for watering in seeds and seedlings to avoid fungal 'damping off' disease).
* Always apply water directly to the soil or compost, not the leaves, which helps to avoid fungal diseases.
* Use automatic or semi-automatic systems with a timer to control time and duration of watering.
* Avoid using sprinklers or fine-spray watering lances: they use lots of water and much of it is wasted through evaporation.
* Do not water lawns during dry spells.

▲ Water has many uses in the garden. Here it is used as a carrier to apply natural slug-controlling eelworms (nematodes) to the soil around early potatoes.

▼ Making a shallow, saucer-shaped depression around new plants and filling it with water ensures that it soaks deep into the soil around their roots.

Simple watering techniques

Water stored in a tank or butt can be transferred to where it is needed in different ways. The simplest way is to fill either a bucket or a watering can and carry the water to the plants that need it. Various semi-automatic devices are also available for watering containers. These turn empty plastic drink bottles into mini reservoirs; water seeps through a spike pushed into the compost, or through an adjustable dripper, over several hours.

▲ Pot-grown plants can be stood in a saucer so the compost can draw up water through holes in the base of the pot.

▲ When full, this large 1,500-litre (330-gallon) recycled water tank produces enough pressure to run a semi-automatic watering system.

▼ If using an automatic system, fit a timer so that watering takes place at the optimum time of day, which is during the cooler night-time period.

DIFFERENT WATERING TECHNIQUES

▲ **Watering can** – use a can to pour water around plants or for watering containers; put a 'rose' over the spout for a fine spray of water.

▲ **'Leaky pipe'** – water seeps through pores in the recycled rubber pipe, which is permanently buried 5–10cm (2–4in) deep in the soil or beneath a mulch.

▲ **Drip waterer** – an adjustable dripper regulates the flow of water to the compost (soil mix) from a plastic bottle reservoir.

▲ **Porous pot** – a buried terracotta pot, fed by a low-pressure water supply (such as a large tank of water) releases moisture into the soil or compost.

▲ **Bottle-top waterer** – a screw-on attachment recycles an empty plastic bottle into a handy waterer for use on young plants and delicate seedlings.

▲ **Watering spike** – this screws on to a plastic bottle and is pushed into the compost, where it slowly releases water over several hours.

A body of stored water can produce enough pressure to make water flow along a garden hose, provided the water level remains above the final outlet (water will not flow uphill). The larger the body of water, the greater the pressure; raising tanks on a base at least 30cm (12in) off the ground can help. This makes it possible to use a garden hose to water directly from a tank, or to fill up a tank or butt elsewhere. The low water pressure makes it easily controllable by placing a thumb over the hose end (or use an attachment).

Advanced systems

Some semi-automatic systems operate using filtered, tank-only pressure water. Dripper pipes, tapes or tubes are laid on the soil (usually in a food garden), and dispense water through holes or nozzles over their entire length. They are easily moved around. A network of porous terracotta pots, linked by plastic tubing, will also operate from a tank. Water fills the buried pots, then percolates into the soil or compost.

Drip irrigation systems carry water to individual plants or containers through plastic pipes to special drip nozzles, and they need fitting with a non-return valve. Using a timer allows watering for a set period. These systems usually need mains tap water pressure to operate, so are less eco-friendly than those using stored rainwater.

A recycled rubber 'leaky pipe' releases water, under pressure, through its pores. It is covered with soil or a mulch, so evaporation losses are minimal, making it an efficient way of watering permanently planted beds and borders.

FOOD GARDENING

Growing at least some of your own fresh, chemical-free and seasonal food is the most planet-friendly of all gardening activities. This chapter explains why home-grown food is so important in helping to reduce your environmental footprint, illustrates what 'food miles' are, and shows how to plan and create an attractive food garden from scratch. Clear step-by-step advice is given for sowing and planting vegetables, growing potatoes, container fruits and tree fruits, and for raising sprouting seeds and microgreens. There are suggestions, too, for beautiful yet productive ways of using vertical growing space.

◀ When you grow your own fresh food, you know everything that has happened to it during its journey from your garden or allotment to your plate.

▲ Kept cool and dry, summer-grown winter squash stores for months.

▲ Potatoes are both an easily grown and highly rewarding food crop.

▲ Bite-size cherry tomatoes can be grown in pots and hanging baskets.

Planet-friendly food

Growing at least some of your own vegetables, fruits and herbs is probably the most eco-friendly gardening activity there is. Home-grown food gathered from a garden or allotment travels only a short distance, requires minimal energy input and has a negligible environmental footprint. Garden-grown organic food is free of pesticide residues and is at its nutritional best when eaten.

Food and our environment

The range of fresh vegetables, salads, fruits and herbs on offer in any modern food store is impressive. Our globalized food industry means that fresh produce from every part of the world is now offered almost all year round – even when it is out of season where it is purchased and eaten.

A good example is strawberries. We traditionally eat these fruits during summer, when the plants naturally flower and produce fruit, but they can now be eaten on every day of the year, even in the depths of winter. Modern food systems have delivered incredible choice, but they have also helped to disconnect us from the changing seasons.

Although a globalized food system could be considered a sign of progress, it is increasingly associated with considerable costs in environmental terms, and the growing demand for food is having an accelerating impact on the world around us.

▲ Strawberries were once iconic summer fruits, but globalized food production means they are available every day of the year.

▲ Home-grown food may not resemble 'perfect' supermarket produce, but it has only a tiny environmental footprint.

The energy intensity of food

Fresh food that has been grown organically uses no synthetic, oil-derived fertilizers, pesticides or fungicides. It has travelled the shortest possible distance, does not need refrigerating, has received

WHAT ARE FOOD MILES?

The distance food travels from where it is grown to where it is eaten is measured in food miles (1 mile is equivalent to 1.6km). The further away it is grown, the higher the food miles and the more energy-intensive the food.

This illustration shows the relationship between the chain of events that make up our current globalized food system, and a home food garden. On the far right is a flourishing, eco-friendly food garden, where much of the produce is grown and then eaten only steps away from where it is harvested. Food which cannot practically be home-grown is bought fresh

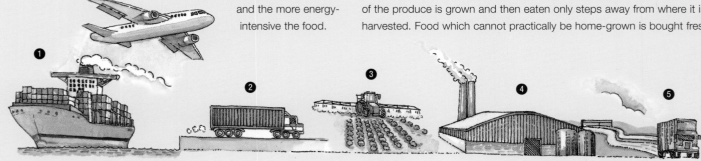

1 Food travels thousands of miles by air, sea and road. Transport emissions release greenhouse gases which are contributing to global warming.

2 Road transport increases the demand for new road networks, leading to the destruction of natural habitats and increases in air pollution.

3 Food grown as a single-crop monoculture requires high inputs of oil-derived, energy-intensive synthetic fertilizers, weedkillers and pesticides.

4 Processing and packaging food is energy-intensive and creates waste when cosmetically less-than-perfect produce is rejected.

5 Additional road transport carries both processed and unprocessed fresh food to supermarkets, adding further to pollution from vehicle emissions.

▲ Food is often transported over long distances to be processed and packaged – often far from where it is produced – before being trucked back to or close to its origin, where it is finally sold in shops and supermarkets.

▲ Excessive, resource-hungry packaging is eliminated entirely when you grow your own planet-friendly food. These apples are picked and eaten straight from the tree.

minimal processing and comes with little or no packaging, and therefore has a low energy intensity. In contrast, food that has been grown using synthetic fertilizers and biocides, has travelled long distances, needs power-hungry refrigeration and is highly processed and packaged – and subsequently marketed – has a high energy intensity.

Food with a high energy intensity has almost always travelled the furthest distance, while low energy-intensity food has travelled the shortest. An apple picked in season from your garden has

a much lower energy intensity than one imported, out of season (organically grown or not), from the other side of the world. The distance food travels is measured in 'food miles', which are explained in the illustration 'What are food miles?'.

Environmental footprints

An environmental footprint is a measure of the resources, such as land, water and energy, needed to grow food. Because food with a high energy intensity demands many different inputs, it has a large environmental footprint. Food you grow yourself has low energy intensity, giving it a tiny environmental footprint, and this is the main reason why food gardening is a key part of more sustainable living.

A major concern with globalized food production is the impact on supplies of fresh water. When we import food crops, we also import the 'virtual water' it took to grow them. Food crops requiring a lot of water are said to have a large water footprint, while that of garden produce, grown using harvested rainwater, is only small. Because many crops are grown in countries with limited water supplies, exporting virtual water can damage fragile ecosystems.

Turning part of your garden over to growing food helps to reduce the energy intensity of what you eat and lightens your environmental footprint.

from the local farmers' market or greengrocer, who in turn stock food (often organically produced) from local market gardens. Some locally, regionally or nationally sourced seasonal food is occasionally available in the out-of-town, car-dependent supermarket. But most of the food available here derives from the chain of events which stretch away to the

far left. This highly industrialized part of our 'food chain' is vulnerable to unexpected shocks and disruption. If there is a break in the supply of foodstuffs due, for example, to fuel shortages or natural disasters, then supplies in supermarkets can quickly dwindle. In contrast, a home food garden increases self-reliance and makes us personally more resilient.

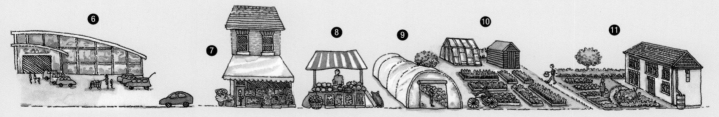

6 Supermarkets use energy around the clock, keeping some food cool and the store warm and lit. Customers' cars emit greenhouse gases.

7 Local greengrocers often sell locally grown as well as imported food, and might be reachable by public transport networks, by bicycle or on foot.

8 Farmers' markets offer mostly seasonal, locally grown food that is often produced organically without using synthetic fertilizers or pesticides.

9 Small-scale market gardens often offer fresh and local produce via an organic box scheme.
10 An allotment within walking or cycling distance

is ideal if gardening space at home is limited.
11 Low energy-intensity garden produce involves no food miles and contains no pesticide residues.

Planning a food garden

A garden dedicated to growing food will be more successful if you start by drawing up an overall plan and then develop it in stages. This phased approach brings a gradual improvement to the soil, encourages the gardener to perfect sowing and planting techniques with easy-to-grow crops, and allows time to identify the best spots for growing long-term crops, such as fruit.

Assessing the garden

In a new or existing garden where you have decided to start growing food, the first step is to look at what is already in place. It helps to sketch out a plan of the garden and record basic measurements, such as how wide and long it is. You can then mark the areas covered by paving or paths, the layout and shape of existing beds or borders, where fences are and the position of any trees or a shed. Use a tape measure to make the plan as accurate as possible, but do not worry if some measurements are approximate – these plans can be modified as the garden develops.

Sun and shade

It is important to identify those parts of the garden that receive most sun and those that remain in shade. Sheltered sunny fences can be used to grow warmth-loving fruits, while compost bins and sheds can go in the shadier spots.

Taking photographs is a simple way to record where the sun falls. On a bright day, preferably in summer, when the sun is high in the sky (midday is ideal), take photographs from different points in the garden, including ones from upstairs windows and from each corner of the plot. Mark on the plan where the sunny and shady spots are.

▲ Aubergines (eggplants) thrive in a sunny spot.

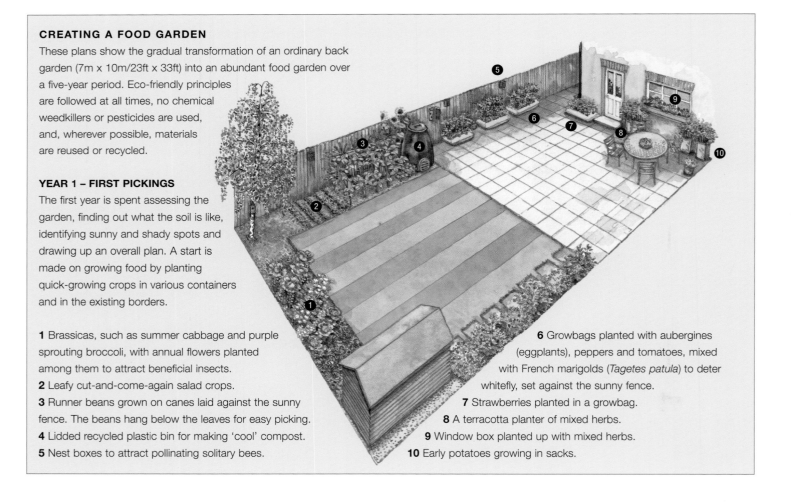

CREATING A FOOD GARDEN

These plans show the gradual transformation of an ordinary back garden (7m x 10m/23ft x 33ft) into an abundant food garden over a five-year period. Eco-friendly principles are followed at all times, no chemical weedkillers or pesticides are used, and, wherever possible, materials are reused or recycled.

YEAR 1 – FIRST PICKINGS

The first year is spent assessing the garden, finding out what the soil is like, identifying sunny and shady spots and drawing up an overall plan. A start is made on growing food by planting quick-growing crops in various containers and in the existing borders.

1 Brassicas, such as summer cabbage and purple sprouting broccoli, with annual flowers planted among them to attract beneficial insects.
2 Leafy cut-and-come-again salad crops.
3 Runner beans grown on canes laid against the sunny fence. The beans hang below the leaves for easy picking.
4 Lidded recycled plastic bin for making 'cool' compost.
5 Nest boxes to attract pollinating solitary bees.

6 Growbags planted with aubergines (eggplants), peppers and tomatoes, mixed with French marigolds (*Tagetes patula*) to deter whitefly, set against the sunny fence.
7 Strawberries planted in a growbag.
8 A terracotta planter of mixed herbs.
9 Window box planted up with mixed herbs.
10 Early potatoes growing in sacks.

YEAR 3 – FULL OF PROMISE

The lawn has gone, bringing an end to energy-intensive and polluting lawn mowing. The paved area has been reduced in size and the soil (especially the compacted ground below the slabs) is being improved using local green waste compost. The lifted slabs are being reused as paths, a reconditioned greenhouse (a gift from a neighbour) has been added (and re-glazed with new glass), and the first raised beds are producing food.

1 Compost bin made from recycled pallets.
2 Leaves rotting down in a leaf-mould cage.
3 Black plastic sheeting smothers the remaining lawn.
4 One-year-old cordon fruit trees trained at a 45-degree angle and supported by taut horizontal wires.
5 Tomatoes, with whitefly-deterring French marigolds (*Tagetes patula*), in the 1.8 x 1.2m (6 x 4ft) greenhouse.
6 Water butt filled from a rainwater diverter on a downpipe.

7 Annual and perennial flower borders attract beneficial insects.
8 Crops provide a growing quantity of food mile-free produce that has not been sprayed with chemicals.
9 Raised beds made with rot- and maintenance-free recycled plastic, separated by wood-chip paths.
10 No-dig maincrop potatoes grow through a sheet mulch laid over the remaining lawn, which smothers and kills all but the toughest weeds.

YEAR 5 – EDIBLE ABUNDANCE

The structure of the garden is now complete and includes a fruit cage to protect the currants and raspberries from birds, more raised beds, a pond and a log pile to attract wildlife. The compost-making capacity has been increased with an extra bin (and could be expanded to a third if needed). Fresh, planet-friendly and low energy-intensity food is being harvested from the garden all year round, helping to reduce the household's overall environmental footprint.

1 Another leaf-mould cage has been added.
2 A log pile creates a wildlife habitat.
3 Black, red and white currants and raspberries grow in a 2 x 2m (7 x 7ft) fruit cage.
4 Cordon fruit trees crop heavily.
5 Rhubarb and asparagus grow permanently in 1 x 1m (3 x 3ft) square beds to which plenty of garden compost has been added.
6 Bed planted with a mixture of herbs.

7 Up off the ground, fast-growing salad leaves are safe from slugs in the window box.
8 Blocks of annual vegetables are rotated between beds each year to avoid a build-up of soil diseases.
9 Self-seeded pot marigolds (*Calendula*) grow among the vegetables and draw in beneficial insects, such as hoverflies.
10 Wildlife is attracted to a small pond 50cm (20in) in diameter. Frogs and toads breed here in spring, helping to boost the local population.

Sowing vegetables

There are different ways of sowing seeds, depending on their size and how they grow. Although you can sow vegetable seeds in various types of container, then plant them out in the garden, most can be sown directly into the soil where you want them to grow until harvest time. Crops such as parsnips, which are grown for their roots and dislike being disturbed, are best treated this way.

Preparing the soil

Any soil preparation, such as working in soil improvers, should be done several weeks before sowing. Use a rake to break up large clods of soil and to produce an even and fine surface tilth: the smaller the seed, the finer the tilth should be. Larger seeds, such as broad beans, can be sown in soil with a rougher finish.

If the soil is dry (in greenhouses and polytunnels it can become very dry during summer), water it thoroughly first and cover it with a sheet of cardboard or plastic to retain moisture.

Never sow seeds when the soil is wet, frozen or sticks to your boots. Vegetables are usually sown outdoors from spring, when the soil feels warm to the touch, through to autumn.

Sowing techniques

Most vegetable seeds can be sown in a narrow V-shaped groove, also called a drill. The depth of the groove depends on the seed size – smaller seeds are sown in shallower grooves and vice versa.

▲ As young vegetable and salad plants grow, they quickly fill the available space. Some will need removing (thinning out) regularly to allow the others to mature.

SOWING IN A SOIL GROOVE

1 You can make a simple wooden soil groove (drill) former from a piece of door frame that is narrower along one edge. Mark it into divisions 1cm (½in) apart.

2 To make a soil groove, press the wooden former into the level, raked surface and rock it from side to side. Use the guide marks to check the depth.

3 If the soil is dry, water the bottom of the V-shaped groove. This gives quicker seed germination and encourages the seedling roots down into the soil.

4 Lay the wooden former along the groove and use it to sow seeds at the correct spacing (check the seed packet). These are 3cm (1¼in) apart.

5 Cover the seeds by floating your fingers over the surface and drawing loose soil into the groove (do not firm the soil). Label with the name and date.

SOWING IN A WIDE GROOVE

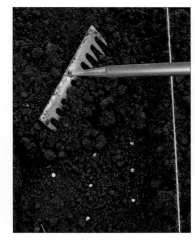

1 Larger seeds such as these peas can be sown in a wide groove (drill) around 25cm (10in) wide and 5cm (2in) deep, which is formed using a rake and working to taut garden line.

2 Sow the large pea seeds individually, spacing them so there is an equal distance of 5–7.5cm (2–3in) each way between the seeds. Three rows of seeds are ample for this groove.

3 Mark the position of the groove at each end, then use the head of the rake to carefully draw loose soil back into the groove, covering the seeds without disturbing them.

▲ Large seeds can be sown in individual, evenly spaced holes made using a dibber. Lay a wooden former on the soil and use it to make holes at the desired spacing. Cover the seeds with soil afterwards.

If you are sowing in long rows across a large area, make a groove using a hoe blade drawn through the soil following a line or board edge to get a straight line.

In narrow or raised beds, where you work from the paths, the tip of a trowel blade, a short stick or even a finger make good grooves. If you are sowing many short rows, a home-made wooden former is quick and simple to use. It also acts as a guide to how far apart and how deep to sow seeds (or space young plants), and is shown in the sequence 'Sowing in a soil groove'. Some seeds, such as peas, are sown in wider grooves, as shown in the sequence 'Sowing in a wide groove'. Large seeds can be sown in individual, evenly spaced holes made with a dibber or trowel.

If seeds have been sown close together in a groove, some of the seedlings will need removing to give the others room to grow. Water the soil first and then gently uproot or nip off every other seedling, so those remaining are just touching. Several such thinnings might be necessary, depending on the type of vegetable (check seed packets for final spacings).

Pelleted seeds and tapes

Small seeds are sometimes coated in inert clay to make sowing easier. When the pellet is sown it disintegrates, leaving the seed free to grow.

Check the seed packet and avoid seed coatings that contain any pesticides or fungicides. Seed tapes are strips of biodegradable paper, containing evenly spaced seeds, which are laid along a soil groove and covered over. The paper rots, and the resulting plants do not need thinning.

▼ These broad (fava) beans were sown directly into the soil at the correct spacing. As they grow larger, the plants will fill out the available space.

Planting vegetables

Vegetable plants that you raise yourself in pots or cells on a sunny wall, or in a greenhouse or polytunnel, will eventually need planting either in the soil or in containers of compost (soil mix). Crops sown directly into the soil need transplanting when they are large enough. Planting time is always exciting – the young plants you have nurtured will now grow to maturity and produce food.

Preparing to plant

Always cultivate the soil to remove any weeds, and add soil improvers several weeks before planting. Vegetables can be planted, depending on the type of crop, from spring, once the soil is workable and warm, right through to autumn. Check planting distances for each crop before you start.

Young vegetable plants grown in pots, multi-cell trays or coir plugs should have a dense mass of fast-growing roots by planting time. This is called the root-ball. To check how well developed it is, gently tap a plant out of its pot, or ease one from its cell. The pale roots should just be starting to grow against the inside of the pot or cell.

The roots should hold the compost (soil mix) together. If only a few roots are visible and the compost falls away, put the plant back in its pot and grow it on for a few more weeks. If a thick dense mass of roots are circling the pot, the plant needs either planting immediately or moving into a larger pot. Plants that run out of root room will stop growing and can take longer to establish after planting. When roots appear through the sides and

base of biodegradable paper or coir pots, they are ready to plant. The pot is not removed and eventually rots down into the soil.

Always water plants thoroughly before planting. If the compost feels dry and sticks to the pot or cell, if the plant feels light in weight or it is wilting, soak the root-ball in water until no more air bubbles appear. How to plant is shown in the sequence 'Planting a pot-grown vegetable'.

▲ To plant into large pots and tubs, first fill the container with compost (soil mix), make a hole for the root-ball, plant, firm in, and water.

PLANTING A POT-GROWN VEGETABLE

1 Use a trowel to take out a planting hole roughly twice the width of the root-ball and the same depth. Use your fingers to make small holes.

2 Water the plant first (this is a sweet pepper) and then remove its pot. Place the root-ball in the hole and check it is level with the surrounding soil.

3 Push some loose soil in around the root-ball and press down gently with your fingertips to firm it in. Put any plant supports in place at this stage.

4 Draw some of the soil away from the base of the plant to form a shallow depression, then pour water into this so it soaks down around the roots.

▼ Pea roots are starting to grow through this biodegradable pot made from cow manure. The whole pot can be planted and will rot down in the soil.

STARTER OR 'PLUG' PLANTS

Young vegetable plants grown in small individual cells of compost (soil mix) are known as starter or 'plug' plants. They are convenient if you do not have the facilities (or time) to raise plants from seed. Mail order is the commonest way of obtaining them; look for those from an organically accredited grower.

Starter plants are planted on arrival and root disturbance is minimal. Open the packaging, water any dry plugs and put them in a shady spot. Plant into small holes made with your finger or a dibber (shown in the sequence), firm gently and water thoroughly. If you cannot plant them out immediately, grow them on in pots of peat-free compost.

1 Unpack and water young starter or 'plug' plants on arrival.

2 Plant each mini root-ball in a hole and firm in using your fingertips.

Hardening off

Plants grown under cover need acclimatizing to the cooler and more exposed conditions outdoors by hardening off. Do this by standing them outdoors during the day and bringing them back indoors at night, for a period of about ten days. Towards the end of the period, unless frost is forecast, they can be left out day and night (cover with fleece on cold nights). Crops grown in a greenhouse or polytunnel do not need hardening off.

Care after planting

Mulching the soil stops it from drying out and prevents weeds from growing. Try to avoid further watering until the plant is growing strongly. This encourages new roots to grow down into the soil or compost and not stay near the surface, where they are prone to drying out. Further watering should be done infrequently but thoroughly, so that the water soaks deep into the soil.

If the crop climbs or needs support, push sticks or canes into position before or just after planting. Twiggy sticks should be pushed in after you plant out peas so that they grow up through them.

Transplanting vegetables

Vegetable plants such as lettuces, which are sown outdoors, then lifted when young and replanted, where they will grow until harvesting, are called transplants. Root crops are not usually transplanted.

Transplant vegetables when it is cool and overcast. Water them first, loosen the soil around the roots and carefully lift them out. Make a planting hole just big enough for the roots, push soil around them, gently firm and water in thoroughly. The leaves often wilt in the sun – this is normal until new roots grow.

▼ These vegetables were all sown elsewhere in the garden, then transplanted as young plants into this bed, where they will grow until they are finally harvested.

▲ Lettuce is a quick-growing salad vegetable which can easily be sown in rows and thinned out, transplanted, or planted as starter or 'plug' plants.

Sprouting seeds and microgreens

You do not need a garden to grow your own sprouting seeds or microgreens – a warm spot indoors is all they require. Both seeds and microgreens produce fresh food in a matter of days, are easy to grow, come in many different flavours, and are rich in health-promoting minerals, vitamins and proteins. This eco-friendly food can be raised all year round and eaten raw.

Sprouting seeds

When seeds start to germinate and grow they produce a small root and a tiny shoot. Seedlings grow quickly at this stage and are very tender. Sprouting seeds (also called seed sprouts) are usually ready to eat in two to seven days when they are approximately 6–40mm (¼–1½in) long. Both the shoot and the seed are eaten.

The seeds are not sown in compost (soil mix) but are soaked or moistened with water and sprouted in warm conditions, with or without light. Bringing them into natural light just before you eat them improves their flavour. Sprouted seeds are a very eco-friendly food for harvesting all year round, needing only water and the background warmth of your home or an unheated greenhouse to grow.

Always use seeds intended for sprouting, ideally from an organically accredited supplier, and always wash them thoroughly in a sieve (strainer) before putting them to sprout. Vegetable seeds treated with chemical pesticides and fungicides should never be eaten. Sprouting works best either in a home-made sprouter such as a glass jar, or in a tiered sprouter as shown in the sequence 'How to sprout seeds'.

▲ A selection of sprouted seeds: (**1**) sunflower; (**2**) rocket (arugula); (**3**) cress; (**4**) alfalfa; (**5**) wheatgrass; (**6**) fenugreek; (**7**) onion; (**8**) adzuki beans; (**9**) radish; (**10**) red cabbage; (**11**) red mustard; (**12**) mung beans; (**13**) peas.

Sprouted seeds can be eaten in sandwiches, salads and stir fries. Avoid eating large quantities of raw sprouted seeds from the pea and bean (legume) family, such as mung beans, fenugreek and peas, in one go. These contain traces of toxin, which is harmless in small amounts.

▲ By making fresh sowings every few days, a tiered sprouter allows you to grow a continuous succession of fresh sprouting seeds.

HOW TO SPROUT SEEDS

1 Some seeds (these are fenugreek) benefit from being soaked overnight in clean tap water. Check each type of seed for any specific instructions.

2 Tiered sprouters allow you to produce lots of sprouts in a small space. Spread the seeds (dry or pre-soaked) out evenly over one of the tiers.

3 Pour fresh tap water over the seeds to moisten them. Excess water runs through the slatted tier to any seeds below. Repeat this 2–3 times a day.

4 Fenugreek is ready to eat when the sprouts are approximately 2.5cm (1in) long. Gather the shoots and rinse them thoroughly under a tap before eating.

▼ The simplest way to sprout seeds is in a glass jar topped with a mesh cover. They should be rinsed several times daily.

GROWING MICROGREENS

1 Put 1cm (½in) of fine-grade vermiculite in a small clean tray. Vermiculite is a sterile, inert growing medium which supports the roots of the microgreens as they grow.

2 Using a bottle top waterer with a fine spray attachment, wet the vermiculite with tap water until it just begins to drain from the base of the tray.

3 Put some seeds (these are mustard) in the palm of your hand, sowing them thickly but evenly over the surface of the moist vermiculite. Do not cover.

4 Using the bottle top waterer or a fine mist sprayer, wet the seeds using tap water. Spray several times daily to keep the seeds moist.

5 Keep the tray in a warm, well-lit spot such as a windowsill. When the microgreens are 5–7cm (2–3in) tall, harvest them with clean scissors.

CHOOSING WHAT TO GROW

The following can all be grown as sprouted seeds and/or microgreens.

Sprouting seeds:
Adzuki beans
Alfalfa
Beet
Chickpeas
Fenugreek
Mung beans
Sunflower
Wheatgrass

Microgreens:
Broccoli*
Chervil
Cress*
Peas (various)*
Mustard*
Radish*
Red cabbage
Rocket (arugula)*

* = Suitable for both sprouting seeds and microgreens

Microgreens

These are fast-growing young seedlings with intense flavour, which are eaten when they have their first two seed leaves (cotyledons) and are 2.5–7cm (1–3in) high. They are sown on to compost, vermiculite or moist paper towels, and kept on a bright windowsill indoors or in a greenhouse. If you do sow them on to compost, you will need to take extra care when watering and harvesting to make sure the compost does not soil the sprouts. They need moisture, warmth and light to grow and are best sown from spring to autumn, when temperatures and light levels are high. They will grow indoors in winter, but only very slowly. Microgreens are usually ready in five to fifteen days and are simply snipped off and eaten. The best way to grow microgreens is shown in the sequence 'Growing microgreens'.

Storing sprouted seeds and microgreens

These tasty ingredients should be eaten as soon as they are ready, but they can be stored in a refrigerator for a few days. Put the sprouted seeds or snipped microgreens into sealed containers or tightly tied plastic bags. If they begin to discolour, compost them. Microgreens will grow tall and leggy, turn yellow and lose their flavour if you leave them too long before cutting.

► You do not need a garden to grow food – microgreens will grow on a sunny windowsill in a warm room indoors. These are at the optimum stage for cutting and eating.

Vertical vegetables and fruits

One of the most enjoyable aspects of food gardening, especially in a small garden, is finding ways of making the most of every available growing space. While many crops grow close to the ground, others will climb naturally up supports or over other structures, or can be trained against walls and fences. Containers and hanging baskets also help to make use of vertical growing space.

Beautiful and productive

Growing vegetables and fruits upwards into the space above the ground not only maximizes your returns, it also creates eye-catching features. Using vertical space is sometimes the most effective way to grow crops that you do not have room for anywhere else. As well as looking attractive and producing food, some crops can also be functional: a row of cordon or espalier apples makes an edible, attractive and constantly changing alternative to a hedge or fence.

A simple teepee of sticks covered with climbing beans is not just productive, it is beautiful too. Training apples or other tree fruits, or guiding

▼ This eye-catching feature is formed from apples that have been trained up and over a sturdy metal arch at the entrance to another part of this food garden.

trailing vegetables over an arch creates a highly decorative feature which also bears fruits and will look good whatever the season. Even peas become ornamental when supported by an imaginatively woven framework of twiggy sticks.

Upright cordon tree fruits, which form narrow vertical columns of flowers and then fruits, can be grown as the centrepiece of a bed in a decorative kitchen garden or potager, where vegetables, fruits and herbs are intermingled, or in a container.

The space next to a wall or fence can be utilized for vertical food gardening. Climbing beans thrive against a warm, sunny wall, and will climb up sticks, trellis, strings or netting. Tree and bush fruits can be trained vertically as cordons, espaliers or fans.

Temporary structures

The most basic type of support for fast-climbing vegetables, such as beans and squashes, is a group of sticks or canes arranged in a circle and tied together at the top. Sticks from your garden or from a local coppiced woodland will give your

▲ Runner beans climbing up a teepee of thick poles tied at the top make a simple but beautiful vertical focal point in a more ornamental food garden.

MAKING A HOME-MADE STRAWBERRY TOWER

1 Turn a used compost (soil mix) bag inside out and fill it with peat-free potting compost, then puncture some drainage holes around the base.

2 Work out how many plants the bag will take. Each plant should be no less than 15cm (6in) apart. Cut cross-shaped planting holes in the top and sides.

3 Plant up the young plants by passing their root-balls through the pre-cut holes and into the compost, which should be firmed in around them.

◀ Redcurrants can easily be trained as single-stemmed cordons against a sunny wall or fence, which makes both finding and picking the fruits extremely easy.

▶ This modular growing system allows you to grow vegetables, herbs and flowers against a sunny wall. This one is planted with oriental vegetables.

Hanging baskets and containers

Crops can also be grown downwards into vertical space by using hanging baskets. Crops that are happy to flop and hang, such as bush tomatoes, grow well in baskets, and in wall- or fence-mounted planters. Food crops in baskets need more careful watering, but are less prone to attack by pests such as slugs, and flowers can be planted among them to attract beneficial insects.

Narrow and upright containers or 'towers' of compost (soil mix) will grow a range of edible crops. These can be purchased or you can make your own. The best way to plant a do-it-yourself strawberry tower is shown in the sequence below.

Flat, wall-mounted planters can be filled with herbs, salads and bush tomatoes. They are fitted with a reservoir, which sits on the top of the planter and feeds water and liquid plant food to special nozzles buried in the compost, so they use water efficiently. The planters should be kept flat at first, to allow crops to develop strong root systems before being hung up. They can be used singly or in groups to create an 'edible wall'.

structures a distinctive look. Sturdier support is needed for heavier crops such as squashes, which produce heavy fruits, and can be made from thicker sticks fixed together with wire or screws.

Permanent supports

Fruit grown on walls or fences, or over arches or other structures, needs a permanent means of support that can carry plants weighed down with fruit. Metal is a good, long-lasting choice for an arch.

On walls and fences, galvanized wire, fixed horizontally, is a durable way to support cordons of both tree and bush fruits such as red or white currants. Wires are also useful for supporting cane fruits, such as blackberries, whose stems can be fanned into attractive patterns.

▲ Bush tomatoes and nasturtium (*Tropaeolum majus*), with its edible flowers and leaves, mingle together in this hanging basket that utilizes vertical cropping space.

4 Sink a flower pot into the top of the bag and water into this until it drains from the base of the bag. Use the pot for subsequent watering/feeding.

5 Stand the planted bag in an open, sunny spot, checking that it will remain upright without any extra support. Turn the bag daily to ensure even growth.

6 When the plants are growing strongly, water regularly and feed weekly with a high-potash liquid plant food to encourage flowers and fruits.

7 Fruiting can be encouraged by pollinating the flowers using a small soft-bristled brush to dust pollen between the flowers. Bees will also do this job.

8 To protect the fruits from birds, drape some netting over the bag as they ripen. Pick the fruits regularly and keep watering and feeding while the plants are cropping.

Growing potatoes

Fresh home-grown potatoes taste delicious and are easy to grow almost anywhere. Ultra-early crops can be raised indoors in containers in a unheated porch, greenhouse or polytunnel. Outdoors, they can be grown in pots or sacks next to a sunny wall, or planted in rows in your eco garden or allotment. To grow a lot of potatoes, you need plenty of space.

Types of potato

Potatoes are a frost-tender crop which is planted in spring. Potatoes fall into two groups according to when you harvest them. Earlies are eaten when the tubers are immature, as new potatoes, while the tubers of maincrops are usually left to mature before being harvested. Earlies are ready from late spring onwards if grown under cover, or from early summer outdoors. Maincrops are eaten from summer onwards and can be stored for autumn and winter use. Second-cropping varieties are planted in late summer and harvested as new potatoes from mid-autumn until mid-winter.

Choosing varieties

There are hundreds of potato varieties, ranging from unusual heritage (heirloom) types such as the blue-fleshed 'Congo' to modern, disease-resistant 'Sárpo Mira', which resists attack by potato blight (a fungal disease that also affects tomatoes). Potatoes usually have white or red skins, sometimes with colourful blue or red spots. Those with a waxy texture are good for boiling; a floury texture is ideal for baking and roasting.

▲ 'Sárpo Mira' is one of a new breed of eco-friendly maincrop potatoes that is naturally resistant to potato blight disease. It also grows well on drier soils.

Potatoes are bought as seed potatoes, which are not seeds, but tubers grown specially for planting. Always buy those certified as disease-free. Some eye-catching heritage varieties are available as virus- and disease-free mini-tubers, which produce vigorous, high-yielding plants.

▲ Once growing strongly, potato haulms (leafy tops) form a dense, shade-casting canopy which prevents annual weeds from germinating and helps smother and weaken any perennial weeds.

GROWING POTATOES IN SOIL RIDGES

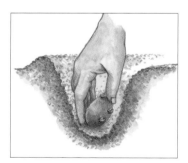

1 To grow potatoes outdoors, prepare the soil in advance and plant chitted seed potatoes in rows of holes 15cm (6in) deep. Plant from early to mid-spring when the soil is easily workable.

2 As soon as the leafy shoots (haulms) begin to push through the soil, use a draw hoe to start pulling loose soil up into a ridge (a technique known as earthing up) to just cover the shoots.

3 Draw more soil up each time new leaves appear, until the ridge is approximately 30cm (12in) high. The plants will produce flowers on leafy shoots, and then tubers appear and swell inside the ridge.

4 To harvest, carefully slide a fork underneath the plant (as deep as possible to avoid puncturing the tubers), grasp hold of the shoots and lift the entire plant upwards and out of the soil.

WHAT IS 'CHITTING'?

Encouraging young shoots or 'chits' to grow before planting encourages earlier crops. Arrange tubers with their rose end (the end with most tiny buds) upwards in a tray in a cool, frost-free, bright spot. Plant when the chits are 2.5cm (1in) long.

▲ 'Chits' are made up of shoots and embryonic roots.

◄ Garden fleece can be used to protect the first leafy shoots of potatoes if ground frost is forecast. Use a double thickness and anchor with stones.

◄ Heritage (heirloom) potatoes come in a striking range of skin colours, some of which are carried through into the flesh. The variety names often give clues to some of the intriguing stories behind them:
(**1**) 'Aura'; (**2**) 'Fortyfold';
(**3**) 'Shetland Black';
(**4**) 'Mr Little's Yetholm Gypsy'; (**5**) 'Puritan';
(**6**) 'Highland Burgundy Red'; (**7**) 'Vitelotte';
(**8**) 'Red Craigs Royal';
(**9**) 'Congo'; (**10**) 'Salad Blue'.

Soil, situation and spacing

To grow potatoes under cover, plant them in a large pot, barrel or sack using peat-free compost (soil mix), or straight into a covered soil bed. Container growing is shown in the sequence 'Growing early potatoes in a plastic sack'.

Outdoors, choose an open, sunny position that is not prone to late spring frosts. Potatoes grow best in fertile, slightly acid soil. In the autumn before planting, improve the soil by working in well-rotted garden compost or one-year-old animal manure. Never grow potatoes on freshly manured ground.

Space earlies 30–38cm (12–15in) apart in rows 38–50cm (15–20in) apart, and maincrops 38cm (15in) apart in rows 75cm (30in) apart. Growing potatoes in soil ridges in a garden or allotment is shown in the illustrated sequence opposite.

VARIETIES

Earlies:
'Rocket' – white skin; heavy, early crops in containers.
'Sárpo Una' – pink skin; blight-resistant.
'Swift' – white skin; short bushy growth, ideal for containers.

Maincrops:
'Axona' – red skin; a blight-resistant 'Sárpo' variety.
'Desiree' – red skin; resists drought, good all-rounder.
'Sárpo Mira' – red skin; blight-resistant.

GROWING EARLY POTATOES IN A PLASTIC SACK

1 Put 15cm (6in) of peat-free compost (soil mix) in the base of the sack (puncture some holes in its base) and plant three seed potatoes, just covering them.

2 When leafy shoots appear, add more compost until the leaves are just buried. Roll up the sides of the sack as it gradually fills up. Water as needed.

3 Once the shoots emerge from the the sack, top it up with compost to within 2.5cm (1in) of the top. Water regularly and give a weekly liquid feed.

4 Keep the plants well watered. Tubers will begin to grow inside the sack – you can usually feel them. To harvest, empty the sack or cut it down one side.

Fruit in containers

You do not need a large garden to grow useful amounts of fresh and nutritious fruit that has zero food miles. Many bush and tree fruits can be grown in good-sized containers, which can be kept on sunny patios, in courtyards and on balconies. Plants in pots and tubs need more care and attention than those planted out in the garden, but are beautiful, rewarding and productive.

Choosing fruits

Many fruits grow successfully in containers: both tree fruits such as apples or cherries, and bush fruits such as blueberries, cranberries, gooseberries or black, red or white currants. Apricots, figs, grapes, nectarines, olives, peaches and plums are also suitable.

One of the main reasons for growing fruit in containers is lack of space. Tree fruits, which naturally grow into good-sized trees, are often grafted on to a dwarfing rootstock, which limits the plant's overall size and results in a much smaller tree. Check when you buy to find out the plant's eventual size and shape.

Bush fruits are not grafted, and their size is largely determined by the size of container used. A general rule with containerized fruit is: the smaller the pot, the smaller the plant and the fewer the fruits. When you grow fruit in containers, try to strike a balance between using the largest containers that you can easily move around. The two step sequences show how to pot up tree and bush fruits.

◄ This collection of apple trees is being grown on dwarfing rootstocks, which restricts their final size. These heavy terracotta pots give them stability.

▼ Redcurrants are a bush fruit that will grow well in a large half barrel.

PLANTING A BLUEBERRY IN A POT

1 For stability, use a terracotta pot. Place some flat stones over the drainage holes in the pot's base and add some peat- and lime-free (ericaceous) compost (soil mix).

2 Pot-grown plants can be potted up at any time, but spring and autumn are ideal times. Choose a strong, well-branched plant with plenty of young shoots.

3 Sit the root-ball on some compost in the pot, then add more and firm it in. Check that the root-ball is sitting level and is 2.5cm (1in) below the pot rim.

4 Water thoroughly until water drains from its base. Stand in an open, sunny spot, water regularly and give a high-potash liquid feed weekly during spring and summer.

Containers and compost

Because plants are often heavy when fruit-laden, wide-based terracotta, stone or wooden containers are preferable to more lightweight plastic ones. These are generally more stable, although you can add extra weight to a plastic container by using stones as a drainage layer.

Start with a container at least 30cm (12in) wide and deep; any smaller and the compost (soil mix) will dry out rapidly in summer. As the plant grows it can gradually be potted into a larger size container. A deep container 45–50cm (18–20in) in diameter is a good final size, as larger and heavier containers are harder to move around.

In containers the plant's roots are entirely reliant on the compost used for nutrients and water. Use a quality peat-free, loam-based compost formulated for long-term container growing. For acid-loving fruits, such as blueberries and cranberries, use a peat- and lime-free ericaceous compost.

Care and maintenance

Containerized fruit needs regular watering and feeding. Watering at least once a day is vital when young fruits are setting; if the roots dry out the fruit will drop off. Apply a home-made liquid feed weekly, from spring until autumn. In autumn and winter, only water if the compost dries out.

POTTING UP A DWARF APPLE TREE

1 Pot-grown apples can be planted year-round but spring and autumn are ideal times. Choose a heavy, flat-bottomed pot and cover the drainage holes with flat stones.

2 Check for plenty of thin, pale and actively growing roots just circling inside the pot. Avoid trees with dark, thick and woody roots circling round and round inside a split pot.

3 Put some peat-free potting compost (soil mix) in the base of the pot and firm it to leave no gaps. Stand the root-ball on the compost to check its depth in the pot.

4 After firming in, the top of the root-ball should be level with the compost, which should be 2.5cm (1in) below the pot rim to help when watering.

5 Give the pot a thorough soaking after potting, then stand it on pot feet to help keep the drainage holes clear and stop the compost becoming waterlogged.

6 Keep the tree well watered, and give a weekly high-potash liquid feed starting when the buds burst into growth in spring, until the end of summer.

◄ Blueberries produce useful crops in pots over several months. Their fruits are ready for picking when they turn from green to dark blue and begin to soften. Ripe fruits can be eaten fresh from the bush or they will store in a sealed container in a refrigerator for several weeks.

When the roots fill the container, pot on into a larger one, preferably in autumn, allowing enough space to add at least 5cm (2in) of fresh compost around the root-ball. When the plant is growing in its final pot, it can be top-dressed each spring by removing the top 5cm (2in) of old compost and replacing it with a fresh layer.

If containers freeze solid in winter, the plants in them will die and terracotta pots or tubs may crack as the compost expands. During severe cold weather, move plants to a sheltered position and/or wrap the container in bubble plastic or old blankets.

Growing tree fruits

Nothing beats being able to pick and eat your own apples, pears, cherries or other fruits straight from the tree. Planting tree fruits with dwarfing rootstocks, which keeps them small and compact, is the easiest way to include fruit in an eco garden with limited space. Tree fruits can be grown as mini orchards among your flowers and vegetables, or trained against walls and fences.

▲ Pears are relatively easy to grow in a garden and, where space is limited, can be trained as space-saving espaliers and cordons.

▼ This apple has been trained against a fence in horizontal tiers, and is known as an espalier.

What are tree fruits?

Tree fruits are those that naturally grow into trees, including apples, apricots, cherries, figs, peaches, mulberries, nectarines, pears and plums. They have a single main stem (trunk) and a framework of branches shaped by training and pruning. Tree fruits are long-lived, often cropping over decades.

Most tree fruits produce their flowers in spring, and these need protection, especially from air frost. The flowers are followed by fruits, which are ready to pick during summer and autumn. Some tree fruits can be stored; certain apple and pear varieties will keep for many months. Others are eaten when they are ripe, or stored in other ways, such as by freezing or bottling, or making them into preserves.

Types of tree

Young, vigorous trees become established more quickly than older ones. The type of tree you buy depends on how you intend to grow it. One-year-old 'maiden whips', which just have a single stem, can be grown and trained into any shape, while one- to two-year-old 'feathered maidens', with a main stem and some side branches, are ideal as freestanding bushes and single-stemmed cordons. Young trees bought part-trained as fans or espaliers are often three or more years old.

ROOTSTOCKS EXPLAINED

Most tree fruits comprise two separate plants joined together by grafting: the 'scion' or top part of the plant, forming the trunk and branches, and the 'rootstock', the roots on to which the scion is grafted. The point where they join shows as a bump on the stem just above the soil. The

rootstock determines the ultimate size of the tree: dwarfing rootstocks produce smaller, quicker cropping trees, which are valuable in smaller gardens, and are also used for trained fruits.

'M27' is the most dwarfing apple rootstock, producing trees only 1.8m (6ft) tall that start cropping a few years after planting; they usually need staking and are also suitable for container growing. 'M26' and 'M9' also produce small apple trees. Other dwarfing rootstocks include 'Pixie' for plums, 'Gisela 5' for cherries and 'Torinel' for apricots. Always check which rootstock has been used when buying trees.

Fruits trees are available as bare-root or container-grown plants. Bare-root trees are lifted when they are dormant (after leaf fall), supplied with no soil on their roots, and planted between late autumn and early spring. The technique is shown in the sequence 'Planting a bare-root fruit tree'. Container-grown trees can be planted all year round but need regular watering if planted in spring or summer while their roots are establishing.

Specialist fruit suppliers offer the widest range of varieties. For the eco garden, search out varieties that succeed in your area, including those known to be naturally disease resistant. Where possible, obtain trees from an organically accredited grower.

▲ Fan trees are trained against a wall or fence. Their branches radiate out from their short trunk.

▲ Stepover apples are single-stemmed cordons grown horizontally, 30–45cm (12–18in) above the ground.

▲ Plums can be grown as small garden trees using 'Pixie' dwarfing rootstock, and can also be fan-trained against sunny walls and fences.

Shapes and forms

Tree fruits can, through training and pruning, be grown in a range of shapes and forms. Most trees are grafted on to rootstocks, which governs their final size. Trees can be trained as freestanding bushes of different shapes, or against walls and fences as cordons, espaliers or fans. Bush trees are pruned in winter, while more restricted forms, such as cordons, are summer-pruned.

Pollination

In order for fruits to develop, the flowers must be pollinated. This happens when pollen from the male parts of the flower is transferred to the female parts, and is usually carried out by insects such as bees. Although some tree fruits are self-fertile

(meaning they pollinate themselves), others must be grown near a different variety that flowers simultaneously, so that cross-pollination (the exchange of pollen between flowers on different trees) can take place. Always check the pollination requirements of a variety before planting.

Soil and situation

The soil should be well drained, with a slightly acid to neutral pH. Incorporate a soil improver before planting. Tree fruits succeed best in a warm, sunny position, sheltered from strong winds, so avoid spots that are prone to spring frosts, which can damage the blossom. In colder areas, grow tender fruits such as apricots, peaches and nectarines against a sunny, sheltered wall or fence.

▼ These pear trees, on a dwarfing rootstock, are being grown as single-stemmed cordons, at an angle of 45 degrees, against a sunny fence.

PLANTING A BARE-ROOT FRUIT TREE

1 Dig out a planting hole wide and deep enough for the roots. Check the planting depth: the dark 'soil mark' on the trunk must be level with the soil.

2 Drive in a tree stake, then, holding the tree at the correct depth, pull loose soil (mixed with organic matter) over the roots. Firm in by treading.

3 When the hole is filled in and the soil firmed, take a tree tie and use it to fix the tree firmly to the wooden stake, 30–45cm (12–18in) above the ground.

4 Water the tree thoroughly to settle the soil in around its roots. To prevent weeds, mulch a 60cm (2ft) diameter circle with organic matter, such as leaf mould.

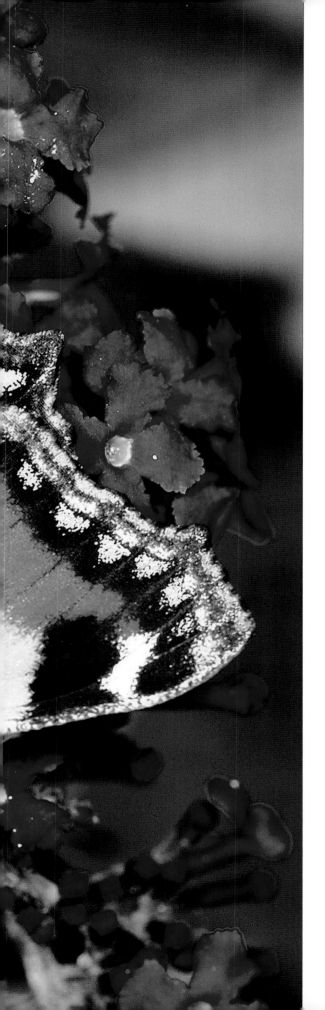

BOOSTING BIODIVERSITY

Although the gardener shapes and tends it, an eco garden remains part of the wider natural world. Some wildlife will visit it regularly, often making its permanent home and reproducing there. This chapter is all about increasing the number and variety of living things that inhabit an eco garden. Advice is given on how to create wildlife-friendly habitats in the garden, which flowers to grow for attracting pest-controlling beneficial insects, and how to maximize the value of self-seeding plants. Step-by-step sequences show the best way to make a simple pond, how to turn your lawn over to wildlife and how to build an insect hotel for free.

◄ The small tortoiseshell butterfly (*Aglais urticae*) is one of the many beautiful insects you will attract when you garden with biodiversity in mind.

▲ These dry logs provide a welcome winter resting place for adult butterflies.

▲ A healthy, balanced eco garden contains myriad life, including spiders.

▲ Fast-moving hoverflies are attracted to simple, single flowers rich in nectar.

Why garden biodiversity matters

A garden plays host to an amazing number of living things, from plants and the more obvious wildlife such as birds and mammals right down to the microscopic organisms inhabiting the compost heap. Gardening in a thoughtful, eco-friendly way, by creating a mixture of habitats, will enrich the variety of life that any garden supports and help it play its part in sustaining global biodiversity.

What is biodiversity?

In its broadest sense, biodiversity is the variety of life on Earth at all levels, from entire ecosystems and specific habitats to individual species and their respective genes. We can also think of biodiversity as the entire living fabric of planet Earth, of which we, as gardeners, are each custodians of only a tiny fragment. However, we usually think about garden biodiversity mostly in terms of individual species – the overall number and variety of living things we encounter there.

Wildlife flourishes in a garden with many different types of wildlife-friendly habitat. Gardens containing a multitude of different species, where synthetic pesticides are not used, will contain some or all of the following: trees, shrubs, hedges, flowers, a pond, a compost heap, some long grass, bird feeders, nest boxes for birds and/or

▼ Gardens containing different types of plant and habitats, where no synthetic pesticides are used, teem with a whole variety of insect, bird and animal life.

insects, and piles of rotting logs. Such gardens, which mirror natural habitats, if only on a small scale, are said to be rich in biodiversity.

Excessively tidy gardens, covered mostly by hard surfaces, gravel, decking or close-mown lawn, with few flowers, and where chemical pesticides and weedkillers are routinely used, will have far fewer species. Such gardens – which are far less interesting to be in – simply contain much less life and are described as having poor biodiversity.

In an eco garden the gardener is part of its biodiversity, and there is plenty you can do to boost this biodiversity further, enriching not just your own plot, but also the wider natural world.

The importance of biodiversity

Human beings are altering the face of the planet. Changes to the way we use land – increasing agricultural intensification, the expansion of towns, cities and roads, the loss of natural habitats such as tropical rainforest – are all increasing the pressure on our planet's biodiversity. Over half the land surface of the Earth has been changed by human activity. Agriculture affects more land area than any other human activity, and we are also having profound effects on the world's oceans. Many species of plant and animal are being driven

▲ Growing plants that wildlife eat is a simple way to boost garden biodiversity. This lesser goldfinch (*Carduelis psaltria*) is feeding on a seeding sunflower head.

▼ Many garden flowers are just as – if not more – attractive to insects as wild flowers. This bedding dahlia is a favourite with bees and butterflies.

▲ These creamy-grey hoverfly larvae are eating a colony of aphids (greenfly), a sap-sucking plant pest. This avoids the need to resort to using either synthetic or natural insecticides. The pale, capsule-shaped hoverfly eggs are still to hatch out.

▼ Bumblebees are among the more visible – and audible – indicators of a biodiversity-rich garden. To attract them, grow simple pollen- and nectar-rich flowers. This is green alkanet (*Pentaglottis sempervirens*).

to extinction by man-made pressures at an ever-increasing rate; for example, a quarter of the world's bird species are already thought to be extinct.

Increasing your garden's biodiversity will not only make it a more enjoyable place to be, because there is so much more activity to watch; it also helps sustain a balanced garden ecosystem where life of all shapes and sizes can flourish.

Garden food chains

Eco gardens buzzing with life play a vital part in nature's food chains. Smaller animals feed on larger animals, which are themselves eaten by larger ones. Boosting garden biodiversity strengthens many different kinds of food chain.

A pond, for example, will add a self-contained aquatic ecosystem to your garden. The larvae of many flying insects, including gnats, midges and hoverflies, live in ponds. These are eaten by other pond-dwellers, such as the predatory larvae of dragonflies, or by greater water boatmen (backswimmers). When the insect larvae mature into adults, they become food for insect-eating birds such as swallows and flycatchers. In turn, small birds are eaten by birds of prey such as sparrowhawks.

Less obvious food chains work hard for the eco gardener. When aphids, a sap-sucking pest, attack your plants, adult hoverflies start to lay their eggs among the aphid colonies on the affected plant's leaves. When they hatch, the hoverfly larvae eat the aphids, and serious damage is avoided. Using insecticides (chemicals which kill insects) effectively breaks the links in natural food chains. With no aphids, there will be fewer hoverflies, making plants vulnerable to unchecked pest epidemics.

▼ Piles of flat stones set among long grass in a open spot provide the perfect habitat for the common lizard (*Zootoca vivipara*) to bask in the sun.

▲ Adult hoverflies (which can hover motionless in the air) feed on simple, nectar-rich flowers and seek out colonies of aphids (greenfly) in which to lay their eggs.

▲ Greater water boatmen (backswimmers) live in garden ponds and feed on insect larvae and tadpoles. They hang suspended, just below the surface, diving to hunt prey.

Every garden counts

It would be easy to think that your own garden cannot make a meaningful contribution to boosting biodiversity. Gardens are frequently overlooked in assessments of how our living environments can be made 'greener', especially in towns and cities. Much emphasis is placed on the value of urban public parks, even though gardens have been proved to be far richer in biodiversity.

But although an individual garden represents only a tiny fraction of the Earth's living fabric, there are hundreds of millions of gardens worldwide. Together they form a giant, interconnected network of individual pockets of garden life, each with its own distinct character, and each of which is home to an array of different species.

Encouraging wildlife

Adding plants and features that imitate natural habitats is the most effective way of attracting more wildlife to your eco garden. Some will live, feed and breed, spending their whole lives there, while others will just pass through it at different times of the year. Wildlife-friendly features can be attractive, are easy to incorporate and no garden is too small to include some.

▲ Nectar-rich teasel (*Dipsacus fullonum*) attracts bees and butterflies in summer, then, in winter, birds such as goldfinch, which feed on its seeds.

▼ Log piles mimic decaying wood on a forest floor. As the logs rot, add new ones to the top.

Your garden nature reserve

Gardens in which wildlife finds it desirable to live do not have to be wild, untidy and overrun with weeds, or involve a lot of hard work. Wildlife-friendly habitats can be included in any garden and yours might already have some of them. A habitat is simply the natural home or environment where wildlife usually lives. Loss of biodiversity in the wild is closely linked to loss of habitat, caused either by its destruction or by changes in how we use land.

Nurturing a garden with wildlife in mind is rather like planning a good-looking nature reserve. Instead of designating a dull corner as 'for wildlife' (it will not stay there anyway), try to encourage its presence throughout your garden.

Lessons from nature

Encouraging garden wildlife is not difficult if you connect what happens in your garden to what goes on in the natural world around us.

Growing trees and shrubs in the garden mimics a natural woodland habitat, whereas a small pond attracts the same kind of wildlife found in natural ponds. Leaving part of your lawn unmown, so that grasses grow tall and lawn weeds can bloom,

▲ Growing trees in your eco garden will attract woodland birds such as the nuthatch (*Sitta europaea*).

brings a patch of grassland to your own back garden. Putting up a nest box attracts birds that normally raise their young in holes in trees. Growing a diverse mixture of nectar- and pollen-rich flowers attracts beneficial insects, which then pollinate crops or feed on plant pests.

Types of habitat

The following are the most important habitats worth including in an eco garden. The effort required to make each one varies. For example, adding a pond requires some initial work, but only minimal attention afterwards. For some long grass, all you need do is stop mowing your lawn.

● Trees and shrubs Adding trees and shrubs, preferably those with autumn fruits or berries, adds an important extra dimension to your garden. For birds especially, this means somewhere to shelter, roost and nest. More insects will be attracted too, as will spiders, which spin their webs among the shoots. Fallen leaves encourage less obvious wildlife: earthworms, slugs and snails, millipedes, woodlice, springtails, bacteria and fungi. All of these play a part in breaking down dead leaves and incorporating them into the soil. They are also an important source of food for larger garden wildlife.

▲ The shallows at the edge of a pond teem with life both in and out of the water.

▲ Small mammals, slow worms and lizards all weave in and out of cracks in this drystone slate wall.

▼ Nest boxes emulate holes in trees where many garden birds, such as tits, will build their nests.

▲ Depending on the time of year, this mixed boundary hedge of hazel, hawthorn and privet provides food and shelter for insects, nesting birds and mammals.

- **A fish-free pond** Ponds teem with life of all kinds and help to increase the amount of wildlife throughout a garden. The most wildlife-friendly ponds have both deep and shallow water (30cm/12in at the deepest is ideal), are fish-free, located in a sunny spot and include both oxygenating and marginal plants. A log pile on the edge of a pond increases its appeal for wildlife.
- **A pile of logs** Adding log piles mimics a fallen tree decaying on a forest floor. As well as providing shelter for frogs, toads, slow worms and lizards, rotting wood is home to a huge number of species, including spiders, solitary wasps, centipedes, millipedes, woodlice, earthworms, flatworms, slugs, snails and ground beetles. Make log piles as large as possible, avoid disturbing them and add more logs as they rot.
- **Mixed hedges** Hedges make an attractive garden boundary and also provide birds with shelter, nest sites and food, while flowering hedges provide nectar for insects. Ground-dwelling wildlife, such as small mammals, move safe and unseen along a hedge bottom. A mixed hedge of evergreen and deciduous plants, particularly autumn-fruiting shrubs, will be most attractive to wildlife. Do not trim hedges when birds are nesting.
- **Drystone walls** Walls built without mortar, with numerous cracks and crevices between the stones, are an ideal habitat for reptiles such

as lizards, which enjoy basking on the hot sun-warmed stones. Small mammals live in drystone walls, and solitary bees will nest there.
- **A compost heap** Reptiles and amphibians, as well as mammals such as hedgehogs, will all make their home in a compost heap, which is also a habitat for hundreds of other smaller species. Wildlife-friendly heaps are those built directly on to the soil, or contained by a structure that is open around its base, allowing wildlife to get in and out.
- **Some undisturbed long grass** Maintaining closely mown, weed-free lawns uses energy and resources, and petrol lawn mowers cause noise and air pollution. By letting grass grow long you can create wild areas of long grass and wild flowers that will attract a variety of wildlife, particularly insects such as butterflies.

▼ Open-sided compost heaps built on the soil are home to many animals, including hundreds of species of beetle.

Attracting beneficial insects

Boosting the population of beneficial insects in the garden brings many rewards. Bees will help pollinate crops while ladybirds and hoverflies will feed on plant pests, meaning there is no need to use chemical pesticides. Some insects, such as butterflies, are stunningly beautiful and fascinating to watch. Growing lots of nectar-rich flowers will make the eco garden a magnet for useful insects.

What are beneficial insects?

Any insects that work to our advantage in an eco garden are known as beneficial insects. Pollinating insects, such as hive and wild bees, pollinate vegetable and fruit crops, helping to ensure a good 'set' of fruits and pods. Growing lots of flowers attracts bees of all types, but you can also

▼ This border is packed with annual flowers chosen for their insect-attracting qualities. They are mostly simple, single flowers rich in nectar and pollen.

encourage wild solitary bees to become residents by providing them with simple nest boxes, as shown in the sequence 'Making a solitary bee nest box'. Other useful insects, such as ladybirds and lacewings, will take up residence in your garden if provided with an insect hotel.

The adults and larvae of many predatory insects feed on the pests that can attack plants. Adult hoverflies lay their eggs among aphid colonies and a single larva will eat around a thousand aphids. Anthocorid, capsid and damsel bugs, earwigs, lacewings, social and solitary wasps, ground and rove beetles and predatory mites all eat plant pests.

Some insects parasitize pests. Tiny ichneumon wasps lay their eggs in or on pest caterpillars. After they hatch, the wasp larvae feed on the caterpillar and eventually kill it. Encouraging healthy populations of natural predators and parasites in a garden creates a natural balance, meaning that pests rarely cause lasting harm to the plants.

Choosing plants

Insects visit flowers to gather nectar and pollen to feed both themselves and, in some cases, such as with bees, their offspring. Aim to grow a diverse mixture of annual and perennial plants, trees and shrubs that flower over many months, so that at least some are in flower all year round, especially early and late in the growing season. The Oregon grape (*Mahonia aquifolium*) flowers in late winter and is a valuable food source for queen bumblebees emerging from hibernation; the flowers of ivy (*Hedera helix*) provide an autumn top-up for butterflies before they hibernate for the winter.

Insects prefer simple, single and scented flowers, rather than double, highly modified and scentless ones, and they find cultivated garden plants just as attractive as wild or native species. When choosing seeds or plants, try to avoid double or pollen-free varieties where the nectar- and pollen-bearing parts of the flower have been lost. Do not forget moths: night-scented flowers

▲ Dahlias with simple, single and accessible flowers, with a distinct central 'eye', are highly attractive to insects. This red admiral butterfly is drinking nectar.

▼ The bright flowers of pot marigold (*Calendula officinalis*) are a magnet for bees and hoverflies, but you need to remember to grow those cultivars with simple, single blooms.

▲ This insect hotel will attract adult lacewings.

such as climbing honeysuckle (*Lonicera*) and flowering tobacco (*Nicotiana*) will keep the eco garden buzzing after dark.

Two particular plant families contain many varieties that attract beneficial insects: the Compositae or daisy family, and the Umbelliferae or umbel family. Plants from the daisy family commonly have flowers with a central disc surrounded by a ring of petals. Pot marigold (*Calendula officinalis*), a hardy annual, is one of the best and easiest of the daisy family to grow. It is a favourite of bees and hoverflies, and quickly self-seeds. The umbel family has open, flat heads of smaller flowers resembling

▲ Among these aphids are pale, capsule-shaped hoverfly eggs. One hoverfly larva can eat 50 aphids per day.

MAKING A SOLITARY BEE NEST BOX

1 Use any size of food can, ensuring that there are no sharp edges. Drill some holes along one side of the can to drain any rainwater which might get inside.

2 Fix the empty can to a wall, fence or post using a screw in its base. Choose a sheltered spot that receives full sunshine for most of the day.

3 Collect some dry and hollow plant stems with a variety of hole sizes ranging between 4mm (⅛in) and 10mm (½in) in diameter.

4 Check the depth of the can and cut the stems into lengths. Each can should contain a variety of hole sizes to attract different bee species.

5 Fill the can up with cut-to-size stems. Fill the last few gaps carefully so that all the stems are packed in tightly together, which helps stop them falling out.

6 It might take one to two seasons before bees find the box and start nesting. Stems sealed with a pale 'plug' of mud show they are in residence.

an inside-out umbrella. Fennel (*Foeniculum vulgare*) is one of the best perennial umbels, attracting masses of hoverflies and other insects.

Plants with tubular flowers, such as foxglove (*Digitalis*), attract insects such as bees, which use their long tongues to gather nectar. Lists of insect-attracting annual, biennial and perennial plants are given in the directory of eco-friendly plants.

BIOLOGICAL PEST CONTROLS

You can boost your garden's population of beneficial insects and other pest-controlling organisms by using biological pest controls. These predatory or parasitic insects, mites and nematodes, which target specific types of pest, are obtained by mail order and used under cover or outdoors. Some biological controls are found naturally in gardens, while others are introduced. They are applied to plants live, as pupae, or, in the case of nematodes, mixed with water and either sprayed on to plants or watered on to the soil. They work alongside naturally occurring beneficial organisms, will not upset the balance of your garden's ecosystem and are a safe, non-chemical way to tackle pest outbreaks. Effective biological controls include those for aphids, caterpillars, chafer grubs, leaf miners, mealybugs, slugs, thrips and whitefly.

◀ The predatory mite *Phytoseiulus persimilis*, a natural biological control for spider mites, is applied using a vermiculite carrier.

Self-seeding plants

Many of the garden plants that draw beneficial insects and other wildlife to an eco garden produce copious amounts of seed once they finish flowering. These seeds fall to the ground and, in many cases, will germinate and grow into new plants if left alone. Many such 'self-seeders' have nectar-rich flowers and some produce seeds that are eaten by birds during autumn and winter.

Plants for free

Self-seeding plants are those that propagate themselves by producing often large numbers of seeds, which fall on to the soil, where they germinate and grow without further help. The resulting seedlings can be left to grow, flower, produce seeds and repeat the whole cycle over again. With some flowers, such as pot marigolds (*Calendula officinalis*), you might need to buy only a single packet of seed. Once they are established in your garden they will perpetuate themselves from year to year by self-seeding, giving you a free and endless supply of flowers and seeds.

> **SELF-SEEDERS TO ATTRACT WILDLIFE**
> The following plants will attract beneficial insects and produce food for seed-eating birds:
> Pot marigold (*Calendula officinalis*)
> Brook thistle (*Cirsium rivulare* 'Atropurpureum')
> Teasel (*Dipsacus* spp.)
> Buckwheat (*Fagopyrum esculentum*)
> Sunflower (*Helianthus annuus*)
> Honesty (*Lunaria annua*)
> Poppies (*Papaver* spp.)
> *Verbena bonariensis*

▲ Borage (*Borago officinalis*) attracts both honey and bumblebees, and produces large black ripe seeds which are very easy to collect.

Nooks and crannies

Self-seeding plants make good use of spots around the garden where it is difficult or undesirable for other plants to grow. The tiny, prolific seeds of Welsh poppy (*Meconopsis cambrica*) and foxglove (*Digitalis purpurea*) will find their way into any nooks and crannies in garden walls, especially drystone structures, where they grow happily, often with very little soil. These plants often look more attractive and natural because they have found their own spot in which to grow. Sweet-scented alyssum (*Lobularia maritima*) will seed itself into the gaps between paving, where it helps to break up straight lines. The main aim of growing self-seeders is to let them do their own thing.

▼ Honesty (*Lunaria annua*) has large, rounded seed pods containing flat seeds which are eaten by birds.

▼ You can collect your own seeds and sow them where you wish. These tiny and prolific seeds are of Welsh poppy (*Meconopsis cambrica*).

▲ Self-seeded orange nasturtium, yellow pot marigold and red orache (*Atriplex hortensis* var. *rubra*) in a food garden. The plants grow in the gaps between crops.

Introducing self-seeders

There are several ways to establish self-seeders. You can sow them in rows or scatter them randomly in selected areas, such as in borders, or in gravel paths. To encourage them in walls, simply flick some seeds into holes and crevices. Alyssum seeds can be mixed with dry soil and brushed into the gaps between paving.

To introduce self-seeders to a food garden, where they attract beneficial insects, either sow them in rows between the crops or grow them in pots and plant them out. Once they have self-seeded, young plants will spring up everywhere without any further input. Sometimes self-seeders flourish in one garden but not another; those plants best suited to your particular garden will thrive and you are unlikely ever to be without them.

Most self-seeders are hardy annuals, meaning they germinate in spring (or the previous autumn) and are not usually killed by frost. Frost-tender plants do not self-seed so easily and it is better to raise these under cover and plant them out.

Getting to know seedlings

Self-seeding plants do not always grow where we want them to, so it is important to know what they look like. Being able to identify them at the seedling stage is extremely useful, especially in borders where other plants are growing, and in food gardens. It is usually possible to pull up or hoe off any unwanted self-seeders (along with any weed seedlings), leaving behind those you do want to grow on and flower. The seedlings of some common self-seeders are shown in the table 'Identifying self-sown seedlings'.

Even if some self-seeders grow large before they are spotted, most are easy to pull up by hand, or can be transplanted to another spot. To avoid excessive self-seeding, remove the spent plants or trim off any faded flowers before they produce ripe seeds and begin to shed them.

▲ Welsh poppies are a valuable source of nectar in early spring.

IDENTIFYING SELF-SOWN SEEDLINGS

When you grow self-seeders you will soon learn how to recognize them by identifying their seed leaves (cotyledons) and their first few true leaves.

▲ Borage (*Borago officinalis*) Broad seed leaves are followed by bristly true leaves that smell of cucumber.

▲ Pot marigold (*Calendula officinalis*) The glistening seed leaves are fleshy, while the true leaves feel slightly sticky.

▲ Californian poppy (*Eschscholzia californica*) The thin and wispy seed and true leaves have a distinct grey-green tinge.

▲ Buckwheat (*Fagopyrum esculentum*) Large and distinctive kidney-shaped seed leaves on tall and fleshy pink-tinged stems.

▲ Poached egg plant (*Limnanthes douglasii*) The bright green seed leaves have long stalks and are followed by finely divided true leaves.

▲ Fiddleneck (*Phacelia tanacetifolia*) Long, hairy and slightly drooping thin, narrow seed leaves are followed by feathery, divided true leaves.

Making a simple pond

Adding a small pond to your garden will dramatically increase the kind and range of wildlife you start to find there. A pond is a unique kind of habitat that is home to a dynamic underwater world, and helps to maintain a well-balanced garden ecosystem. You can make an attractive wildlife-friendly pond quickly and easily using any suitably sized recycled container that will hold water.

▲ The slow-moving common toad (*Bufo bufo*) returns to the same pond each year to breed.

▼ This small wildlife-rich pond in a half barrel is actually in a flower border.

Life in a pond

Ponds are self-contained aquatic ecosystems teeming with all sorts of wildlife both in and out of the water. Some animals depend totally on a pond, spending their entire life cycle there, while others, such as frogs and toads, visit them to breed before returning to other habitats on land. Tadpoles, the young of frogs and toads, spend their entire early life in a pond before maturing into froglets and toadlets.

Many eye-catching insects begin to appear when you add a pond: adult dragonflies and damselflies will feed on smaller insects breeding in a pond, and their own larvae live there, too. Other pond wildlife includes beetles, water boatmen (backswimmers), alder flies, pond and water skaters, caddis fly and mayfly larvae, water snails and leeches. Mammals, birds and insects such as bees visit ponds to drink, and birds will bathe there.

CHOOSING OXYGENATING PLANTS

Good choices for your pond:

Water starwort (*Callitriche stagnalis*)

Hornwort (*Ceratophyllum demersum*)

Water milfoil (*Myriophyllum spicatum*)

Curled pondweed (*Potamogeton crispus*)

Water crowfoot (*Ranunculus* spp.)

Invasive plants to avoid:

Water fern (*Azolla filiculoides*)

Australian swamp stonecrop (*Crassula helmsii*)

Floating pennywort (*Hydrocotyle ranunculoides*)

Water primrose (*Ludwigia grandiflora*)

Parrot's feather (*Myriophyllum aquaticum*)

A pond increases the number of insects whose larvae live in water, meaning more food for spiders, adult damselflies and dragonflies, and insect-eating birds such as swallows. Gardens with ponds will have more wildlife in general, helping to boost biodiversity and strengthening garden food chains.

Pond size

The size of a pond is not too important, and it does not need to be deep. About 30cm (12in) of water is ideal for most kinds of pond life, although it is vital to include some shallow areas so that pond-loving creatures can drink at the edges and climb out if they fall in by accident. Deep ponds with steep sloping sides are not wildlife-friendly. Large stones or cobbles make good shallows; arrange them so that some are mostly out of the water, with others almost submerged.

A number of small, easy-to-install ponds might be even more beneficial to wildlife than building a large (and potentially expensive) one. The step sequence shows how a small wildlife pond can be made for free, using recycled and reclaimed materials. Its main components are a reused plastic container, stones and some weathered slate.

▲ Ponds are home to much wildlife, such as these young newts.

Avoiding fish

Ponds containing fish are much more dull than fish-free ponds in terms of biodiversity. Fish will eat almost anything, from tiny water fleas (Daphnia) to insect larvae and tadpoles, all of which will thrive and grow to maturity in a fish-free pond.

Plants for ponds

Wildlife in a pond needs shelter to breed, feed and hide from predators. Marginal plants are grown around the edge of a pond, either in the mud or in containers standing in the water. Taller marginal plants such as bulrushes (*Typha* spp.) provide dragonfly nymphs with the ideal habitat to crawl up when they leave the water and turn into adults.

Submerged oxygenating plants live below the water surface, help keep the water clear and provide hiding and egg-laying places for aquatic animals. Oxygenators should always be included in a pond, whatever its size. Certain oxygenators have become seriously invasive and ecologically

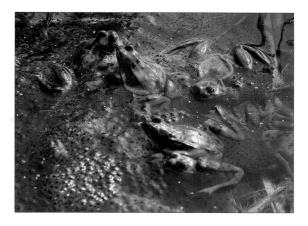

▲ Frogs (*Rana temporaria*) move into ponds to breed noisily in early spring. They produce masses of frogspawn, which develops first into tadpoles and later into froglets.

damaging weeds in streams and waterways, and should not be used. These are listed in the panel. More pond (and bog) plants are described in the directory of eco-friendly garden plants.

MAKING A QUICK AND EASY WILDLIFE POND

1 Bury a watertight container (this one is 40cm/16in wide and 30cm/12in deep) just below the soil surface. Check it sits level.

2 Use pieces of stone to make a 'staircase' on one side, which any animals that accidentally fall in can use to climb out.

3 Hide the edge of the container with pieces of overlapping stone, leaving plenty of crevices where frogs and toads will live.

4 Using water from another healthy garden pond will kick-start it into life, but avoid using water from ponds containing fish.

5 To establish a small clump of marginal plants, fill one of the crevices on the edge of the pond with a handful of garden soil.

6 Plant a suitable, non-invasive marginal plant in the soil-filled crevice. As it grows, it will provide valuable cover for wildlife.

7 Add a few stems of a non-invasive oxygenating plant such as hornwort (*Ceratophyllum demersum*) to help keep the water clear.

8 Wildlife will start to take up residence in the pond within weeks. If the level falls, top up with rainwater (not tap water).

Transforming your lawn

Letting your lawn go 'wild' and grow into areas of tall, long grass with wildflowers scattered through them will help to boost the wildlife in your eco garden. It will also reduce work and avoid the polluting, high-energy inputs usually associated with manicured, well-watered and weed-free lawns. You can add more flowers by planting young plants and bulbs.

The problem with lawns

Traditional lawns are routinely treated with synthetic chemical weedkillers and fertilizers, and watered and mown regularly, all of which consumes vast amounts of energy and resources. Lawn treatments, as well as the fuel needed to run petrol-driven lawn mowers, are derived primarily from fossil fuels such as oil. Burning these releases carbon dioxide, the main greenhouse gas responsible for global warming. Lawn mowers also create local pollution as noxious fumes and noise. Keeping a lawn constantly green requires large amounts of energy-intensive mains water, while lawn fertilizers can be responsible for polluting water supplies with nitrates and phosphorus.

Lawn weeds are usually treated with hormone weedkillers. Concerns over the effect of these types of weedkiller on human health has led to some countries banning their domestic use. Clippings from a weedkiller-treated lawn can also damage the growth of other garden plants.

The traditional lawn might be attractive to look at, but it comes with a high environmental cost and is usually devoid of all but passing wildlife.

Letting grass grow

The more of your lawn you turn over to tall, undisturbed grasses and wildflowers, the more wildlife it will attract. Fast-moving ground beetles (which eat slugs) and hunting spiders, as well as other beneficial insects, thrive in long grass. Wild plants once treated as weeds will be able to grow, flower and produce seeds, which will attract other wildlife. Log piles and ponds can be included in areas of long grass to add more habitats.

To make your existing lawn into a more planet-friendly, flower-rich one, simply stop mowing, feeding and watering it, or using weedkiller. Decide if any paths will weave through it, or whether you want to create a few islands of longer grass and wildflowers, surrounded by mown paths. If you are unsure about what the results might look like, leave a small area unmown to begin with, then gradually add to it.

Any wild plants already present will flower during spring and summer, letting you see what you already have. If wildflowers are sparse, using plug plants available from specialist suppliers is an effective way to enrich your grassy areas. You can also collect seeds from existing wildflowers and raise your own. Some suitable plants are listed

▲ Spring-flowering snakeshead fritillary (*Fritillaria meleagris*) thrives in unmown grass where the soil is moist but well drained. Flowers can be white or purple.

▼ Ground beetles move about in long grass and will eat slugs when hunting for food after dark.

FLOWERS FOR WILD AREAS

Perennials:

Harebell (*Campanula rotundifolia*)

Hogweed (*Heracleum sphondylium*)

Field scabious (*Knautia arvensis*)

Ox-eye daisy (*Leucanthemum vulgare*)

Primrose (*Primula vulgaris*)

Selfheal (*Prunella vulgaris*)

Bulbs:

Crocus spp.

Snakeshead fritillary (*Fritillaria meleagris*)

Snowdrops (*Galanthus* spp.)

Bluebell (*Hyacinthoides non-scripta*)

Wild daffodil (*Narcissus pseudonarcissus*)

TURNING LAWN INTO LONG GRASS

1 Wildflowers such as this ox-eye daisy are readily available by mail order as young starter or 'plug' plants for planting from spring to autumn.

2 Use sand poured from a bottle to mark out an area of lawn which will be allowed to go 'wild', where you are intending to plant some wildflowers.

3 Use a pointed dibber to make random planting holes at varying spacings over the area, and always plant in odd-numbered, unevenly spaced groups.

4 Carefully push the young plants into the dibber holes and firm them in. Afterwards, use a watering can to give the planted areas a thorough soaking.

5 The wildflowers will soon become established, some eventually forming clumps among the long grass, and will spread themselves further by self-seeding.

▲ Battery-powered electric lawn mowers are one of the most eco-friendly options for cutting a lawn.

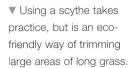

▼ Using a scythe takes practice, but is an eco-friendly way of trimming large areas of long grass.

in the panel 'Flowers for wild areas', and how to plant them is shown in the sequence 'Turning lawn into long grass'.

Cutting the grass

Mown grass paths around or through wild patches allow you to watch the wildlife without stepping into the long grass. Paths can be winding and sinuous, or follow more geometric lines. Using a push mower, powered by human energy, or an electric model powered from a renewable energy source, will ensure any mowing is as planet-friendly as possible. Push mowers are simple and quiet to use and involve regular physical exercise.

Your wild areas will be more successful if the grass is cut, usually in late summer, once any flowers have faded. Cutting and removing the

grass prevents the soil from becoming too rich and fertile, which encourages grasses rather than flowers. Cut small areas using shears or a hand-held sickle. For larger areas, use an electric line trimmer (powered by renewable energy) or, preferably, a scythe, which is quieter to use, entirely pollution-free and less lethal to wildlife – you can usually hear any animals moving about in the grass and let them move away before you cut. Line trimmers also cause less obvious pollution: the cutting line (often nylon) fragments in use, and is then left lying around on the ground.

After cutting, leave the material to dry out for a couple of weeks so that any maturing seed-heads ripen and shed their seeds, which will drop to the ground. It can then be raked up and composted, or used as a weed-smothering mulch.

▼ A sickle is a useful and eco-friendly way of cutting smaller areas of long grass in late summer, after any flowers have faded and shed their seeds.

▼ Allowing parts of your lawn to grow long not only creates a striking contrast with any closely mown areas, but also makes it more wildlife-friendly.

Building an insect hotel

Beneficial insects outnumber the other wildlife in your eco garden many times over. You can attract them by growing lots of nectar-rich flowers, but you can also encourage them to stay around for longer by providing somewhere for them to breed and to shelter during the winter. An insect hotel is easy to make from scrap wood and other recycled materials.

Potential guests

Home-made insect hotels attract a range of different species. Some of the most common are solitary bees, which include the leafcutter (*Megachile* spp.) and mason bee (*Osmia* spp.). Rather than forming colonies with a queen and workers, solitary bees make individual nests for their larvae. Those that favour hollow plant stems and holes in dead wood will readily use a purpose-built insect hotel. If you have brick walls in your garden, you might also see solitary bees nesting in any crumbling mortar. Although less conspicuous than honey bees and noisy bumblebees (neither of which use insect hotels), solitary bees are also useful pollinators of vegetable and fruit crops.

Other important beneficial insects that use insect hotels are solitary wasps. These also make individual nests. They help keep garden pests in check by catching and paralyzing aphids, caterpillars, flies and leafhoppers, which they use to feed their larvae. Solitary wasps are smaller than the larger social wasps, and harmless.

During winter, hibernating insects need a dry and sheltered hiding place. Ladybirds and lacewings will use hotels, especially if they have a mixture of hollow plant stems of different diameters. Spiders will also spin their webs near insect hotels.

Hotel design

You can make a simple insect hotel, suitable for solitary bees and wasps, by drilling holes in a block of wood measuring at least 10–15cm (4–6in) square, which has not been treated with preservative or painted. The solid blocks found in wooden pallets are ideal. Drill holes at least 10–15cm (4–6in) deep, and in varying diameters of between 4mm (⅛in) and 10mm (½in) – but no larger – randomly over one side of the block, but

▲ Many reused and reclaimed materials make good homes for garden wildlife. Here, old wooden pallets, bricks, tiles and drilled wooden blocks and logs have been used.

▼ A very simple hotel for solitary bees and wasps can be made easily from an untreated wooden block drilled with smooth, appropriate-sized holes.

▼ Adult lacewings are welcome in an eco garden because they prey on aphids (greenfly). They will hibernate in your garden during winter in an insect hotel.

▼ Solitary red mason bees (*Osmia rufa*) are up to 15mm (½in) long, with distinctive reddish-brown hairs. They nest in holes in walls and also use insect hotels.

▲ Adult two-spotted ladybirds (*Adelia bipunctata*) will use an insect hotel for winter hibernation, often gathering in groups. Both adults and larvae eat aphids (greenfly).

without drilling right through. Use sharp drill bits, as solitary bees and wasps prefer the entrance holes to be smooth, without any splinters. Different diameter holes attract a wide range of bee and wasp species. Remove any sawdust, then fix the block on a sunny wall, fence or post, 90–150cm (3–5ft) above the ground.

Constructing a five-star insect hotel using everyday materials, with a mixture of different-sized nest holes, nooks and crannies, is shown in the sequence 'Making an insect hotel'.

Ready-made insect boxes are widely available, but always check that any intended for use by solitary bees include a mixture of different diameter holes, with none larger than 10mm (½in).

Signs of visitors

You will know if solitary bees and wasps are using your hotel because, after filling a nest hole with food and laying an egg, they will seal up the entrance. Solitary bees do this using either mud or chewed plant material, making the seals appear cream- or straw-coloured. Leafcutter bees use circles of live green leaves to seal their nests.

Hibernating insects are less obvious, tending to hide away at the back of holes and crevices during the winter months. Do not be tempted to dismantle the hotel to check for their presence.

Seasonal management

Insect hotels need little care. To safeguard the survival of any nests and hibernating residents during winter, it is a good idea to take the hotel indoors by mid-autumn. Rain can wash away the

MAKING AN INSECT HOTEL

1 Use some untreated pallet wood to make a rectangular box 60cm (24in) long, 20cm (8in) wide and 15cm (6in) deep, which is open on one side.

2 In the base of the box, drill some evenly spaced 1cm (½in) diameter holes to allow any rainwater that gets into the insect hotel to drain away.

3 Gather materials: hollow plant stems, bee nest boxes made from cans, rolled cardboard, drilled wooden blocks, log sections and square sections.

4 Use the square wood sections to form loose compartments, then fill the remaining spaces with the materials, which should fit snugly inside the box.

5 Pack hollow plant stems tightly between the larger materials to hold them firmly in place and provide even more potential bee and wasp nesting sites.

6 Fix the completed insect hotel securely to a sunny wall, fence or post so that its top is between 1.2m (4ft) and 1.8m (6ft) from the ground.

seals on nests, and hungry birds such as tits and woodpeckers may peck at them. Any cardboard or plant stems will rot if they get wet.

Either move hotels under the wide eaves of a building, to protect them from driving rain, or store them in a cold and dry shed or garage. Never put them in a warm place or insects will emerge prematurely and die. Return them to their usual positions by early spring when temperatures rise.

▶ Solitary mason bees have nested in these old bamboo canes. After laying an egg in each chamber, they seal it with a mortar-like plug of mud or plant material.

SUSTAINABLE LANDSCAPING

The materials used to create an eco garden – to make paths, fences, screens and other features – all have an impact on the environment. The origins of these materials, their effect on natural, often distant, landscapes, how far they have travelled and the energy they consume are all important considerations. This chapter defines sustainable landscaping and explains how to shrink your gardening footprint. Advice is given on sourcing reclaimed and recycled materials; making rainwater-absorbing paths; planting a wildlife-friendly living roof; choosing chemical-free fencing materials; and making a living garden 'fedge'.

◄ Simple garden structures such as this garden bench made with locally sourced timber will last many years and will have only a modest 'gardening footprint'.

▲ These reclaimed granite setts can be used indefinitely for a variety of purposes.

▲ Roofs can be used to grow plants and create extra wildlife habitat.

▲ Wood is an attractive and versatile material that locks up carbon.

What is sustainable landscaping?

Making a new garden or reshaping an existing one requires thought, planning, some physical energy, and the use of various materials. Where those materials came from, how they were acquired and the amount of energy it took to make them all determine their environmental impact. Using low-impact, sustainable landscaping materials will help to reduce your gardening footprint.

Defining sustainability

When taking on a brand new garden, or inheriting or changing an existing one, the gardener usually decides to modify its layout and the way it looks and works – perhaps by removing or adding new features and planting new trees, shrubs and other plants (often called 'soft landscaping'). The total effect is landscaping, or garden-making. Hard surfaces, such as paving, might be replaced with a variety of different plants, and with wildlife-friendly features such as a pond, or a food mile-free edible garden can be created. All of the garden, or just part of it, might be changed.

Gardening in an eco-friendly way adds another important dimension to the landscaping process: sustainability. Being mindful of the environmental impact of the materials used when making any changes allows the gardener to create ecologically harmonious gardens without depleting finite and often irreplaceable natural resources.

Sustainable garden landscaping can be defined as the sensitive use of appropriate, eco-friendly materials to create a new garden or change an existing one. These are materials that meet the present needs of the gardener, but avoid any adverse impacts on wider natural ecosystems and communities, both now and in the future.

▼ Quarrying stone has a dramatic and irreversible effect on natural landscapes. Whole mountains can be destroyed.

A gardening footprint

Just as an environmental footprint is a measure of the resources needed, for example, to manufacture a product or to grow a food crop, a gardening footprint is an assessment of the inputs needed to make and subsequently maintain a garden. In an eco garden, the aim is to shrink the size of this footprint, preferably to a mere toeprint, in order to avoid any negative and potentially damaging impact on the wider natural world.

The greatest contribution to a garden's footprint occurs when a new garden is created from scratch, or an existing one is changed, because this is when most materials and energy (derived from fossil fuels such as oil) are used. Afterwards, as it matures over time, a garden, especially one tended in an eco-friendly way, can bring significant environmental benefits, helping to shrink its initial footprint. Sustainable landscaping helps to minimize a garden's footprint from the start.

Perhaps the most effective way to keep your garden's footprint small is to resist gardening fads and trends, and not to keep changing it every few years to try to keep up with fleeting gardening fashion. This will also benefit its resident wildlife.

▲ Woven shoots of living willow – a natural, renewable landscaping material – create a beautiful boundary marker in this wildlife-friendly garden.

▼ Transporting materials by air, road and sea burns fossil fuels derived from oil, which releases the polluting global-warming gas carbon dioxide.

▲ An eco-friendly hand-made seat created from locally grown oak and willow required few inputs other than human labour and ingenuity.

▼ A carefully planned eco garden, made with its potential gardening footprint in mind and using only sustainable landscaping materials of known origin, can be highly attractive.

Industrial gardening

Many garden materials are the products of a highly industrialized, global gardening industry, and often come at considerable cost to the environment. Some of the less visible impacts of producing landscaping materials include:

• **Extraction** Quarrying stone and other non-renewable raw materials destroys irreplaceable natural habitats. Materials sourced from overseas, such as stone, raise ethical concerns over workers' rights in developing countries, where labour safeguards might be weaker than they are elsewhere. Whether it is morally right to exploit other people's landscapes in order to satisfy individual gardeners' needs is also questionable.

• **Transport** Moving often heavy raw or processed materials over long distances uses oil-derived fuels, which release carbon dioxide, the main greenhouse gas responsible for climate change. Road transport encourages the building of more infrastructure and diminishes natural countryside. The exhaust fumes cause harmful pollution.

• **Deforestation** Illegally logged tropical hardwoods from unmanaged forests are commonly used to make garden furniture. Felling tropical rainforest removes its ability to act as a carbon dioxide-absorbing 'sink' and destroys biodiversity.

• **Processing and manufacturing** This requires energy derived from the burning of the finite and non-renewable fossil fuels, oil, coal and natural gas, creating pollution in the form of both carbon dioxide and other atmospheric pollutants, as well as liquid and/or solid waste.

▲ These steps are made from reclaimed slate, while the rail and fence are made from untreated green oak and sweet chestnut, two durable and long-lived hardwoods.

Identifying sustainable materials

Finding sustainable, eco-friendly materials for use in garden landscaping can be challenging, but they all share one or more of the following characteristics. Sustainable materials are usually:

• Reclaimed, often from other gardens, and can be reused again indefinitely.

• Made from renewable and natural local raw materials, such as wood, or from waste materials which can be usefully recycled, such as plastic.

• Not responsible for damage to landscapes or communities elsewhere in the world.

• Responsible for minimal or zero waste, producing no harmful pollution during their manufacture.

• Sourced as locally as possible to (or even from within) your own garden, often for free, needing only minimal transport.

• Easily recyclable or reusable, perhaps indefinitely, or biodegradable at the end of their life.

• Durable and extremely long-lived, needing little or no ongoing preservation or maintenance.

Choosing sustainable materials

Reusing existing landscaping materials, especially those from your own garden, will always be the most low-impact option. Other good sources of pre-used materials include reclamation yards, community recycling projects, online 'gifting' sites, or even a neighbour. A range of 'new' (recycled) sustainable materials is also available, especially those made from recycled plastic.

▲The raised beds and table in this food garden are made from untreated green oak.

▼ Stakes made out of recycled plastic milk bottles.

Reuse to save energy

The best way to keep your gardening footprint as small as possible is to reuse landscaping materials. Although most reused materials required high energy inputs when they were first extracted or made, natural stone, bricks, blocks, granite setts, pavers, quarry tiles and concrete slabs all use far less energy when they are used again. For example, if you reuse paving slabs from your own garden, the only energy required will be the renewable human kind needed to lift, carry and re-lay them. Similarly, if you source landscaping materials from a local reclamation yard or community recycling project, some energy will be needed to transport them, but it will be a fraction of that used in the original extraction and shipping or manufacturing process. Knowing that you are using materials that have been pre-loved is also deeply satisfying.

Wood

Natural and sustainable, wood is a potentially long-lived landscape material that locks up atmospheric carbon, releasing it only when the wood rots or is burnt. It can be used for fencing and seating, for raised beds, as plant supports or for making paths. Hardwoods, such as oak (*Quercus* spp.), require no preservative treatment and last for many years outdoors. Softwoods, such as pine (*Pinus* spp.), are used widely for making landscape products such as fence panels, and are usually impregnated with chemical preservatives to prolong their life. In your eco garden, try to use hardwoods, or if softwoods are the only option, buy untreated wood and use an eco-friendly preservative. Softwoods are widely available, but hardwoods are often only available from local sawmills, from specialist suppliers or reclamation yards.

Wooden railway sleepers (railroad ties) treated with the preservative creosote have long been used in gardens, but should avoided because of creosote's potential carcinogenic (cancer-causing) properties. Hardwood green oak planks, made from untreated oak (*Quercus* spp.), are an attractive, long-lived and safe alternative, and can be used to make sturdy raised beds.

Recycled products

Many materials considered as waste can be recycled into versatile landscaping products, making use of a valuable resource while relieving pressure on landfill. High-density polyethylene (HDPE) plastic milk bottles can be recycled into products that are durable, do not rot or splinter, need no preservative treatment, are extremely long-lived and can be recycled indefinitely. Although an energy-intensive base material is used (the bottles are derived from crude oil), the energy needed for the recycling process is less than that required to make the original bottles. HDPE cartons are plentiful and are collected in many areas through household recycling schemes.

▲ Reclaim yards are an excellent source of often unique sustainable landscaping materials that you simply will not find anywhere else.

Recycled plastic can be made into planks, raised beds, stakes, compost bins, decking, boardwalks, hand rails, benches, walkways or nest boxes, and comes in various colours and textures. Products with a wood-like finish can be hard to distinguish from real wood and will blend easily into a garden setting. Other materials, such as uPVC, which is used for making window frames and conservatories, can also be recycled into useful gardening products such as modular raised beds.

Avoiding cement

Cement, which is used in building mortar and concrete, is manufactured using an energy-intensive process and is responsible for up to 10 per cent of global carbon dioxide emissions. Lime mortar is a more eco-friendly material that can be used for building garden structures, as well as for laying paths and paving. It needs less energy to make, so it produces lower carbon emissions, and actually absorbs carbon dioxide as it sets.

Materials for free

One of the most interesting ways of obtaining materials, other than searching reclamation yards, is to join a free online 'gifting' community, such as *www.freecycle.org* or *www.ilovefreegle.org*. Originally set up to encourage the reuse of all kinds of materials and reduce waste, these internet-based networks allow people to offer items they no longer want, and also post requests for things they do want; items are not sold but given away, and no money is exchanged. This can be a very effective way of locating all kinds of sustainable landscaping materials, including the quirky and unique.

▼ In this wildlife garden, a bathtub and enamel sink reclaimed from a skip (dumpster) make an eye-catching water feature.

▲ Skips (dumpsters) can be a rich source of eco-friendly gardening materials, such as bricks, paving slabs and timber, but always ask for permission before you dive in.

Skips (dumpsters) can also be a rich source of useful, and free, landscape materials which would otherwise go to landfill. Before taking anything you find in a skip, always ask the person responsible for it for their permission – they might even have other materials to dispose of which you can use.

▼ This earth-friendly garden combines old and 'new' sustainable materials. The wall is made from 'gifted' reclaimed slate, the path from slate chippings sieved from quarry waste and the black path edging is recycled plastic derived from milk bottles.

Eco paths and paving

Paths encourage people to move around the eco garden, while paved areas create spaces for benches, seats and tables, or somewhere to stand pots and containers. Both can be made using sustainable, reclaimed or recycled materials. Using permeable materials helps gardens to absorb rainwater, especially during storms, which can reduce the risk of flooding in towns and cities.

Choosing materials

Many common path-making materials, such as gravel and stone or slate chippings, are extracted by quarrying or marine dredging before being processed and transported, often over long distances. This destroys natural landscapes, uses energy and generates pollution, as does quarrying natural stone to use for paving. Pebbles and stones should never be removed from beaches (or any other natural habitat) for garden use.

In an eco garden, it is always worth considering what materials are available closer to home. Any existing stone or concrete slabs can be lifted and re-laid as paths throughout the garden, which also helps to break up areas of wildlife-unfriendly hard surfacing. If the soil is very stony, the stones can be raked and/or sieved out and used to form paths edged with wooden or recycled plastic boards, making good use of a free material that might otherwise go to landfill. Wood chippings are often free to collect on roadsides, and can be laid over a natural or recycled weed-blocking fabric for low-cost paths between raised beds in

▼ Garden paths made from recycled materials, such as this one using a colourful montage of broken ceramic tiles and glass pebbles, can be individual and highly attractive.

◄ Recycled aggregates are often more planet-friendly than the original materials they are made from: (**1/2**) crushed ceramic industry waste is available in various grades and different shades, and is a useful and hard-wearing material for paths and other areas of regular foot traffic; (**3**) crushed brick is made from old house bricks and comes in various grades; (**4**) cockle shells, a seafood industry by-product, make a novel path surface; (**5**) slate chips are reclaimed from the slate industry.

a food garden. Hard-wearing stone or slate chippings can be sieved from quarry spoil heaps.

Reused materials are the most sustainable option for paved areas; natural or synthetic stone or concrete slabs, bricks, pavers and blocks can all be found in reclamation yards. If you do buy new paving materials, choose those made from recycled ingredients. These still use some energy-intensive materials, such as cement, but do not directly encourage the quarrying of natural stone.

Recycled aggregates

Waste bricks, concrete, stone and ceramics, which have been crushed and/or graded into different sizes, can all be used to make paths or driveways. Recycled aggregates are an attractive alternative to gravel and utilize materials that would otherwise go to waste. Various colours, textures and grades are available; finer grades are ideal for paths and they can also be used as a mulch.

Other recycled and novel materials for making paths include seashells, a seafood industry by-product, and broken glazed ceramic tiles, which can be made into eye-catching designs.

▼ These reclaimed granite setts have been grouped together to act as miniature stepping stones, allowing water to flow between them from one pond to another.

▲ The edge of this pond has been paved with reclaimed broken concrete slabs, following a random pattern. Plants are self-seeding into the cracks between the slabs.

Soaking up rainwater

One way to make an eco garden even more environmentally friendly is to ensure it soaks up as much water as possible during storms and periods of intense and/or prolonged rainfall. Paths and paved areas, including driveways, with tightly sealed joints between the paving materials, do not absorb water, but instead shed it into drains, which then feed into the neighbourhood drainage network. These networks can soon become overwhelmed during intense rainstorms, often leading to localized or sometimes more widespread general flooding in towns and cities.

These practical measures will ensure that your garden absorbs as much rainfall as possible:
• Keep hard, paved surfaces to a minimum.
• Use porous materials for garden paths (such as stones or recycled aggregates) so that rainwater passes through them into the soil below.
• When using solid paving materials, instead of sealing the joints between them with mortar, fill them with recycled sharp sand or grit instead, so that water can soak in. Self-seeding and beneficial insect-attracting plants such as alyssum (*Lobularia maritima*) will colonize the cracks.
• On a large area, leave out some of the paving units and either plant them up, or fill them with a porous aggregate, so that rainwater can soak into them rather than running off into the drains.
• Where feasible, lay solid path and paving materials on a bed of sand or hardcore, rather than on solid mortar or concrete, so water can percolate through; most garden paths can be laid straight on to leveled and firmed soil.
• Consider installing permeable paving (see panel).

▼ Flooding in urban areas can be eased if gardeners install paths and hard surfaces that encourage rainwater to soak through into the soil.

HOW PERMEABLE PAVING WORKS

Permeable paving is a special system that encourages the absorption of rainwater or snow melt. It uses interlocking paving units (often concrete blocks) which are designed so that a gap remains between them. This gap is filled with the same free-draining material on to which the units are laid. When it rains, water drains between the paving units, then soaks down through the drainage layer and into the soil. Permeable systems are used for driveways or other high-traffic areas. Owing to their specific nature, they require expert installation.

1 Paving units with gaps.
2 Fine drainage aggregate (below and between units).
3 Coarse drainage aggregate.
4 Permeable landscape fabric.
5 Soil.

▼ Paving blocks in permeable systems have grooves on their sides keeping a gap between them.

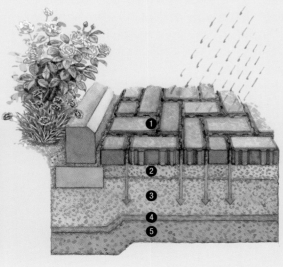

Living or green roofs

Growing a layer of plants on the roof of a garden shed, summerhouse or verandah will give it not just a whole new look, but also create a wildlife-friendly habitat that is attractive to beneficial insects. A living roof is straightforward to install, easy to maintain and, if you only have a small garden, can even be used for growing useful plants such as herbs.

What is a living roof?

A living or green roof is simply a roof with a layer of vegetation added to it. The most familiar examples are roof gardens found on the tops of buildings, from private homes to offices. They require specialist construction, are planted with a wide range of plants and need regular maintenance. Expert advice from a structural engineer must be sought before embarking on planting a roof garden.

More modest, self-build and low-maintenance living roofs can be planted on garden sheds, porches, verandahs, log stores, summerhouses, pet shelters, play houses and even bird tables. These structures generally have thin, lightweight roofs that are not intended for walking on. In most cases, where a structure is generally sound, it should be capable of supporting the weight of a simple living roof, and it is usually easy to strengthen it further if necessary. The roof must also be completely waterproof. In a simple living roof the plants grow in a layer of well-drained, lightweight growing medium, as shown in the panel 'How to make a living roof'.

Excess rainwater not absorbed by the growing media and plants can be directed into normal guttering and stored in a water butt. Living roofs absorb a surprising amount of water, especially during summer, releasing any excess only slowly (it quickly rushes off a bare roof).

▼ Adding a living roof to a garden office helps to replace any habitat lost in the construction of the building.

Advantages of living roofs

As well as making an otherwise dull surface attractive, a living roof will:
• Help replace any habitat lost in the construction of the building on which the roof is planted.
• Boost biodiversity in the eco garden by increasing the range of plants; the roof can be planted with flowers to attract beneficial insects.
• Support a 'mini meadow' containing plants that thrive in poorer, drier soil, and in more stressful conditions than are found in the rest of the garden.
• Provide a a habitat for wildlife, such as insects, which in turn provide a food source for birds, helping to strengthen the garden's food chain.
• Have an insulating and temperature-regulating effect on summerhouses, keeping them cooler in summer and warmer in winter.
• Absorb water during a rainstorm, reducing the rate at which rainwater enters the drainage network, which can help alleviate flooding.
• Provide extra growing space in a small garden for useful plants such as herbs.

▲ This small shed roof is planted with a living roof of various succulents, such as houseleek (*Sempervivum* spp.), the nectar-rich flowers of which attract insects.

▼ Sedum is a drought-resistant, low-maintenance perennial that is ideal for a living roof. It can be bought as a pre-grown mat.

▲ Fleshy-leaved houseleeks (*Sempervivum* spp.) will grow happily on sun-baked tiled roofs, surviving without rain for many months at a time. They flower in summer.

Planting options

The best ways to establish plants in a living roof are by sowing seeds, laying living sedum matting, or planting young 'plug' or pot-grown plants. Wildflower seed mixtures are widely available and are best sown in spring or autumn to allow them time to establish, as this is more difficult in dry summer conditions. Sedum, a reliable and drought-tolerant perennial, can be grown from cuttings but is usually obtained as a ready-grown mat that is rolled out over the growing medium. Plant larger plugs and pot-grown plants in spring or autumn, rather than in summer. Low-growing, creeping, mat-forming plants are generally the most suitable ones for a living roof.

Maintenance

Living roofs, once established, are not usually watered or fed, unless they include plants grown specifically for harvesting, such as herbs. The only regular jobs are to remove weeds or fallen leaves.

▼ Young 'plug' plants are best planted in a living roof in spring to give them time to establish before drier summer conditions. Alternatively, plant in autumn.

◄ This bird table has been attractively eco-fitted by covering its previously plain roof with a piece of ready-grown living sedum matting. Although covering only a small area, the sedum flowers attract many different and beneficial insects.

HOW TO MAKE A LIVING ROOF

This slice through a simple living roof planted with purple-flowered chives (*Allium schoenoprasum*) and lemon thyme (*Thymus citriodorus* 'Variegatus') shows its various different layers.

On a gently sloping or flat roof a recycled timber frame is used to contain the growing medium; on steeper roofs a lattice of timbers is used to create planting pockets, preventing slippage of the growing medium. The edges of the waterproof layer should overlap into the guttering.

1 A slate chipping mulch 10mm (½in) deep, to conserve moisture and prevent weeds.

2 Growing medium 10cm (4in) deep, comprising a 50:50 mixture of recycled crushed brick and gritty soil-based (peat-free) compost (soil mix). Expanded clay granules can also be used.

3 The permeable membrane allows drainage but stops the growing medium and roots from entering the drainage layer.

4 A drainage layer 2.5cm (1in) deep, made up of lightweight polystyrene chips or recycled plastic products. This layer is not essential on a small sloping roof.

5 A waterproof layer (for example a plastic sheet) laid over the roof surface.

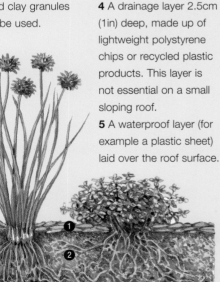

Sustainable fences and screens

Wood is the most commonly used fencing material, and choosing locally sourced, long-lasting hardwoods will help to make a garden more eco-friendly. Many other natural, plant-derived materials, some of which you can easily grow yourself, can be used to make attractive screens or plant supports. For a wildlife-friendly cross between a fence and a hedge, you could plant a living 'fedge'.

Fencing materials

Although wood is potentially the most eco-friendly material to use for garden fencing, much of the available wood is the familiar, mass-produced panel-type fencing made from softwoods, such as pine (*Pinus* spp.). These products are routinely treated with synthetic preservatives containing copper and fungicides to prevent rotting, which can leach into the soil when the wood eventually decays. Another disadvantage of softwood fencing is that it requires regular, usually annual treatment of preservative – often made using a cocktail of oil-derived chemicals in energy-intensive processes – to prolong its life. A local forestry product supplier might offer untreated softwood panel fencing, which you can then treat yourself using an eco-friendly preservative based on natural and non-toxic plant oils.

Hardwoods are the preferred choice of fencing material for an eco garden. Even though they are more expensive to buy, hardwoods are naturally decay-resistant, owing to their high tannin content, so require no preservative treatment. They are virtually maintenance-free and long-lived; oak (*Quercus* spp.) and sweet chestnut (*Castanea sativa*) will last 20 to 40 years, sometimes even

longer. Oak can be used for fence posts, fencing, paving and compost bins. Sweet chestnut makes durable fence posts and beautiful fences or pergolas.

Always try to source local, sustainably grown fencing materials, or enquire where other products on offer have come from. Wooden fencing that is certified as derived from responsibly and sustainably managed forests (rather than from illegally logged wild natural forest) usually carries an internationally recognized logo, such as the 'tick tree' symbol used by the Forest Stewardship Council (FSC). Using reclaimed hardwood and making your own fences is another sustainable option.

▲ This fence of sweet chestnut (*Castanea sativa*) paling requires no chemical preservative treatment, and blends into the surrounding woodland.

▼ Tough and durable oak fencing develops a silver-grey sheen, needs no preservative treatment and lasts for many decades.

Screens

While fences make a permanent, solid boundary for a garden, screens tend to be more open in nature. They can be used to divide a garden into different parts or to screen off unsightly elements such as fuel tanks. Like fences, screens can also be used to support climbing plants, giving them a dual function. You can obtain ready-made woven screens made of hazel (*Corylus* spp.) and willow (*Salix* spp.), or from other natural materials such as reeds and heather, none of which require any

▼ Woven willow screens can be beautiful, but they tend to be short-lived outdoors, lasting for only a few years.

HOW TO MAKE A GARDEN 'FEDGE'

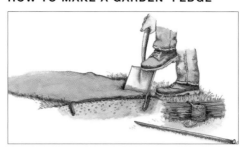

1 Anchor a 90cm (3ft) wide strip of weed control fabric by pushing 15cm (6in) of it on each side into slits in the ground made using a spade.

2 Use a pointed metal rod to make 30cm (12in) deep holes 40cm (16in) apart and at an angle of 45 degrees to the ground.

3 At the same angle, push each of the dormant, 2cm (¾in) diameter willow rods into the holes until they reach the bottom of the hole.

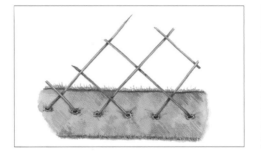

4 Make more holes between the first row of rods and push in more rods so they are 20cm (8in) apart. Weave the rods together.

5 Tie the interwoven rods together where they cross over using jute twine. This holds them in place while they take root and start growing.

6 Weave the thin tops of the rods around a rod laid horizontally at the desired height of the 'fedge' and bind with jute twine.

preservative. Hazel and willow might be available from local woodsmen offering little-travelled and planet-friendly sustainable coppice products.

Bamboo screens are usually made with much-travelled imported canes, but it is easy to grow bamboo, both for making do-it-yourself structures and for use as supports for climbing plants such as beans. *Phyllostachys bissetii* and *Pseudosasa japonica* are two cane-producing species; three-year-old canes, which have been dried for six months under cover, are the most durable.

Growing a willow 'fedge'

A 'fedge' is a fence-cum-hedge made of suitable varieties of vigorous-growing willow (*Salix* spp.). Long, woody cuttings (rods) are planted between late autumn and early spring. These form decorative, leafy screens that attract wildlife and need little maintenance once established, other than winter pruning. Willow roots can grow into drains and building foundations, so always plant a 'fedge' at least one and a half times its eventual height away from any buildings. The sequence shows how to make a 'fedge'.

▲ You can easily grow your own bamboo canes for making into eco-friendly screens and plant supports. Dry, three-year-old canes are ideal for this purpose.

◀ An established willow 'fedge' makes a living, ever-changing division between different parts of a garden. Once growing, the lattice of rods is self-supporting.

DIRECTORY OF ECO-FRIENDLY PLANTS

Choosing what to grow in your eco garden requires more care and thought than might usually be applied when selecting plants. Eco-friendly flowering plants tend to be those with simple single blooms, rather than complex double blooms, which are less attractive to insects. Plants that provide wildlife habitats are also good choices, as are food garden plants with natural resistance to pest and diseases. Plants that provide bees with pollen and/or nectar are indicated by ✹. Plants that attract beneficial insects are indicated by ✤.

◀ Tall verbena (*Verbena bonariensis*) is a summer-flowering perennial that is usually grown as an annual. Its nectar-rich flowers will attract clouds of butterflies.

▲ Poached egg plant (*Limnanthes douglasii*) readily self-seeds.

▲ Common honeysuckle (*Lonicera periclymenum*) attracts moths at night.

▲ Birds will feed on the large red and juicy hips of *Rosa rugosa*.

Eco-friendly annuals

Fast-growing annuals, which complete their life cycle within a year, are among the most valuable of all eco garden plants, and many will freely self-seed. Some flower within weeks of sowing and immediately start attracting bees and other beneficial insects. Always choose those varieties with simple, single flowers, which are rich in insect-accessible nectar and pollen.

Calendula officinalis
Pot marigold
Family: Asteraceae
A fast-growing annual with slightly sticky, pale green leaves and flat, disc-like flowers, often with dark eyes that are a magnet for bees and hoverflies. Sow the large seeds outdoors in mid-spring (or in autumn for early flowers the following spring). 'Nova' and 'Daisy May' are good single cultivars. Allow to self-seed among crops in a food garden. 30–45cm (12–18in).

Dahlia 'Fascination'
Bedding dahlia
Family: Asteraceae
Bees and butterflies flock to the large flowers, up to 10cm (4in) wide, held above the bronze leaves of this tuberous-rooted perennial, grown as a half-hardy summer flowering annual. Sow in mid-spring under cover or buy ready-grown plants, choosing single cultivars in mixed colours. Tubers can be stored frost-free over winter. 'Bishop's Children', 'Mignon Mixed' or 'Romeo' are all good choices.

▲ *Dahlia* 'Fascination'

Deadhead regularly to promote flowering. 45–60 x 60cm (18–24 x 24in).

Dianthus barbatus
Sweet William
Family: Caryophyllaceae
This fragrant, short-lived perennial is often grown as a biennial in borders; its flattish

flowerheads make beautiful and lasting cut flowers. Sow under cover in early to mid-spring for late summer and autumn flowers, or sow in late spring to early summer for blooms the following year. The cultivars 'Monarch Mixed' and 'Single Mixed' attract nectar-seeking bees and butterflies to their single blooms. Up to 70 x 30cm (28 x 12in).

Eschscholzia californica
California poppy
Family: Papaveraceae
Fast-growing, drought-tolerant hardy annuals with finely cut, pale blue-green leaves and short-lived but prolific poppy-like flowers up to 7cm (3in) across followed by narrow seed pods. Sow outdoors in spring. Prefers poor, dry soil in full sun; self-seeds prolifically in paths, especially in the cracks between paving and on hot, sun-baked gravel areas. A favourite plant of hoverflies seeking nectar. Choose single-flowered cultivars, e.g. 'Golden Values' (yellow), 'Ivory Castle' (white) or 'Single Mixed'. Up to 30 x 15cm (12 x 6in).

▼ *Calendula officinalis*

▼ *Dianthus barbatus*

▼ *Eschscholzia californica*

▲ *Helianthus annuus*

▼ *Limnanthes douglasii*

▲ *Lobularia maritima*

▼ *Nicotiana sylvestris*

Helianthus annuus
Sunflower
Family: Asteraceae
Sunflowers produce either a single large flowerhead (up to 60cm/24in across), or a branching head with multiple blooms. Sow in spring, outdoors or in pots and plant out. The flowers are rich in pollen and nectar (avoid growing 'pollen-free' cultivars as these have much less insect-appeal). Birds eat the seeds in autumn and winter, so leave plants in place until spring. Try 'Hallo' (multi-headed), 'Titan' (huge single heads) or 'Pastiche' (mixed shades and ideal for using as a cut flower). Up to 5m x 60cm (16ft x 24in). ✱ 🦋

Limnanthes douglasii
Poached egg plant
Family: Limnanthaceae
The nectar-rich, yellow-centred white flowers of *Limnanthes* appear from spring onwards above glossy and divided yellow-green leaves. Sow the large black and easy-to-handle seeds outdoors in spring. It self-seeds readily and forms low-growing clumps which can be left to fill gaps along the edges of beds in a food garden. Self-sown seedlings will overwinter and flower early the following spring. The cultivar 'Spanish Omelette' contains two-tone, white and yellow flowers. 15cm (6in). ✱ 🦋

Lobularia maritima (syn. *Alyssum maritimum*)
Sweet alyssum
Family: Brassicaceae
Grows as low mounds of grey-green leaves and small, honey-scented flowers. Makes a good edging plant, or can be dotted around a food garden. Half-hardy; sow under cover in early spring, planting out after frosts. 'Rally Formula Mixed' contains pale yellows and ochres. 5–30 x 20–30cm (2–12 x 8–12in). ✱ 🦋

Nicotiana sylvestris
Tobacco plant
Family: Solanaceae
Night- and day-flying moths are attracted to this half-hardy annual's tubular, nectar-rich flowers which flood the night-time garden with scent. Useful for the backs of borders. Sow under cover in spring, then plant after frosts. *N. langsdorffii* reaches 1.5m (5ft) tall and has scented yellow-green flowers. 1.5m x 60cm (5ft x 24in). 🦋

Papaver somniferum
Opium poppy
Family: Papaveraceae
Both honey bees and bumblebees make noisy visits to the 10cm (4in) wide blooms of this tall and hardy, self-seeding annual with blue-green leaves. Sow outdoors in spring. Produces seeds in pepperpot-like seed pods which attract birds such as finches. Avoid cultivars with double blooms. 1.2m x 30cm (4ft x 12in). ✱ 🦋

▼ *Papaver somniferum*

Eco-friendly perennials

Perennials are hardy plants which live for two years or longer and flower annually when they are mature. The most familiar are herbaceous perennials, which produce new flowering stems each year that die back in autumn; they then lie dormant over winter, sending up new shoots in spring. Perennials are invaluable in an eco garden because they flower unfailingly, often for many months.

Anchusa azurea 'Dropmore'
Blue bugloss
Family: Boraginaceae
Forms clumps of hairy, grey-green leaves below shoots carrying lots of amethyst-blue flowers which are adored by bees. Good border plant. Deadheading after the first flush of flowers encourages a second showing. 'Loddon Royalist' is a strong-growing cultivar 90cm (3ft) tall, with deep blue flowers. 'Little John' reaches just 45cm (18in) tall, and has deep blue flowers. 60–90 x 60cm (2–3 x 2ft). 🐝

▲ *Anchusa azurea* 'Dropmore'

▼ *Cirsium rivulare* 'Atropurpureum'

Astrantia 'Hadspen Blood'
Hattie's pincushion
Family: Apiaceae
Pretty, clump-forming plants with lobed leaves that are ideal for borders in sun or dappled shade. The umbrella-like flowerheads comprise small flowers surrounded by papery bracts, both deep red in colour, which are much visited by bees. Can be dried for use indoors. Divide large clumps in spring. *A. major* subsp. *involucrata* 'Shaggy' has long, green-tipped bracts; *A. major*

▲ *Astrantia* 'Hadspen Blood'

▼ *Geranium* x *magnificum*

'Sunningdale Variegated' has striking cream-edged leaves and pink bracts. 30–90 x 45cm (1–3ft x 18in). 🐝

Cirsium rivulare 'Atropurpureum'
Ornamental thistle
Family: Asteraceae
Watch the tall stems of this non-invasive thistle sway under the sheer weight of visiting bees. An attractive border plant, it needs regular deadheading to prolong its flowering period. Divide large clumps in spring. Its pincushion-like flowerheads, measuring 3cm (1¼in) across, are deep crimson. Stop deadheading in late summer to allow the seedheads, which are eaten by birds, to form. 1.2m x 60cm (4 x 2ft). 🐝🦋

Geranium x *magnificum*
Hardy geranium
Family: Geraniaceae
Find a sunny spot for this clump-forming herbaceous perennial. Bees flock to the deeply veined violet-blue, saucer-like flowers, 5cm (2in) wide, which appear non-stop throughout the summer. The lobed leaves take on reddish autumn tints. Shade-loving *G. macrorrhizum* 'Ingwersen's Variety' is a good ground cover plant 45cm (18in) tall, with soft pink flowers from late spring, making it a valuable source of early nectar for bumblebees. 60cm (2ft). 🐝

Iris sibirica
Siberian iris
Family: Iridaceae
There are many different cultivars of *Iris sibirica*, in a wide range of flower colours. Plants form clumps of narrow, grass-like leaves. In early summer, tall stems carry

▲ *Iris sibirica*

▲ *Leucanthemum vulgare*

▲ *Nepeta racemosa*

up to five blue-violet flowers with paler markings and striking dark veins. Grows happily in fertile border soil, or in damp ground near a pond. *I. bulleyana* is similar, growing 45cm (18in) tall. 50–120cm (20–48in).

Leucanthemum vulgare
Ox-eye daisy
Family: Asteraceae
From a low, spreading mound of dark green leaves, tall solitary flowerheads appear, each 2.5–5cm (1–2in) across, comprising a yellow centre surrounded by white petals. Ideal for growing in long, unmown grass in a 'wild lawn', these are a magnet for butterflies and hoverflies. Plants raised from summer-saved seed and planted in late summer or autumn will flower the following summer. 30–90 x 60cm (1–3 x 2ft).

Nepeta racemosa
(syn. *N. mussinii*)
Catmint
Family: Lamiaceae
The sound made by the sheer number of bees visiting the flowers of catmint will draw this plant to your attention. The lavender-blue flowers appear in summer

on long, slightly floppy, spreading stems. The leaves are hairy and have a 'catmint' fragrance. Divide in spring or autumn; trim in spring. *Nepeta* 'Six Hills Giant' is similar but grows 90cm (36in) tall and wide. Up to 30 x 45cm (12 x 18in).

Phlomis russeliana
Sticky Jerusalem sage
Family: Lamiaceae
This sun-loving perennial, with its felted leaves, has dense, striking whorls of hooded yellow flowers up to 4cm (1½in) long, in which bees forage furiously. A good choice for a sun-baked, dry garden as an attractive ground cover. Flowers appear non-stop from late spring to autumn.

▼ *Phlomis russeliana*

Leave the dead flower stems for winter interest, cutting them down in spring. Up to 90 x 75cm (3ft x 30in).

Verbena bonariensis
(syn. *V. patagonica*)
Tall verbena
Family: Verbenaceae
Butterflies flock to the sweetly scented heads of lilac-purple summer flowers up to 5cm (2in) across, carried on the tall, branching stems. Also attracts moths. Easily grown from seed, or from cuttings taken in spring, and often treated as an annual, it will readily self-seed. Blooms from midsummer until the first frosts. Up to 2m x 90cm (7 x 3ft).

▼ *Verbena bonariensis*

Eco-friendly shrubs and climbers

Shrubs and climbers are long-lived hardy plants with woody stems, usually producing several branches from their base at or near ground level (trees have a single stem). Shrubs either keep their leaves all year round (evergreen), or drop them in autumn (deciduous). Shrubs provide food such as pollen, nectar and autumn/winter fruits, nesting sites and year-round shelter for wildlife.

Buddleja davidii
Butterfly bush
Family: **Loganiaceae**
In late summer this fast-growing deciduous shrub attracts clouds of butterflies and other beneficial insects to its elongated, nectar-rich and honey-scented flowerheads from late summer. Grow it in a mixed border with insect-attracting perennials. Prune in spring. Pink- and lilac-coloured B. davidii cultivars are usually the most attractive to insects. B. alternifolia and B. crispa are also insect-attractants. 3 x 5m (10 x 16ft).

Ceanothus 'Pershore Zanzibar'
Variegated California lilac
Family: **Rhamnaceae**
A striking evergreen shrub which is best grown against a sheltered sunny wall. Its golden-yellow leaves have a dark green central splash. Clusters of small, powder-blue flowers, which appear among the colourful foliage in late spring and early summer, are popular with bees and other insects. The cultivar 'Autumnal Blue' has sky blue flowers in late summer and autumn. Up to 3m (10ft).

▲ Ceanothus 'Pershore Zanzibar'

▼ Cotoneaster horizontalis

▼ Buddleja davidii

▲ Helianthemum 'Ben Ledi'

▼ Hypericum olympicum

Cotoneaster horizontalis
Herringbone cotoneaster
Family: **Rosaceae**
This deciduous shrub will clamber up against a wall, or spread over the ground. The branches, borne in a herringbone pattern, are covered with small dark leaves which turn vivid red in autumn. In spring, bees are drawn in large and noisy numbers to the small, pinkish-white sweet-scented and nectar-rich flowers. The flowers are followed by spherical red fruits 6mm (¼in) long, which are eaten by birds. 1 x 1.5m (3 x 5ft).

Helianthemum 'Ben Ledi'
Rock rose
Family: **Cistaceae**
An evergreen, low-growing and ground-covering shrub for the edges of paths and borders, which thrives in dry soil and full sun. Good for seaside gardens. A succession of deep pink, yellow-eyed flowers bloom from late spring onwards. They are rich in nectar and attract foraging bumblebees. Other cultivars include brick red 'Henfield Brilliant' and pink 'Rhodanthe Carneum'. 20–30 x 30cm (8–12 x 12in).

▲ *Lonicera periclymenum*

▲ *Rosa* 'Ballerina'

▲ *Solanum crispum* 'Glasnevin'

Hypericum olympicum
St John's Wort
Family: Clusiaceae
Look out for honey bees gathering pollen and nectar among the long, filament-like stamens of the yellow flowers, which are up to 6cm (2½in) across. The leaves of this deciduous shrub are grey-green. *H. olympicum* f. *uniflorum* 'Citrinum' has lemon-yellow flowers. *H.* 'Hidcote' makes a semi-evergreen bush up to 1.2m (4ft) tall and wide, with large golden yellow flowers produced in succession for many months. 25 x 30cm (10 x 12in).

Lonicera periclymenum
Common honeysuckle
Family: Caprifoliaceae
The white to yellow, red-flushed flowers of this vigorous deciduous climber will fill your garden with a heady and powerful fragrance after dark. Moths, including the larger hawk moths, feed on the flowers' nectar at night, and other insects visit by day. Let honeysuckle scramble through a hedge or up into the boughs of a tree. Birds eat the glossy red berries that follow the flowers. The cultivar 'Serotina' has creamy-white flowers streaked with red-purple. Height up to 7m (23ft).

Rosa 'Ballerina'
Hybrid musk/polyantha rose
Family: Rosaceae
This spectacular, disease-resistant rose has a spreading habit and large heads of pink, white-centred flowers, which bees find irresistible. The flowers appear from spring to autumn. All roses with open, single flowers are the preferred eco garden choice; species or cultivars where a cluster of golden stamens are obvious are the most insect-friendly. 1–1.5 x 1–1.2m (3–5 x 3–4ft).

Solanum crispum 'Glasnevin' (syn. *S. crispum* 'Autumnale')
Chilean potato vine/tree
Family: Solanaceae
A warm sunny wall is the ideal position for this fast-growing and semi-evergreen climbing shrub, which needs training on trellis or wires. In summer it produces heads of fragrant purple-blue flowers 15cm (6in) wide, which are attractive to bees of all kinds. The flowers bear a striking resemblance to those of the potato plant, hence the common name of potato vine. *S. jasminoides* 'Album' is similar, but with fragrant pure white flowers. Height up to 6m (20ft).

Weigela 'Florida Variegata' (syn. *W. florida* 'Variegata')
Weigela
Family: Caprifoliaceae
A colourful deciduous shrub for a mixed border, its pink flowers, 3cm (1¼in) long, are produced in spring and early summer along arching shoots, and are much visited by bees in search of an early source of nectar. The leaves have pretty creamy-white margins and make a good foil for darker flowers. For pink flowers set as a striking contrast against dark bronze-green foliage, choose *W. florida* 'Follis Purpureis', which grows up to 1m (3ft) tall. 1.2–2m (4–7ft).

▼ *Weigela* 'Florida Variegata'

Eco-friendly hedging plants

Hedges are living barriers or screens made up of attractive hardy evergreen or deciduous shrubs, and sometimes climbers. They are used to mark out a garden's boundary. Eco-friendly hedges contain a diverse range of flowering and fruiting plants. Birds, bees, beneficial insects, small mammals, spiders and other creatures will all live and feed in, on and below a species-rich hedge.

Berberis darwinii
Barberry
Family: Berberidaceae
This upright evergreen shrub flowers in mid- and late spring and is an invaluable and reliable early source of nectar for bees, when few other spring flowers are available. Its orange flowers are held in hanging clusters 5cm (2in) long among glossy, dark green spine-toothed leaves. It also provides dense and safe cover for birds. *B. x lologensis* 'Apricot Queen' is similar, with dark orange flowers opening in spring. 3m (10ft).

Cotoneaster lacteus
Cotoneaster
Family: Rosaceae
Throughout winter, the arching branches of this evergreen shrub carry clusters of red fruits 6mm (¼in) in diameter, which birds such as blackbirds and thrushes will eat during freezing spells. The leaf undersides are felted yellow-white. In spring the scented white flowers attract honey bees and bumblebees. Prune carefully, in late winter, using secateurs to maintain the hedge shape. *C. simonsii* also makes a dense, semi-evergreen hedge. 4m (13ft).

Crataegus monogyna
Hawthorn
Family: Rosaceae
In late spring this thorny deciduous shrub's white flowers fill the air with a sweet honey fragrance, and are much visited by noisy foraging bees. The flowers are followed by fruits 6mm (¼in) in diameter which turn red in autumn, and are a valuable winter food source for many garden birds such as blackbirds, redwings, starlings and thrushes. It is easily trimmed into a dense, formal hedge, making it popular with nesting birds. 10 x 8m (33 x 26ft).

▲ *Crataegus monogyna*

Hebe 'Great Orme'
Hebe
Family: Scrophulariaceae
This evergreen shrub, with its narrow, glossy leaves, makes an excellent insect-friendly informal hedge that needs little if any pruning. Its spikes of flowers 5–10cm (2–4in) long in pink, fading to white, bloom non-stop from midsummer to mid-autumn. Thrives in coastal areas.

▼ *Berberis darwinii*

▼ *Cotoneaster lacteus*

▼ *Hebe* 'Great Orme'

▲ *Ilex aquifolium*

H. x franciscana 'Variegata' flowers in summer and autumn and has pale mauve flowers set against cream-edged leaves. 1.2m (4ft). 🐝 🦋

Ilex aquifolium
Common holly
Family: Aquifoliaceae
Eventually making a dense, spiny and bird-friendly evergreen hedge, this shrub has small white flowers in spring, followed by bright red berries which persist throughout winter and are eaten in severe cold snaps by thrushes and other birds. The cultivar 'J. C. van Tol' is self-fertile, so it will reliably produce berries without being close to other hollies. Up to 25 x 8m (82 x 26ft). 🐝

Prunus spinosa
Blackthorn
Family: Rosaceae
One of the first deciduous shrubs to flower, its white flowers stud the leafless stems in early spring, providing welcome nectar for bees. It makes a tough and spiny informal wildlife hedge and is less suitable for formal pruning; it forms a good impenetrable boundary for a large garden with wild areas. Spherical black fruits or 'sloes' 15mm (½in) wide ripen in autumn. 5 x 4m (16 x 13ft). 🐝

Pyracantha 'Orange Glow'
Firethorn
Family: Rosaceae
The persistent and eye-catching orange berries of this thorny evergreen shrub stand out against its dark green leaves, although hungry songbirds will often strip the berries during winter cold snaps. Honey bees and bumblebees visit the sweet-scented clusters of white flowers in late spring. Mature hedges are a good habitat for nesting birds. The cultivar 'Soleil d'Or' is similar, but has golden yellow berries. 3m (10ft). 🐝 🦋

Rosa rugosa
Rugosa rose
Family: Rosaceae
Disease-resistant and thriving in poor soil, this tough deciduous species rose makes a low-maintenance multipurpose hedge.

▲ *Pyracantha* 'Orange Glow'

▼ *Prunus spinosa*

Its prickly stems carry wrinkled, leathery leaves and deep pink cup-shaped flowers 7cm (3in) across, throughout the summer. Bees visit them for nectar. Large reddish-orange hips follow in autumn and are eaten by birds. *R.* 'Roseraie de l'Hay' has salmon-pink flowers 10cm (4in) wide. 1–2.5m (3–8ft). 🐝

Viburnum lantana
Wayfaring tree
Family: Caprifoliaceae
Ideal for a multi-species wildlife hedge, this upright deciduous shrub has grey-green leaves that turn red in autumn. Domed heads of small white flowers open in late spring, followed later by oblong red, and finally black, fruits. Succeeds on alkaline (lime-rich) soil. *V. opulus* (Guelder rose) has white spring flowers and fleshy red fruits. 5 x 4m (16 x 13ft). 🐝

▲ *Viburnum lantana*

▼ *Rosa rugosa*

Eco-friendly trees

Trees are evergreen or deciduous hardy, long-lived woody plants, usually with a single stem (trunk) from which other branches arise. They are an integral part of a garden's framework. In an eco garden, trees offer roosting or nesting sites and winter food for birds, and provide spring and summer pollen and nectar for bees and other beneficial insects. Some bear edible fruits.

Amelanchier lamarckii
Juneberry
Family: Rosaceae
This deciduous small tree or shrub carries heads of nectar-rich white flowers 13cm (5in) long in mid-spring, followed by sweet and juicy black edible fruits in mid- to late summer. Its green 7cm (3in)-long leaves turn fiery red and orange in autumn. *A.* x *grandiflora* 'Ballerina' flowers profusely and has red-purple autumn foliage. 10 x 12m (33 x 39ft).

▲ *Amelanchier lamarckii*

▼ *Arbutus unedo*

Arbutus unedo
Strawberry tree
Family: Ericaeae
In autumn this glossy-leaved evergreen tree carries clusters of white, bell-like flowers followed by round red, strawberry-like edible fruits, which ripen the following spring. The reddish-brown bark is flaky, adding to this tree's appeal during winter. Needs acid or neutral soil. Much visited by bumblebees searching for nectar. *A. unedo* can reach 8m (26ft) tall;

▲ *Betula pendula*

▼ *Cercis siliquastrum*

A. x *unedo* f. *rubra* has dark pink flowers. Compact-growing 2m (7ft) 'Elfin King' is ideal for a smaller garden.

Betula pendula
Silver birch
Family: Betulaceae
An elegant deciduous tree which grows well on dry, sandy soils. It has an open canopy of branches, casting dappled shade, where birds will perch during the day and roost at night. The pretty bark is white and peeling, becoming cracked at the base of the trunk on older trees. In spring, male catkins 6cm (2½in) long appear. The leaves turn yellow in autumn. 25 x 10m (82 x 33ft).

Cercis siliquastrum
Judas tree
Family: Fabaceae
The pink flowers of this multi-stemmed, slow-growing deciduous tree appear before the leaves in late spring and early summer, often on the thicker main branches. They are a useful food source for bees. In autumn its blue-green heart-shaped or kidney-shaped leaves turn to shades of rich yellow. *C. siliquastrum* f. *albida* has white flowers, while those of the cultivar 'Bodnant' are dark purple-pink. 10m (33ft).

Elaeagnus umbellata
Autumn olive
Family: Elaeagnaceae
Tolerant of exposure, this deciduous small tree or large shrub has leaves 10cm (4in) long which are silvery when young, later becoming bright green. In early spring, bumblebees and other wild bees flock to its highly fragrant, silvery yellow-white

▲ *Elaeagnus umbellata*

flowers, which are 1.5cm (½in) long. These are followed by small round edible fruits which ripen from silver to red by autumn. Also useful as part of a scented hedge. 4 x 6m (13 x 20ft). 🐝

Eucryphia glutinosa
Eucryphia
Family: Cunoniaceae
This beautiful evergreen (or semi-evergreen) upright tree has dark green glossy foliage and flowers in mid- and late summer. The cup-shaped white flowers are 6cm (2½in) wide with a central boss of gold-tipped stamens; they attract so many bees that the entire tree can appear to be buzzing and is often heard before

▼ *Eucryphia glutinosa*

it is seen. *E.* x *nymansensis* 'Nymansay' is similar and grows 15m (50ft) tall. 10 x 6m (33 x 20ft). 🐝

Halesia carolina
Snowdrop tree
Family: Styracaceae
This unusual slow-growing deciduous tree or large shrub produces its bell-shaped, hanging flowers, which are 2cm (¾in) long, in late spring, just before its leaves appear. The winged fruits that follow are edible, with a pea-like flavour, and should be eaten when young and tender (usually midsummer). Both honey bees and wild bees visit the flowers, which can also be eaten in salads. The leaves turn yellow in autumn. 8 x 10m (26 x 33ft). 🐝

Salix caprea 'Kilmarnock'
Kilmarnock willow
Family: Salicaceae
The yellow-grey catkins of this small, deciduous weeping tree appear in mid- and late spring on bare downswept stems, and provide an early food source for foraging bees. The leaves turn yellow in autumn and the bare stems add winter interest. Many willows grow very large, but 'Kilmarnock' allows a bee-friendly tree to be grown in any average-sized garden. 1.5–2 x 2m (5–7 x 7ft). 🐝

▼ *Salix caprea* 'Kilmarnock'

▲ *Halesia carolina*

Sorbus aucuparia
Mountain ash
Family: Rosaceae
A hardy deciduous tree with divided, herringbone-like leaves that take on dazzling shades of red and yellow in autumn. Heads of fragrant, creamy-white flowers appear in late spring, and are much visited by bees. These are followed by heavy clusters of round, orange-red berries which, as they swell and ripen, often weigh the branches down. Many different birds feed on the berries throughout autumn and winter. *S. aucuparia* var. *xanthocarpa* (syn. 'Fructu Luteo') has orange-yellow autumn fruits. 15 x 7m (50 x 23ft). 🐝 🦋

▼ *Sorbus aucuparia*

Eco-friendly annual vegetables

Modern cultivars of vegetable which have been bred to be resistant to or tolerant of specific plant pests and diseases are ideal choices for an eco-friendly food garden. Equally, some 'heritage' or 'heirloom' vegetable cultivars can be extremely beautiful, as well as resilient and productive, and growing them (and saving seed) helps to maintain the vegetable gene pool for the future.

Allium cepa
(Cepa Group) 'Golden Bear F1'
Bulb onion
Family: **Alliaceae**
This high-yielding globe-shaped onion is very tolerant of downy mildew and botrytis (grey mould), and resistant to white rot disease; it is a good choice for growing on a long-established allotment known to be infected with onion diseases. Red-skinned and red-fleshed cultivars are also available. Sow seed or plant 'sets' (small immature bulbs) in spring, or in autumn choosing cultivars suitable for autumn planting.

Brassica oleracea
(Botrytis Group) 'Clapton F1'
Cauliflower
Family: **Brassicaceae**
A vigorous hybrid cauliflower which, together with the cultivar 'Clarify F1', is highly resistant to soil-borne clubroot disease, which affects all members of the

▼ *Allium cepa* 'Golden Bear F1'

▲ *Brassica oleracea* (Botrytis Group)

cabbage (Brassicaceae) family. Sow seeds from early spring to mid-spring and harvest the cauliflowers from midsummer onward. Using resistant cultivars is the only way to produce a reliable crop on clubroot-infected ground. These cultivars are also available as young starter plants or plug plants.

Brassica oleracea
(Capitata Group) 'Kilaxy F1'
Cabbage
Family: **Brassicaceae**
'Kilaxy F1' is a ball-headed cabbage that is resistant to clubroot disease. It is sown from late winter to mid-spring for harvesting from early autumn to early winter. It is hardy, stores well for long periods and can be cooked or eaten raw. Autumn-harvested, ball-headed 'Kilazol F1' is also clubroot-resistant. For a clubroot-resistant Brussels sprout, grow *B. oleracea* (Gemmifera Group) 'Crispus F1'.

Daucus carota **'Flyaway F1'**
Carrot
Family: **Apiaceae**
'Flyaway F1', 'Maestro F1', 'Nandor F1' and 'Resistafly F1' are all modern F1 hybrid cultivars of carrot bred to resist

▲ *Brassica oleracea* (Capitata Group)

attack by carrot fly (a small fly whose maggots burrow into carrots). Sow seeds outdoors from early spring to midsummer for pulling from early summer to early winter. Early crops can also be grown in soil beds or containers in a greenhouse or polytunnel. Leave any overlooked roots to produce their flat nectar-rich flowerheads the following year – they attract many beneficial garden insects, including hoverflies. 🦋

▼ *Daucus carota*

▲ *Pastinaca sativa*

▲ *Pisum sativum* 'Clarke's Beltony Blue'

▲ *Vicia faba* 'Crimson Flowered'

Pastinaca sativa 'Albion F1'
Parsnip
Family: Apiaceae
Ideal for an eco-friendly food garden, this white-skinned parsnip cultivar is highly resistant to canker and other soil-borne diseases. Sow seeds outdoors from early to late spring, and lift the roots from mid-autumn to late winter. 'Gladiator F1' (early maturing), 'Javelin F1' (slender, tapering roots) and 'Tender and True' (outstanding flavour) are also canker-resistant. Leave a few roots in the ground in spring to flower and attract hoverflies. 🦋

Phaseolus coccineus 'Red Rum'
Runner (green) bean
Family: Papilionaceae
This disease-resistant cultivar of climbing runner (green) bean has the added advantage of producing a reliable crop

▼ *Phaseolus coccineus* 'Red Rum'

even during poor summer weather. The white-flowered cultivars 'White Lady' and 'Moonlight' are also reliable croppers during indifferent summers. Sow outdoors in mid-spring to late spring; protect young plants from frost. For an eye-catching display, 'Painted Lady' and 'St George' have bi-coloured red and white flowers, and 'Celebration' is salmon pink. 🐝

Pisum sativum 'Clarke's Beltony Blue'
Purple-podded mangetout (snow) pea
Family: Papilionaceae
With its beautiful purple pods, this unusual, tall-growing heritage (heirloom) mangetout (snow) pea originates from Northern Ireland in the United Kingdom. Sow in spring. The pods, which appear following the pink-purple flowers, are eaten whole when young. Birds find purple pods less attractive. Other unusual cultivars include 'Golden Sweet', which grows 2m (7ft) tall, with purple flowers followed by obvious, easy-to-pick, lemon yellow pods.

Solanum tuberosum 'Sárpo Mira'
Potato
Family: Solanaceae
One of the most disease-resistant maincrop potato cultivars, giving a reliable crop of red-skinned tubers, even when outbreaks of potato blight (a fungal disease) are severe. With dense,

weed-smothering leafy tops (haulms), little need for feeding, good drought resistance and a long storage period, 'Sárpo Mira' is ideal for an eco-friendly food garden. 'Sárpo Shona' (white-skinned maincrop) and 'Sárpo Una' (pink-skinned early) are also blight-resistant.

Vicia faba 'Crimson Flowered'
Crimson-flowered broad (fava) bean
Family: Papilionaceae
The striking crimson flowers of this heritage (heirloom) cultivar are followed by short pods containing green beans. The flower colour makes this broad (fava) bean ideal for an ornamental or potager-style food garden. Sow the large seeds in spring, or in autumn for early crops the following summer. Most broad bean cultivars have black and white flowers; bees visit them to gather nectar. 🐝

▼ *Solanum tuberosum* 'Sárpo Mira'

Eco-friendly bush and tree fruits

Bush fruits (also called soft fruits) and tree fruits (also called top fruits) are mostly hardy, long-lived deciduous woody trees or shrubs which produce crops over many years. In an eco garden, the most suitable cultivars to grow are those with proven and natural resistance to pests and diseases. New cultivars are introduced regularly and are often listed in plant catalogues.

Fragaria x ananassa 'Florence'
Strawberry
Family: Rosaceae
The flowers of this perennial appear in spring and are followed by initially green, then fleshy, fragrant and sweet-tasting dark red fruits, which ripen from early summer to midsummer. 'Florence' is highly disease-resistant; 'Christine' produces fruits for picking in late spring if grown in a greenhouse or polytunnel; 'Albion' produces fruits in flushes from early summer to mid-autumn. Both 'Christine' and 'Albion' are also disease-resistant. 23cm (9in). 🐝

Malus domestica Redlove® Era®
Eating apple
Family: Rosaceae
This red-skinned cultivar has unusual rosy-red flesh, which is crisp and juicy; fruits can be eaten fresh from the tree or used for cooking (the flesh retains its red colouring). The spring flowers are deep pink. Harvest from early autumn.

▲ *Malus domestica* Redlove® Era®

Highly resistant to apple scab disease. Grow on a dwarfing rootstock (e.g. 'M9') for a small, deciduous tree suitable for a small garden. 2.5 x 1.5m (8 x 5ft). 🐝

Malus domestica 'Sunset'
Eating apple
Family: Rosaceae
Pick the fruits of this disease-resistant cultivar in early autumn. Its golden-skinned,

▲ *Ribes nigrum*

red-streaked fruits are aromatic and well flavoured. It crops heavily and makes a small, deciduous tree if grown on a dwarfing rootstock such as 'M9'. 'Fiesta' (yellow skin, flushed red, mid-autumn picking) and 'Scrumptious' (red skin, early autumn picking) are both disease-resistant cultivars which are also suitable for growing in colder areas. 2.5 x 1.5m (8 x 5ft). 🐝

Ribes nigrum 'Ben Sarek'
Blackcurrant
Family: Grossulariaceae
A deciduous bush which sends up vigorous new shoots from the base of the plant each year. This cultivar only grows 90cm (3ft) tall so is a good choice for a small food garden with limited growing space (it can also be grown in a large tub at least 60cm (2ft) in diameter). It is resistant to foliage diseases such as mildew and produces a heavy crop of large currants in midsummer. Prune in late winter. 'Ben Connan' is also compact, and is disease- and frost-resistant. 90 x 90cm (3 x 3ft). 🐝

▼ *Fragaria* x *ananassa* 'Florence'

▼ *Malus domestica* 'Sunset'

Ribes rubrum 'Blanka'
Whitecurrant
Family: Grossulariaceae
This deciduous bush is trouble-free and carries heavy crops of pale, translucent fruits on long stalks (strigs) ready for harvesting in midsummer. Whitecurrants require only simple pruning and crop reliably for many years. 'Versailles Blanche' makes a strong, upright bush. 'Gloire de Sablon' has pink fruits. Whitecurrants can also be grown as vertical single or double cordons trained against a sunny wall or fence. 1.2 x 1.2m (4 x 4ft). 🐝

Ribes rubrum 'Jonkheer van Tets'
Redcurrant
Family: Grossulariaceae
The sweet juicy fruits of this trouble-free deciduous bush, which are carried on long stalks (strigs), are ready for picking

in midsummer. Prune in late winter. Other cultivars include 'Junifer', 'Redstart' and 'Rovada'. Can be grown as a free-standing bush, or as a space-saving vertical cordon or fan against a wall or fence. Grow in a fruit cage if birds are a problem. 1.2 x 1.2m (4 x 4ft). 🐝

Ribes uva-crispa 'Invicta'
Gooseberry
Family: Grossulariaceae
One of the best cultivars showing resistance to powdery mildew disease, which can affect the leaves of the gooseberry, weakening and killing them. This is a spiny, vigorous-growing deciduous bush with large, pale green fruits that soften as they ripen in early summer. Prune in winter, wearing stout gloves. 'Pax' has red fruits and is spine-free; 'Hinnomaki Yellow' has yellow-green

▲ *Rubus idaeus*

fruits. Both cultivars are disease-resistant. Can be grown as a vertical cordon. 1 x 1m (3 x 3ft). 🐝

Rubus idaeus 'Malling Minerva'
Summer-fruiting raspberry
Family: Rosaceae
These suckering and spiny deciduous shrubs produce fruits on their long canes in summer or autumn. 'Malling Minerva' is spineless and resistant to disease, and its sweet, delicious fruits can be picked continuously over a period of four to six weeks, starting in early summer. 'All Gold' is autumn-fruiting with yellow fruits that have outstanding flavour. Small bumblebees visit the flowers for nectar. The canes usually need supporting with wires. Height 1.2–2m (4–7ft). 🐝

Vaccinium 'Bluecrop'
Highbush blueberry
Family: Ericaceae
Grow these deciduous shrubs either in acid (lime-free) soil or in large containers of peat-free ericaceous (lime-free, low-pH) compost (soil mix). Upright-growing 'Bluecrop' flowers in late spring and its large, pale fruits are ready to harvest in midsummer. In autumn the leaves turn orange-bronze. 'Sunshine Blue' grows 90cm (3ft) tall and wide, making it ideal for containers. Bumblebees visit the flowers. 1.5 x 1.5m (5 x 5ft). 🐝

▲ *Ribes rubrum* (whitecurrant)

▼ *Ribes rubrum* (redcurrant)

▲ *Ribes uva-crispa*

▼ *Vaccinium*

Eco-friendly herbs

Herbs can be hardy annuals, herbaceous perennials or woody shrubs, and they are among some of the most useful of all eco garden plants. As well as their visual appeal and their culinary or other uses, the nectar-rich flowers of many herbs are wonderful for attracting beneficial insects. They all thrive in full sun, and some will readily self-seed, then grow unassisted year after year.

Agastache foeniculum (syn. *A. anisata*)
Anise hyssop
Family: Lamiaceae
The young leaves of this herbaceous perennial can be eaten in salads or added to soups for their distinct aniseed flavour. The spikes of blue flowers 7–10cm (3–4in) long, set among violet bracts, are carried at the tops of the stems. An excellent bee and butterfly plant. The cultivar 'Golden Jubilee' has golden yellow leaves. Raise from seed. 90 x 30cm (3ft x 12in). 🐝 🦋

Allium schoenoprasum
Chive
Family: Alliaceae
A bulbous perennial producing a clump of narrow, cylindrical, dark green leaves which are eaten raw in salads or used as flavouring. Dense heads of pale purple (sometimes white) flowers appear in

▼ *Agastache foeniculum*

▲ *Allium schoenoprasum*

▼ *Anethum graveolens*

summer and are visited by bees gathering nectar. Easily grown from seed, and clumps can be divided in spring. *Allium tuberosum* (garlic chives) has garlic-flavoured leaves and heads of fragrant white flowers. 30cm (12in). 🐝

Anethum graveolens
Dill
Family: Apiaceae
A hardy annual grown for its aromatic, thread-like blue-green leaves and its seeds, which are both used in cooked dishes. In midsummer it produces flat,

▲ *Borago officinalis*

▼ *Foeniculum vulgare*

umbrella-like glistening heads made up of small golden-yellow flowers, up to 9cm (3½in) across. These attract large numbers of adult hoverflies, which will lay eggs among colonies of aphids. Self-sown seedlings are easily recognizable. 90 x 30cm (3ft x 12in). 🐝 🦋

Borago officinalis
Borage
Family: Boraginaceae
This fast-growing hardy annual is a reliable self-seeder that will renew itself from year to year – there is normally no

need to sow it after it is established. Bright blue, star-shaped flowers are carried above bristly, pale green leaves. The large black seeds are easy to collect for scattering elsewhere. An excellent bee plant. *B. officinalis* f. *alba* has white flowers. 60 x 45cm (24 x 18in).

Foeniculum vulgare
Fennel
Family: **Apiaceae**
Beneficial insects are drawn to the flat heads of yellow, nectar-rich flowers, which open in mid- to late summer. The finely divided, hair-like green leaves of this herbaceous perennial are aromatic and used for flavouring food. It can be an aggressive self-seeder, so remove any seedheads before they ripen. *F. vulgare* 'Purpureum' (bronze fennel) has bronze-purple leaves. Divide clumps in spring. 2m x 60cm (7 x 2ft).

Lavandula angustifolia
English lavender
Family: **Lamiaceae**
This compact and sun-loving evergreen shrub is prized for its heads of fragrant pale to deep purple and bee-attracting flowers, 7cm (3in) long, which bloom in mid- to late summer. The flowers are used fresh for flavouring food, or dried

▼ *Lavandula angustifolia*

▲ *Origanum vulgare*

and added to potpourri. There are various cultivars: 'Hidcote' has silver-grey foliage and dark purple flowers, while 'Loddon Pink' is soft pink. Trim plants over in spring using shears. 90cm (3ft).

Origanum vulgare
Oregano
Family: **Lamiaceae**
Butterflies will dance in clouds above the heads of oregano's pink flowers, which appear in midsummer and last into autumn. This woody-stemmed, spreading perennial is grown for its aromatic leaves, which can be eaten raw in salads or used for flavouring. The cultivar 'Aureum'

▼ *Salvia officinalis*

▲ *Thymus* 'Culinary Lemon'

(golden oregano) has golden yellow leaves and pink flowers. Grows well on dry soils and needs full sun. 30–60cm (12–24in).

Salvia officinalis
Common sage
Family: **Lamiaceae**
Although the leaves of this shrubby evergreen perennial are most often used for culinary purposes, its fresh flowers can also be added to salads. Its woolly, aromatic, grey-green leaves are 7cm (3in) long. Spikes of lilac-blue flowers appear in summer and are visited by bees. *S. officinalis* 'Purpurascens' (purple sage) has reddish-purple young shoots. Needs full sun and well-drained soil. 80cm x 1m (32 x 39in).

Thymus 'Culinary Lemon'
Lemon-scented thyme
Family: **Lamiaceae**
Grow this low, mound-forming evergreen shrub, which makes a fragrant path edging, for its strongly lemon-scented small green leaves, which are used for flavouring. During summer, its heads of lavender-pink flowers are much visited by honey bees and bumbebees. *T. pulegioides* 'Bertram Anderson' has bright yellow leaves and pink flowers. *T. vulgaris* (common thyme) is another good species for attracting bees. Up to 30 x 25cm (12 x 10in).

Eco-friendly pond and bog plants

Plants that float on or are submerged in water, or grow in the boggy, damp soil around the edge of a pond, are all valuable additions to an eco garden. Growing some of each, in and around even a small pond, helps to create a range of different habitats above and below water, where wild creatures large and small will live, hunt and breed.

Ajuga reptans
Bugle
Family: Lamiaceae
This creeping evergreen perennial will thrive in the moist soil around ponds and in rain gardens. In late spring and early summer, spikes of dark blue flowers 15cm (6in) tall, which attract bees and butterflies, appear above a carpet of dark green leaves. Increase by replanting sections of rooted stems. 'Burgundy Glow' has dark, wine-red leaves and purple flowers. 15 x 60–90cm (6 x 24–36in) or more. 🐝 🦋

Caltha palustris
Marsh marigold
Family: Ranunculaceae
Wet soil or shallow water at the edge of a pond is ideal for growing this herbaceous perennial. It starts flowering in early spring, producing useful food for bees and other insects just emerging from their winter hibernation. Its dark green, kidney-shaped leaves are a good foil for the waxy, bright yellow buttercup-like

▲ *Caltha palustris*

flowers. Divide in early spring. *C. palustris* var. *alba* has white flowers. 15–40 x 45cm (6–16 x 18in). 🐝 🦋

Ceratophyllum demersum
Hornwort
Family: Ceratophyllaceae
Spending its whole life under water, this submerged aquatic perennial is a good

oxygenating plant for any size of pond; it keeps the water clear and creates a habitat for pond-dwelling wildlife. Its long stems carry whorls of narrow green leaves. In winter it forms resting buds (turions), which sink to the pond bottom, then regrow the following spring. Other oxygenators include *Callitriche stagnalis* (water starwort) and *Myriophyllum spicatum* (water milfoil). Height and spread indefinite.

Eupatorium cannabinum
Hemp agrimony
Family: Asteraceae
Butterflies and other insects flock to the nectar-rich pink, purple or white flowerheads, 10cm (4in) wide, of this tall and potentially invasive herbaceous perennial. Grow it in moist soil near the edge of a pond or in a bog garden. It has red-tinted stems and dark green leaves. Divide clumps in spring. *E. maculatum* (Joe Pye weed) is similar, with flowerheads 15cm (6in) wide on stems up to 2m (7ft) tall. 1.5 x 1.2m (5 x 4ft). 🐝 🦋

▼ *Ajuga reptans*

▼ *Ceratophyllum demersum*

▼ *Eupatorium cannabinum*

▲ *Filipendula ulmaria*

▲ *Lythrum salicaria*

▲ *Mentha aquatica*

Filipendula ulmaria
Meadowsweet
Family: **Rosaceae**
Grow this herbaceous perennial where its roots are moist but not waterlogged. In summer, frothy heads of creamy-white, insect-attracting fragrant flowers appear above feathery leaves. Divide in spring. Birds will feed on the seedheads. *F. ulmaria* 'Aurea' has creamy-yellow foliage; *F. rubra* 'Venusta' (Queen of the prairie) has pink flowers and can reach 2.5m (8ft) tall. 60–90 x 60cm (2–3 x 2ft).

Lychnis flos-cuculi
Ragged robin
Family: **Caryophyllaceae**
A good plant to grow in moist but not waterlogged soil near a pond, in a bog

▼ *Lychnis flos-cuculi*

or in a swale feeding a rain garden. It will also grow in damp soil in 'wild' lawns. The pink or scarlet flowers of this herbaceous perennial are carried on branched, swaying stems in summer, and are visited by bees and other insects. 75 x 80cm (30 x 32in).

Lythrum salicaria
Purple loosestrife
Family: **Lythraceae**
This striking herbaceous perennial prefers to have its roots in permanently wet soil. It adds colour to an eco garden from midsummer through to autumn. Its reddish-pink flowers, 2cm (¾in) wide, are carried in spikes up to 45cm (18in) long. It can be invasive and is unsuitable for small ponds. *L. virgatum* is more compact, with purple-red flowers. 1.2m x 45cm (4ft x 18in).

Mentha aquatica
Watermint
Family: **Lamiaceae**
The lilac-pink flowers of watermint, like those of other *Mentha* spp., are ideal for attracting bees and many other beneficial insects; they appear from summer to early autumn in rounded heads at the ends of the shoots. Plant it with care: this spreading herbaceous perennial can easily overwhelm a small pond, but will colonize the margin of a larger one, creating dense shelter for both adult

frogs and toads, as well as froglets and toadlets. Its soft, hairy leaves are highly fragrant when bruised. 15–90cm x 1m (6–36 x 40in) or more.

Typha minima
Dwarf reedmace
Family: **Typhaceae**
The tall leaves and stems of this aquatic herbaceous perennial are used by the insects that alight near a pond, and by emerging dragonfly nymphs, which crawl up them before transforming into adults. In mid- and late summer, the cylindrical brown flower spikes filled with seeds and fluffy down appear on the tops of tall stems. *T. minima* is the only reedmace (bulrush) suitable for a small pond. 75 x 30–45cm (30 x 12–18in).

▼ *Typha minima*

Calendar of care

Early spring

- Empty compost bins and use the contents as a soil improver. Put any unrotted material back into the empty bin.
- Sow *Calendula officinalis* (pot marigold) under cover for some extra-early flowers which will draw beneficial insects into your greenhouse or polytunnel.
- Buy fresh, undamaged bags of peat-free compost (soil mix) for sowing and potting, avoiding any that are heavy and waterlogged. Store them under cover.
- Mix your own sowing and potting compost using sieved leaf mould or other materials, and store in reused plastic bags.
- Start sowing seeds under cover as light levels increase and temperatures rise.
- Vegetable crops can be sown outdoors; sow fast-growing salads regularly every few weeks throughout summer. Rake the soil to a fine tilth first.
- Mark out some areas of your lawn which will be left to grow long and 'wild' to attract butterflies and other insects.
- Pull up and compost any unwanted self-sown annual or perennial seedlings, or carefully lift and transplant them to another spot in the garden.

▼ Mature and well-rotted garden compost can be sieved and used as one of the ingredients in home-made potting compost (soil mix).

Mid-spring

- Once the soil starts to warm up, spread mulching materials over the surface to conserve moisture and prevent weed seeds germinating.
- Apply plant foods such as pelleted chicken manure four to six weeks before sowing or planting outdoor crops.
- Position new water butts and tanks and attach them to downpipes using a rainwater diverter.
- Set up a wormery using a suitable container, with some composting worms from your compost bin to start it off.
- If you do not have a greenhouse, use a warm sunny wall to start germinating seeds, but protect pots and trays from rain.
- Plant up a living roof on your garden shed (check the roof is sound first).
- Keep greenhouses well ventilated on sunny days, opening both the top and louvre vents; fit automatic openers if you are away from home all day.
- Sow microgreens under cover for a nutritious addition to salads.
- Use a small soft brush to pollinate the flowers of strawberries grown under cover. Dust the pollen between different flowers.

▼ A do-it-yourself wormery is simple to make, using any suitably sized container and some readily available materials and tools.

Late spring

- Plant out half-hardy annuals after the last spring frosts in your area.
- Cut nettle shoots and comfrey leaves for making into liquid feeds.
- Young starter or plug plants ordered by mail should be opened on arrival and planted immediately.
- Protect vulnerable vegetables and other plants from attack by slugs and snails, using physical barriers or deterrents, or use eco-friendly slug pellets.
- Loosen the soil around deep-rooted perennial weeds and lift them out.
- In a food garden, put in any supports for vertical-growing crops such as climbing beans. Do this before sowing/planting to avoid damaging the young plants.
- Leave self-sown annuals to grow and flower among food crops, where they will attract beneficial insects.
- Harden off any frost-tender plants for ten days before planting them outdoors.
- Support ornamental plants and food crops (such as peas) with twiggy sticks pushed into the soil while plants are still young. Guide pea shoots into the supports until their tendrils take hold.

▼ These sweet peas are clambering up a teepee made out of hazel sticks. The plants have tendrils, so they are self-clinging.

Early summer

- Cover crops vulnerable to white brassica butterflies with insect mesh, to prevent butterflies laying their eggs.
- Water the biological (nematode) control for slugs on to moist soil around potatoes. Do this during or immediately after rain.
- Hoe regularly to kill seedling weeds growing between food crops.
- Improve soil by sowing green manures (cover crops) such as fast-growing mustard.
- Start weekly foliar feeding with seaweed extract to keep plants healthy.
- Cut your lawn with a manual mower or an electric-powered mower using renewable energy from a 'green' supplier.
- Use shading to stop the temperatures in a greenhouse or polytunnel from soaring on sunny days. Remove any shading on dull, wet and overcast days.
- Increase watering and liquid feeding as plants grow more strongly; fit container-grown plants with slow-release watering systems that use recycled plastic bottles as the water reservoir.
- Look out for ready-grown insect-attracting plants such as single-flowered bedding dahlias and marigolds (*Tagetes*), and plant these at random in any gaps among crops in your food garden.

▼ Growing *Tagetes tenuifolia* just inside the door of your greenhouse or polytunnel will draw in beneficial insects such as hoverflies.

Midsummer

- Check the undersides of brassica leaves for the yellow eggs of cabbage white butterflies, or young caterpillars, squashing any you find. Do this regularly every few days.
- Sow fast-growing green manures on any patches of soil which are likely to remain bare for more than a few weeks. Do this as necessary until autumn.
- Drown persistent perennial weeds in a barrel of water, or seal them inside empty compost bags until they rot down. Weaken them first by chopping them up and drying them out in hot sunshine.
- Use sheets of cardboard to cover bare soil and keep it weed-free until you are ready to sow or plant.
- Water food garden crops as and when necessary, giving them an infrequent but thorough soaking.
- Make as much garden compost as you can, using garden, kitchen and household waste, plus any offered by neighbours.
- Keep any container-grown fruit plants watered at all times. If they dry out, they will shed their fruits.
- Top up ponds, if necessary, using rainwater; mains tap water can encourage algal blooms.

▼ Crush any eggs/young caterpillars you find on the undersides of the leaves of cabbages and other brassicas using your finger and thumb.

Late summer

- Cut the long grass in a 'wild' lawn using a scythe, making sure no wildlife is sheltering in the grass before you start.
- Immerse a sack of garden compost in water to make a tonic that can be watered or sprayed on to any plants where growth is flagging.
- Make a saucer-shaped depression around any new plants, filling it with water so that it soaks in around the roots.
- Harvest bush (soft) fruits regularly as they ripen. Drape netting over any bushes that are not protected by a fruit cage, to stop birds eating the fruits.
- Fit a large water butt or tank with a semi-automatic watering system, to water plants while you are away.
- If stored rainwater supplies run low, use freshly collected 'grey water' from the kitchen and bathroom, but do not let it come into contact with any of the edible parts of food crops.
- Sow overwintering salad crops such as oriental greens in multi-cell trays for transplanting under cover later on, or sow them direct into soil beds in a greenhouse or polytunnel.
- Harvest food crops regularly to keep them productive over a long period.

▼ Fruits such as raspberries are ready to pick when they feel slightly soft and will pull away easily from the plant, leaving the stalk behind.

Early autumn

• Remove the seedheads of self-seeding annuals and perennials; scatter seeds where you want new plants to grow, or store them for spring sowing.

• Sow overwintering green manures (cover crops) such as field beans, grazing rye and winter tares from now until early winter, or as long as soil conditions allow.

• Plant dwarf fruit trees and bush (soft) fruits in large containers so that their root systems have a chance to grow and develop before winter.

• Do not be over-zealous about tidying your garden; untidy, out-of-the-way areas where fallen leaves gather naturally provide a valuable wildlife habitat.

• To increase the biodiversity of a 'wild' lawn, plant some wildflower starter or plug plants, which will quickly become established and will flower the following spring and summer.

• Use the warm and dry conditions in a greenhouse or polytunnel to dry off and ripen crops such as bulb onions. Then store them in a cool and dry place.

• Harvest autumn-fruiting raspberries continuously to encourage further fruiting.

• Pick apples as they ripen, and store them in a cool place.

▼ Hang bulb onions up to dry in the wind and sun. In wet weather dry them off in a sunny porch, greenhouse or polytunnel.

Mid-autumn

• Make and plant a garden pond so that it has time to settle down and achieve a balance ahead of spring.

• Stretch netting across a pond to stop any leaves from falling in.

• If you garden near the sea, collect any seaweed that has washed up after storms and use it (in a layer 7–15cm/3–6in deep) to mulch bare soil during winter.

• While the soil is still warm, lay a sheet mulch to clear an area of ground of all but persistent perennial weeds.

• Do not be over-zealous about cutting down faded perennial plants; their hollow stems provide overwintering sites for insects such as adult ladybirds.

• Treat wooden garden fences with an eco-friendly, plant-friendly preservative based on natural materials; apply it using a brush, rather than a sprayer, to reduce resource use and prevent drift.

• When the first frost blackens their leaves, cut pumpkins and winter squash, putting them in full sun to ripen their skins, then store in a cool and dry place.

• Add garden waste to your compost bin as fading crops and flowers are cleared.

• Lift and dry maincrop potatoes, then store in hessian (burlap) or paper sacks.

▼ Butterflies such as the speckled wood (*Pararge aegeria*) will feed on rotting apples and other windfall fruits such as plums.

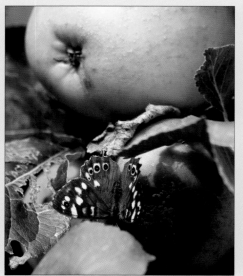

Late autumn

• Collect up fallen leaves and put them in inside-out compost (soil mix) bags, or into a wire cage, to rot down into leaf mould.

• Check over, clean, sharpen and repair any garden tools. Coat them with eco-friendly oil to prevent corrosion.

• Compost every bit of garden waste; chop up tougher plants, crushing any thick stems with a hammer.

• Gather up any unwanted garden materials and sort them into different piles for reusing, recycling or composting.

• Stack up some logs in an unused corner of your garden to create a habitat for different types of garden wildlife.

• Plant and stake dormant bare-root tree (top) fruits, when soil conditions allow, from now until early spring.

• Obtain dormant willow rods from a specialist supplier and plant a living 'fedge' as a garden feature or play area.

• Push your fingers into the soil around overwintering crops growing in a greenhouse or polytunnel. If it is dry and the plants are wilting, water carefully but avoid getting any water on to their leaves.

• Leave fallen and diseased apples for adult butterflies to feed on before entering winter hibernation.

▼ Simple wire cages are all you need to collect large volumes of autumn leaves, which will rot down into rich, soil-improving leaf mould.

Early winter

- Drain water butts and tanks to prevent them cracking during freezing weather, when the water inside will expand as it turns to ice; scrub them out after emptying.
- Wrap your wormery in insulation to stop it freezing, or move it temporarily indoors to a frost-free place, especially during prolonged cold snaps.
- Dig over heavy clay soils, leaving them exposed to winter frosts.
- Start putting out food for birds, topping up feeders regularly from now until late spring. Provide fresh water, too.
- Make a scale plan of a new garden, marking positions of any paths and beds, or a greenhouse or polytunnel. Mark these out on the ground using stakes and string.
- Use a bright windowsill indoors to sprout seeds for use in winter salads.
- Check the fixings holding any supporting wires used for training fruit on walls and fences, and make any repairs.
- Shred woody, non-thorny prunings and other tough stems and use them as mulch around shrubs or as a covering for paths.
- Start feeding birds when their natural food sources, such as hedgerow berries, run low. Wash feeders weekly to reduce the risk of disease.

▼ A metal cage will protect your bird feeders from troublesome mammals such as squirrels, but still allow smaller birds to gain access.

Midwinter

- Scrub clean plant pots and trays using an eco-friendly cleaner, then rinse them in a sterilizing fluid, based on natural plant extracts, to deter disease.
- Make biodegradable plant pots out of newspaper using a wooden mould, ready for spring seed-sowing.
- Draw a sketch of the vegetable beds in your garden or on an eco allotment, then work out a crop rotation plan.
- Build raised beds in a food garden using maintenance-free recycled plastic boards. Construct them using rust-resistant fixings.
- Remove and clean staging from a greenhouse, especially if pests or diseases have been a problem.
- Make an insect hotel out of natural and recycled materials, ready for putting out in the garden in early spring.
- Put aside any garden landscaping materials you no longer want, offering them as 'free' in your front garden, or via an online gifting website.
- Start chitting seed potato tubers in a light, frost-free place.
- Study seed and plant catalogues and order by mail or online. Wherever possible, choose organically grown seeds and plants. Avoid seeds treated with chemicals.

▼ Use egg boxes to chit seed potatoes. Ensure that the end of the tuber with the tiny buds (the rose end) is uppermost in each cell of the box.

Late winter

- Lift and divide herbaceous perennials.
- To remove dirt and any winter build-up of algae, use a stiff-bristled brush to wash down greenhouses and polytunnels with an eco-friendly cleaner. The hard-to-reach top of a polytunnel can be cleaned by two people (one either side) pulling a large cloth sheet back and forth.
- Prune and/or shape bush and tree fruits before their buds start to burst.
- Plant early cultivars of potato, such as 'Swift', in large pots and tubs under cover for extra-early 'new' potatoes in late spring. Cover them with fleece on frosty nights.
- Replace the skin of a polytunnel on a still, sunny day. Wrapping the new cover in black plastic and leaving it in the sun for a few hours warms it up and makes it more pliable and easier to stretch tight.
- Soak the soil in beds in greenhouses or polytunnels ready for spring sowing and planting; it can become very dry, even during the winter period.
- Collect some dry hollow plant stems and pack them inside a food can to make a spring nest box for wild solitary bees.
- When seed orders arrive, keep them in a container with a tightly fitting lid, in a cool, dry place away from heat sources.

▼ Put a solitary bee nest box in a sheltered and sunny position on a wall or fence, or on a post, so that it sits 90–150cm (3–5ft) above the ground.

156

Further information

UNITED KINGDOM
Organizations and public display gardens

Barnsdale Gardens,
The Avenue, Exton, Oakham,
Rutland LE15 8AH,
tel: 01572 813 200
www.barnsdalegardens.co.uk
office@barnsdalegardens.co.uk
Thirty-eight organically run gardens
over 3.25 hectares (8 acres).

Garden Organic,
Coventry CV8 3LG,
tel: 024 7630 3517
www.gardenorganic.org.uk
enquiry@gardenorganic.org.uk
The UK's leading organic growing
charity dedicated to researching
and promoting organic gardening,
farming and food. Membership
organization with extensive organic
display gardens. Home of the
Heritage Seed Library. Also runs
home and community schemes
to promote composting via
www.homecomposting.org.uk.

Hough Garden,
Hough Lane, Alderley Edge,
Cheshire SK9 7JD,
tel: 01625 425 192
Private eco-friendly organic food
garden open by arrangement.

Tatton Park,
Knutsford,
Cheshire WA16 6QN,
tel: 01625 374 400
www.tattonpark.org.uk
tatton@cheshireeast.gov.uk
Fifty acres of gardens, including
a restored kitchen garden.

Suppliers

Alan Romans,
72 North Street, Kettlebridge, Fife
KY15 7QJ, tel: 01337 831 060
www.alanromans.com
admin@alanromans.com
Seed potato supplier specializing in
heritage (heirloom) cultivars, including
'minitubers'. Also sells seeds.

AutoPot Global Ltd,
Brill View Farm, Ludgarshall Road,
Piddington, Oxfordshire OX25 1PU,
tel: 0844 858 1520
www.autopot.co.uk
mail@autopot.co.uk
Automatic/semi-automatic systems for
greenhouse and polytunnel watering.

Bluebell Cottage Gardens
& Lodge Lane Nursery,
Lodge Lane, Dutton, Warrington
WA4 4HP, tel: 01928 713 718
www.lodgelanenursery.co.uk
info@bluebellcottage.co.uk
Peat-free and eco-friendly hardy
herbaceous perennial nursery and
0.6 hectare (1.5 acre) display gardens.

EcoCharlie,
PO Box 77, Petworth, West Sussex
GU28 8AW, tel: 01798 867 780
www.ecocharlie.co.uk
enquiries@ecocharlie.co.uk
Environmentally sustainable ethical,
natural and recycled garden products.

Garden Systems,
103 Burrell Road, Ipswich,
Suffolk IP2 8AD, tel: 01473 400 103
www.ecpgroup.com
sales@gardensystems.co.uk
Garden watering systems.

Harrod Horticultural,
Pinbush Road, Lowestoft, Suffolk
NR33 7NL, tel: 0845 402 5300
www.harrodhorticultural.com
enquiries@harrod.uk.com
Wide range of gardening products,
many suitable for eco gardening.

Just Green,
Unit 14, Springfield Road Industrial
Estate, Burnham-on-Crouch,
Essex CM0 8UA, tel: 01621 785 088
www.just-green.com
info@just-green.com
Natural biological pest control products
and eco-friendly gardening sundries.

Mr Fothergill's Seeds Ltd,
Gazeley Road, Kentford,
Newmarket, Suffolk CB8 7QB,
tel: 01638 751 161
www.mr-fothergills.co.uk
info@mr-fothergills.co.uk
Seeds, plants and gardening sundries.

Organic Plants,
Berwick Road, Doddington,
March, Cambridgeshire PE15 0TU,
tel: 01354 740 553
www.organicplants.co.uk
info@organicplants.co.uk
Organically certified mail-order
fruit, vegetable and herb starter
(plug) plants.

Slug Lady,
www.sluglady.com
farialawrence@yahoo.co.uk
Salt-impregnated card collars to
protect plants from slugs and snails.

Specialist Aggregates,
162 Cannock Road, Stafford,
Staffordshire ST17 0QJ,
tel: 01785 665 554
www.specialistaggregates.com
steve@specialistaggregates.co.uk
Recycled landscape materials,
including crushed seashells.

Suttons Seeds Ltd,
Woodview Road, Paignton,
Devon TQ4 7NG,
tel: 0844 922 0606
www.suttons.co.uk
Supplier of seeds, plants and
gardening sundries, including
paper pot-makers.

The Organic Gardening Catalogue,
Riverdene Business Park,
Molesey Road, Hersham, Surrey
KT12 4RG, tel: 01932 253 666
www.organiccatalogue.com
enquiries@chaseorganics.co.uk
Extensive range of organic seeds
and plants, and eco-friendly
gardening accessories.

Thompson & Morgan (UK) Ltd,
Poplar Lane, Ipswich, Suffolk
IP8 3BU, tel: 01473 695 200
www.thompson-morgan.com
ccare@thompson-morgan.com
Supplier of seeds, plants and
gardening sundries, including
sprouting seeds and microgreens.

VertiGarden,
Sunnyfield Nurseries,
Wraggs Marsh,
Spalding,
Lincolnshire PE12 6HH,
tel: 01406 370239
www.vertigarden.co.uk
sales@vertigarden.co.uk
Modular vertical growing systems
for ornamentals and food plants.

Wild Flower Shop,
Lime Kiln House,
Old Ipswich Road,
Claydon,
Ipswich,
Suffolk IP6 0AD,
tel: 07590 895590
www.wildflowershop.co.uk
enquiries@wildflowershop.co.uk
Mail-order supplier of wildflower
plugs, plants, bulbs and
pond plants from cultivated
UK-grown stock.

IRELAND

Coronet Miniature Apple Trees,
tel: 058 42811
www.coronet.ie
springfieldnurseries@eircom.net
Dwarf apple trees for container
growing; suppliers listed on website.

UNITED STATES
Organizations

Ecology Action,
5798 Ridgewood Road,
Willits, CA 95490,
tel: 707 459 0150
www.growbiointensive.org
bountiful@sonic.net
Research organization offering
information and training in high-
yielding, sustainable growing systems.
Its non-profit project Bountiful
Gardens (www.bountifulgardens.com)
supplies seed of open-pollinated
heritage (heirloom) vegetables
and flowers, and green manures
(cover crops).

International Biochar Initiative,
9B Main Street,
Bowdoinham,
ME 04008,
tel: 914 693 0469
www.biochar-international.org
info@biochar-international.org
Information on using biochar
as a soil improver.

Rain Gardens of West Michigan,
West Michigan Environmental
Action Council, 1007 Lake Drive SE,
Grand Rapids, Michigan 49506,
tel: 616 451 3051 ext. 29
www.raingardens.org
Environmental education progamme
focusing on stormwater and using
rain gardens and native plants
to improve water quality. Lists
demonstration rain gardens.

Rodale Institute,
611 Siegfriedale Road, Kuztown,
PA 19530-9320, tel: 610 683 1400
www.rodaleinstitute.org
Non-profit organization researching
organic farming and growing.
Offers workshops.

SafeLawns.org,
SafeLawns Foundation, PO Box 301,
Cumberland, ME 04021,
tel: 207 252 0869
www.safelawns.org
paul@safelawns.org
Coalition of organizations promoting
the benefits of eco-friendly lawn care.

Sustainable and Urban Gardening,
susan@sustainable-gardening.com
www.sustainable-gardening.com
Website aiming to teach gardening
in a sustainable, eco-friendly way.

Union of Concerned Scientists,
2 Brattle Square,
Cambridge, MA 02238-9105
www.ucsusa.org/food_and_
agriculture/what_you_can_do/
the-climate-friendly-gardener.html
Science-based non-profit
organization working for a safer
environment. Information on climate-
friendly gardening and global warming.

Suppliers
CowPots,
324 Norfolk Road, East Canaan,
CT 06024, tel: 860 824 7520
www.cowpots.com
info@cowpots.net
Biodegradable plant pots made
from composted cow manure.

Fedco Seeds,
PO Box 520, Waterville,
ME 04903, tel: 207 873 7333
www.fedcoseeds.com
Cooperative business offering
organically grown flower and
vegetable seeds.

GREENCulture Inc.,
32 Rancho Circle, Lake Forest,
CA 92630, tel: 877 204 7336
www.eco-gardening.com
Recycled and ecologically sustainable
products, including compost bins.

Renee's Garden,
6060A Graham Hill Road, Felton,
CA 95018, tel: 888 880 7228
www.reneesgarden.com
customerservice@reneesgarden.com
Untreated, open-pollinated flower,
herb and vegetable seeds,
including heritage (heirloom)
and modern cultivars.

CANADA
Organizations
Canadian Organic Growers,
National Office, 323 Chapel Street,
Ottawa, Ontario K1N 7Z2,
tel: 613 216 0741
www.cog.ca
office@cog.ca
National organic growing charity
with a diverse membership.

Society for Organic Urban Land Care,
PO Box 8548, Victoria, BC V8W 1L4
www.organiclandcare.org
info@organiclandcare.org
Information, training and certification
to support urban organic methods.

Suppliers
Greta's Organic Gardens,
399 River Road, Gloucester,
Ontario K1V 1C9, tel: 613 521 8648
www.seeds-organic.com
greta@seeds-organic.com
Certified organic vegetable seeds.

Salt Spring Seeds,
Box 44, Ganges PO,
Salt Spring Island, BC V8K 2W1,
tel: 250 537 5269
www.saltspringseeds.com
dan@saltspringseeds.com
Untreated, open-pollinated and
non-GMO heritage (heirloom)
organically grown vegetable seeds.

AUSTRALIA
Organizations
Cityfood Growers,
PO Box 446, Samford, Queensland
4520, tel. 617 3289 3602
www.cityfoodgrowers.com.au
Paid-for multimedia subscriber
service offering support and
knowledge to home food gardeners.

Commonwealth Scientific and
Industrial Research Organization,
CSIRO Publishing, PO Box 1139,
Collingwood, Victoria 3066,
tel. 03 9662 7666
www.publish.csiro.au/nid/22/sid/59.htm
publishing.sales@csiro.au
Publications covering eco-friendly
sustainable gardens, food and
low-water gardening.

Sustainable Gardening Australia,
6 Manningham Road West, Bulleen,
Victoria 3105, tel. 03 9850 8165
www.sgaonline.org.au
vic@sgaonline.org.au
Non-governmental, non-profit-making
organization raising awareness of
the environmental consequences
of conventional gardening practices,
and providing realistic and sustainable
alternatives. Email newsletter.

Suppliers
Digger's Club,
PO Box 300, Dromana,
Victoria 3936, tel: 03 5984 7900
www.diggers.com.au
info@diggers.com.au
Eco-friendly gardening club
specializing in heritage (heirloom)
seeds and plants, with two
demonstration gardens.

NEW ZEALAND
Organizations
Koanga Institute,
RD 12, Havelock North 4294
www.koanga.org.nz
Supports access to heritage
(heirloom) food plants; offers seeds
grown using sustainable methods,
and workshops.

Organic NZ,
PO Box 36170, Northcote,
Auckland, tel: 09 419 4536
www.organicnz.org
editor@organicnz.org
New Zealand's largest membership
organization supporting organic
food and farming.

Suppliers
Oakdale Organics,
107 Beatty Road, Pukekohe,
Auckland, tel: 09 889 0006
www.oakdale-organics.co.nz
monica@oakdale-organics.co.nz
Organically certified heritage
(heirloom) vegetable and
herb plants.

Weathersfield Organics,
485 Kaipara Coast Highway,
Kaukapakapa, RD 1 0871,
tel: 09 420 3002
www.weathersfieldorganics.co.nz
weathersfield@xtra.co.nz
Certified organic herb and
vegetable starter (plug) plants.

SOUTH AFRICA
Suppliers
Biogrow,
Private Bag X15, Suite 116
Hermanus, 7200, tel: 028 313 2054
www.biogrow.co.za
sales@biogrow.co.za
Eco-friendly plant foods,
bio-stimulants and natural pest,
disease and weed controls.

Kitchen Garden,
6 Arundel Circle, Tokai 7945,
Cape Town, tel: 082 820 9646
www.kitchengarden.co.za
info@kitchengarden.co.za
Seed-sprouting kits and seeds.

Sustainable.co.za,
9b Bell Crescent,
The Green Building,
Westlake Business Park,
Cape Town 7495, tel: 021 701 2028
www.sustainable.co.za
Affordable eco-friendly products,
including those for water
conservation and composting.

Talborne Organics (Pty) Ltd,
229 Voortrekker Road, Monument,
Krugersdorp, PO Box 596,
Paardekraal 1752, tel: 011 954 5763
www.talborne.co.za
info@talborne.co.za
Manufacturer and distributor of
organically accredited fertilizers.

Index

▲ *Eupatorium cannabinum*

▲ *Phlomis russeliana*

ACKNOWLEDGEMENTS

The author and publisher would like to thank the following for allowing photography to take place in their gardens: Nick Hamilton, Barnsdale Gardens; Sue Beesley, Bluebell Cottage Gardens & Lodge Lane Nursery; Garden Organic, Ryton Gardens; Peter Woollam, Hough Garden; Sam Youd, Tatton Park Gardens.

John Walker would also like to thank Richard Ellis for ongoing support during the making of this book.

The publisher would like to thank the following for allowing their photographs to be reproduced in the book (t=top, b=bottom, l=left, r=right, m=middle): Felicity Forster: 16t, 28bl, 107bl, 108bl, 123b. iStockphoto: 8b, 11bl, 45bl, 53m, 61br, 97br, 101bl, 106t, 108tr, 115tr, 116b, 146tr. Colin Leftley: 47tr, 47 panel (cut off seedlings, remove fragments, grow dense crops, use ground cover, use landscape fabric), 58t, 58b, 59 (all), 61tr, 76bl, 84, 106bl, 122bl. Photolibrary: 118bm, 127bl, 140bl, 140bm, 141ml, 141mr, 142bl, 143tl, 143tr, 143bm, 144tl, 144br, 145tl, 146bl, 146br, 151tr. Suttons Seeds Ltd: 146tl. John Walker: 5t, 14bl, 17m, 21m, 44t, 44bl, 47 panel (sow a green manure), 48t, 63ml, 64bl, 74br, 83ml, 101mr, 110br, 114b, 124t, 125br, 127bm, 129tr, 130br.

▲ *Thymus* 'Culinary Lemon'